Sailing to Aus

'Farewell to old England, and now for a nev

These words were written in 1836 by John Brown, bound for the long journey out to South Australia. For him, and hundreds like him, the journey to this new promised land was fraught with difficulty and danger. It was a huge transition, both geographically and culturally, and one way of dealing with this was by writing a diary.

Between 1788 and 1880 some 1.3 million free emigrants arrived in Australia from the British Isles, part of a mass migration from Europe without precedent in human history. Before the advent of photography, the surviving diaries offer snapshots of the lives and experiences of many ordinary men and women who embarked on this adventure.

In this fascinating study, Andrew Hassam analyses these journals and diaries to answer the question: 'How did writing a diary help diarists make sense of such a momentous and absolutely alien experience as emigration by sail, to a continent about which they very likely knew almost nothing?' The stories that emerge are as much to do with the process of life-writing as they are an historical snapshot of a bygone time, and make for fascinating reading for anyone interested in travel writing, autobiography, cultural or social history especially of Australia.

Andrew Hassam is Associate Lecturer in English at the University of Wales, Lampeter.

To Clare

Sailing to Australia

Shipboard diaries by
nineteenth-century British emigrants

ANDREW HASSAM

Manchester University Press
Manchester and New York
Distributed exclusively in the USA and Canada by St. Martin's Press

Copyright © Andrew Hassam 1994

Published by Manchester University Press
Oxford Road, Manchester M13 9NR, UK

Distributed exclusively in the USA and Canada
by St. Martin's Press Inc., 175 Fifth Avenue, New York,
NY 10010, USA

British Library Cataloguing-in-Publication Data
A catalogue record for this book is available from the British Library

Library of Congress Cataloging in Publication Data
Hassam, Andrew.
    Sailing to Australia : shipboard diaries by nineteenth-century
British emigrants / Andrew Hassam.
        p.   cm.
    Includes bibliographical references and index.
    ISBN 0-7190-3929-0. — ISBN 0-7190-4546-0 (pbk.)
    1. British—Australia—Diaries.   2. Immigrants—Australia–
–Diaries.   3. Australia—Emigration and immigration—History—19th
century—Sources.   4. Great Britain—Emigration and immigration–
–History—19th century—Sources.   5. Ocean travel—History—19th
century—Sources.   I. Title.
DU122.B7H37   1994
304.8'94041'0922—dc20
[B]   94—12596

ISBN 0 7190 3929 0 *hardback*
      0 7190 4546 0 *paperback*

Photoset in Linotron Clearface
by Northern Phototypesetting Co. Ltd, Bolton

Printed in Great Britain
by Bell & Bain Ltd, Glasgow

Contents

Preface

This study began almost by accident. Towards the end of 1988, two texts arrived on my desk and together began generating sparks. The first text was the diary of Richard Watt, who emigrated to Brisbane in 1864 on board the Black Ball Line's *Young Australia*. One of the ways in which I had relieved some of the more repetitive tasks of renovating a house in west Wales had been by listening to BBC Radio 4. In September 1987 extracts of Watt's diary had been broadcast and, curious to read the whole diary, I had succeeded by the end of 1988 with the invaluable help of Mrs Joan Leech, the programme's researcher, in tracking down a copy as it was published in 1956–7. The diary manuscript seems later to have been lost; its loss is great since it stands as one of the fullest diaries of the voyage out to have been written. I have returned to it often, and if any reader can locate the manuscript, I would beg them to let the world know in as loud a voice as possible.

The text which found its way to my desk at the same time as Watt's diary was Paul Carter's *The Road to Botany Bay*. It was passed on to me by Gavin Edwards, a friend and colleague at the University of Wales, Lampeter, to whom I am indebted in many other ways, most notably for his help when I was preparing for my own trip to Australia in 1992. Paul Carter's contentious re-reading of the source documents of Australian history initiated me into the rich world of Australian studies and his brief but, to me, revelatory comments on emigrant diaries of the voyage out inspired me to promise a conference paper exploring his approach through Richard Watt's diary. That paper marked the beginning of my research and a road which led three years later to a discussion with Paul Carter himself over an excellent cup of coffee in Melbourne.

My first step was to try to locate emigrant journals in Britain, and I was fortunate to be able to call on the expertise of Kathy Miles, the

Preface

interlibrary loans librarian at the University of Wales, Lampeter, in tracing copies of diaries published in various journals and books. I am grateful for the invaluable help given me by the staff at the National Maritime Museum, Greenwich, in providing me with access to their holdings of manuscript diaries; and I am also indebted to Mr Gordon Read, curator of archives at the Merseyside Maritime Museum, Liverpool, for making available to me his own transcriptions of some of the museum's holdings. A visit to Liverpool to experience the permanent exhibition 'Emigrants to a New World' is a necessity for anyone in the United Kingdom interested in the subject of nineteenth-century European migration.

More papers followed, and during this stage of my research I was lucky enough to find support from Jim Walter and Richard Nile during their tenure at the Sir Robert Menzies Centre for Australian Studies in London. I profited greatly from twice being invited to give a paper at the Centre, and by their publication of one of my papers in 1992.

It was obvious, however, that most of my research material was in Australia, and I owe a huge debt to the National Library of Australia in Canberra for awarding me a Harold White Fellowship for 1992 to enable me to spend five months at the National Library reading its extensive collection of diaries. My thanks are due to Graeme Powell, currently Acting Principal Librarian, Australian Collections, for his assistance, to Margaret Dent for her unfailing enthusiasm, and indeed to all at the National Library not only for their professional assistance but for the friendly atmosphere in which I worked; I lost count of the number of cakes I consumed. My 'fellow Fellows' at the National Library, Ian Britain and Bill Mandle, proved to be excellent office companions, keen to offer scholarly advice and – good cooks both – invitations to dinner.

While in Australia, I had the good fortune to discuss my ideas with a number of scholars, and David Fitzpatrick (ANU/Dublin), David Goodman (Melbourne), Wenche Ommundsen (Deakin), Richard Reid (Australian War Memorial), and Gillian Whitlock (Griffith) each shared with me their own work. I am grateful to David Parker and to Terry Collits for inviting me to give papers at the Australian National University and the University of Melbourne respectively, and to Mark Staniforth, curator at the Australian National Maritime Museum in Sydney and an expert in nineteenth-century Australian immigration, for allowing me access to the resources of the museum and for answering an endless stream of queries going far beyond the call of duty. Shauna Hicks, archivist at the John Oxley Library in Brisbane, has, since my return to Wales, provided me with further valuable material.

None of this, of course, would have seen the light of day without the support of Anita Roy at Manchester University Press, and I am grateful to Anita, the Press, and their academic readers for their advice and assistance.

Acknowledgements

Extracts from unpublished manuscripts are reproduced by courtesy of:
the Council of the Australian National Maritime Museum (as listed in
bibliography); Mrs Ethel Biddle (Maria Steley diary); Keith Brennand
(Stephen Brennand diary); Lt Col R. P. Carter RM (John Carter diary); Alan
J. Cohen (Solomon Joseph diary); Thomas Coram Foundation for Children
(William Wills diary); Anne Cox (J. W. Reeves diary); Steven Cross (Mary
Maclean diary); Cumbria Record Office (Joshua Hughes diary); Devon
Record Office (Frances Thornton diary); Miss N. L. Dunlop (Elizabeth
Ankatell diary); Edinburgh City Libraries (James Espie White diary); Mrs
Mary Emmott (Mary Stack diary); Noel Francis (Edwin Francis diary); Mrs
Mary Gravil (Thomas Coy diary); SS *Great Britain* Project (as listed in
bibliography); the Harris Library, Preston (Daniel Higson diary); Liverpool
Libraries and Information Services (Sir William Bower Forwood diary);
F. W. McClements (Samuel Shaw diary); Sir Humphrey Maud (Andrew
Hamilton diary); the Mitchell Library, State Library of New South Wales
(George Kershaw diary); National Library of Australia (as listed in biblio-
graphy); the Trustees of the National Maritime Museum (as listed in biblio-
graphy); the Trustees of the National Museums and Galleries on Merseyside,
Merseyside Maritime Museum, Archives and Library (John Hedges diary);
John Oxley Library, State Library of Queensland (Maria Steley diary); the
late T. G. F. Patterson (Samuel Pillow diary); Deputy Keeper of the Records,
Public Record Office of Northern Ireland (Elizabeth Ankatell, John Martin,
Samuel Pillow, Samuel Shaw diaries); Lady Randall (George Randall diary);
Mrs A. Ryan (John Martin diary); Mrs Christine Scott (Henry Widdowson
diary); Scottish Record Office (Alexander Turner diary); State Library of
Victoria (Susan Meade diary; Henry White Meade letter, William Thompson
diary); Cdr F. N. Towle RN (Edward Towle diary); G. A. Walpole (Margaret
Walpole diary); Mrs Angela Winston-Gregson (Arthur Clarke diary); Andrew
Wilson (Alexander Turner diary).

Acknowledgements

Every effort has been made to trace the copyright owners of all previously unpublished material quoted; the author would be pleased to hear from anyone claiming copyright not acknowledged above.

Chapters 2 and 3 employ my article, 'Farewell to Old England and now for a new Life and a new Journal: Emigration as Narrative', *Journal of Australian Studies* 36 (March 1993), pp. 23–35 © 1993 Andrew Hassam.

Chapter 4 employs my paper, 'Our Floating Home: Social Space and Group Identity on Board the Emigrant Ship', *Working Papers in Australian Studies* 76. London: Institute of Commonwealth Studies © 1992 Andrew Hassam.

Chapter 5 employs my article, 'As I Write: Narrative Occasions and the Quest for Self-Presence in the Travel Diary', *Ariel* 21.4 (1990), pp. 33–47 © 1990 The Board of Governors, The University of Calgary.

Chapter 6 employs my article, 'Writing the Coastline of Australia: Emigrants' Diaries and the Long Looked For Shores', *University of Toronto Quarterly* 61.2 (1991), pp. 195–206 © 1991 University of Toronto Press Incorporated.

Introduction

We are not quite sure why we *take* photographs. The still photograph is not a way of recording an instant in time as much as a way of intensifying the experience then and there. The camera is an instrument for intensifying the awareness both of the photographer and of those being photographed. For the amateur the film record is incidental. Most people never look at the photographs more than once. Few photographs *capture* the thing anyhow, they are only a note of the thing, an *aide-mémoire*. Holiday photographs are our evidence, because we lack a strong sense of personal credibility. They are evidence not only for our friends that we exist, but for ourselves, evidence that we live. (Frank Moorhouse, *Tales of Mystery and Romance* p. 110)

It may appear slightly perverse to begin a study of nineteenth-century shipboard diaries with a quotation about still photography. Doubly perverse in that the quotation comes from Frank Moorhouse, a twentieth-century fiction writer. But when I read this passage a short while ago it struck me as similar to the position I was working towards with regard to the diaries. Namely, that the cultural function of diaries written at sea by Australian immigrants in the middle years of the nineteenth century needed to be related to the 'then and there' of their moment(s) of composition. My argument is that the diaries actively contributed to the way in which the voyage out was lived. This is not easy to show and it is easier to see how emigrants' diaries have continued to function in various ways in differing contexts: being read by anxious relatives to whom they may have been sent, being published in nineteenth-century newspapers as exemplary tales for intending emigrants, being sold to archives in the twentieth century, and being repackaged and republished in scholarly editions. Like all texts, emigrant diaries have circulated, accruing new meanings as old meanings have worn out and are lost.

It is not possible to retrieve a sense of one of these diaries as new, as maybe only half-written and awaiting the next entry. To try to imagine the ink as having just dried on the page is like trying to imagine the Morris Minor as an innovative design. Yet emigrants' diaries must have had a function on board ship or none would have been written, and no matter how much care emigrants took to copy their diaries and send them home, a diary had already done a good deal of work by the end of the voyage. Like Moorhouse's photographs, the record was perhaps incidental, it was the act of recording that was important, and if the diaries have been passed down in a way that makes them seem inevitable and finished artifacts, we nonetheless have to attempt to guess not so much why they were written, but what the effect of their being written was on the writer. Like ethnographers, we need to be aware that collecting cultural objects is almost worthless without a knowledge of cultural performance, how the objects were used and what their cultural function was. We must ask similar questions of emigrant diaries. How did writing a diary help diarists to make sense of such a momentous and absolutely alien experience as emigration by sail, to a continent about which they very likely knew almost nothing?

I am not going to suggest that the diaries were written out of the same kind of existential angst as the photographs in the Moorhouse passage; nineteenth-century British emigrants were not postmodern subjects and there is nothing in the diaries to suggest that any of the diarists had worries about the intensity of their experiences. There were, of course, anxieties, but they were more about loss of status or public identity, and it is not surprising to find that in the alien world of the voyage out emigrants clung to what they knew. There is nothing like crossing the seas for bringing out a culture's latent chauvinism, and one of the main objectives, for working-class as much as for middle-class British emigrants, was to retain a sense of never having left Britain. They were not keen travellers and on the whole they would rather have stayed at home; they were not explorers, not missionaries, and not holiday-makers, and if they were early participants in the huge European military, economic and colonial expansionism that darkened the world in the late-nineteenth century, they were reluctantly so. Emigrants were emigrants because they wanted a better standard of living, not because they had any great belief in colonisation; most European emigrants, it must be remembered, went to the United

States, a land passing rapidly beyond the influence of the European colonial powers. Possibly the young (and often not so young) men lured to the Australian goldfields were a shade less reluctant to leave family and friends than other emigrants, but most gold-diggers saw themselves as adventurers who would be returning to Britain within a few years weighted down with pockets of gold. Few Europeans in the mid-nineteenth century considered travelling to Australia just for the fun of it; the fun of a three- or four-month voyage under sail to Australia was more than counteracted by the poor diet, inadequate ventilation, lack of privacy, and contagious diseases of the voyage out.

Reluctant travellers they might have been, but travellers of necessity they had to be, and they knew once they stepped on board ship that the voyage out had somehow to be negotiated, both physically and culturally. To be carried off to sea for three or four months out of contact with land was to have made a symbolic break with the old and yet not to have entered the new; it was to be caught between (as they saw it) two worlds and two lives. This sense of transition needed to be contained if it was not to get out of hand, and one way of doing this was to write it down in a book. A book promised that the experience of the voyage could be contained within a cover, that all the upheaval and strangeness of the voyage could be ordered and given a beginning, middle, and an end. The voyage could be made meaningful for those back home to whom a copy of the diary might be sent, and at some point in the future when the promised land had been reached, the diarist would be able to see the voyage as both a completed book and a completed episode. But however it might be seen in the future, writing a diary at sea was a job of work; as in Frank Moorhouse's snapshot, it was not a matter of 'capturing' what already existed, it was more a question of transforming the experience of the voyage into a narrative.

But if diaries are similar to photographs in having an effect in the 'then and there' of their moment of production, the two are entirely different when seen in narrative terms. Snapshot photography was not available to emigrants until after the introduction of Kodak's first box camera in 1888, and where today we might reach for our camera to record such a journey, nineteenth-century emigrants took with them a notebook. A notebook is all very well if it is treated like a camera, with notes being made at the whim of the notetaker, but emigrants were intent on writing the voyage out as a continuous narrative. A narrative needs beginnings and ends, it needs a narrator, it needs to create a sense of its audience, it needs to create a sense of the space from which it is being told; it needs, above all, events to narrate. In the particular circumstances of emigration by sail, each of these aspects of narrative posed problems for the emigrant diarist. My interest is in how diarists resolved these problems, how, for example, they created personas for themselves, or how they filled their diaries when there was nothing to write about. But this interest, as I have already suggested, is not a purely literary one. The relationship between the diary and the way in which the voyage was seen and experienced is such that the construction of the diary was also an attempt to construct the voyage experience. Journeys are already defined as narratives with beginnings and ends, and by bringing out what was already implicit in the idea of the journey, writing a diary was an attempt to frame and control the meaning of the voyage out.

In 1836, immediately prior to setting off for South Australia, John Brown punctuated his diary with the words: 'Farewell to old England, and now for a new Life and a new Journal.' Emigration suggests a new life, and like other emigrants, John Brown was seeing his life in terms of books. The closing of one book meant the opening of a new. Yet the analogy between life and a book could not work: not only does life have no absolute beginnings and endings, emigrants were themselves ambivalent about wanting the analogy to work. Inherently conservative, being forced to emigrate rather than choosing to emigrate, emigrants wanted better lives, but they also wanted lives continuous with the old. On board ship and then in Australia, they very quickly sought to preserve old customs and practices. In such circumstances, the new diary stood in for the new life they both wanted and dreaded; they hoped the new life would be an improvement on the old, yet they resisted any threat to their old way of living. Emigrants wanted to believe that new lives could be started as a new journal might be, but in practice they found that the border between an emigrant and an immigrant, like all borders, was artificial: a complete break was neither possible nor desirable. The diary of the voyage out stands in a complex relationship to the experience of migration, and writing the words 'the end' in a diary does not allow any of us an unqualified entry into a new life.

*

Whenever I mention to friends in Britain my interest in Australian immigrant diaries, the usual response is, 'Did convicts keep diaries?' Either that, or I am told the tale of the colleague who emigrated for £10, the one with whom there was a short, now lapsed, correspondence. In

Introduction

the British popular imagination, there seems to be about one hundred years missing from Australian history, roughly from the 1840s to the 1940s. Partly this is due to few people alive in Britain today having any personal experience of matters Australian dating before 1940; the experience they do have is generally of the colleague who emigrated in the 1950s or 1960s for £10. If I were optimistic I would say that the memory of Australia's convict history is a residual cultural guilty conscience, though I would have to admit there is no way of distinguishing it from a sense of British metropolitan superiority. Added to this, convicts are more colourful than emigrants, they are imagined to have been desperadoes escaping the gallows by the skin of their teeth. Those icons of emigration in the nineteenth century, the gold nuggets and the clipper ships, have more or less gone, leaving a large gap in the British popular imagination. Some people, it is true, still think of themselves as having almost mythical 'cousins' in Australia, but I would doubt that many people in Britain today know much about the scale of nineteenth-century British emigration to Australia.

For the record, there are indeed some convict diaries, though they are few on the ground, and those that do exist are largely untypical of the experience of the bulk of transportees to Australia. John Martin was an Irish political exile, one of the seven 'Young Irelanders' sentenced for their part in the uprising of 1848. He travelled as a privileged 'state prisoner' from Ireland on board the convict ship *Mountstuart Elphinstone* in 1849, and his diary, held in the Public Record Office in Northern Ireland, is worth reading for an insight into the mind of an unrepentant Irish nationalist: '*Sunday July 8* Anniversary of my arrest for felony. Also of O'Dogherty's. Celebrated it at dinner with the help of our modicum of Sherry, which the Captain sends us down on Sundays. Success to Felony! with one whole heart.' There is also the diary of another convicted Irish nationalist, the Fenian Denis Cashman, convicted for treason after the rebellion of 1867 and transported to Western Australia on board the *Hougoumont*; his diary is held in the State Archives of Western Australia, and extracts have been published in Bryce Moore's *The Voyage Out*. But neither diarist can be considered a typical transportee. John Martin was a privileged 'state prisoner' being shipped to Hobart almost ten years after transportation to the main convict destination, New South Wales, had ceased in 1840; and Denis Cashman, another political exile, was travelling on the very last convict ship to any destination in Australia. John Ward's diary for 1841–2 in the National Library of Australia is written by a less privileged transportee, but his account of the voyage out was written after the voyage, and it would surely have been almost impossible to secure either the conditions or the materials for keeping such a diary. If the diary by the convict William Noah on board the *Hillsborough* in 1798–9, listed in Ian Nicholson's *Log of Logs*, is indeed what it seems to be, then it is very rare indeed. This scarcity of convict diaries may also owe something to the level of literacy of the average transportee, though I would guess that a surprising number of the convicts would have been literate enough to have written one, and basic literacy among convicts was higher than might have been expected, as Captain Forbes, the guard commander on the *Guildford*, recorded in his shipboard diary of 1827: 'I observed to day that *every one of the convict boys* can read – So much for the education of the lower orders – It speaks volumes & no doubt future convict ships will owe a great part of their cargo to lessons imbibed at the glorious about-to-be College of Stinkomalee' (22 April 1827). We do not have to know the precise reference here to understand the tenor of Captain Forbes's remarks.

But the size of transportation is tiny compared to the scale of free emigration to Australia. The British government began assisted migration schemes to New South Wales and Van Diemen's Land in 1831 and already by the late 1830s free emigration had overtaken the numbers of transportees, despite the number of transportees itself increasing during this period; between 1835 and 1839, there were about 40,000 free emigrants compared to about 25,000 convicts (Harper 37; Robson 170). Thereafter, while transportation was scaled down during the 1840s, the discovery of gold in 1851 dramatically increased the influx of free migrants, with the population of Victoria expanding sevenfold from 77,345 in 1851 to 540,322 in 1861 (Rickard 35). In total, the number of convict arrivals in Australia from the first fleet in 1788 to the end of all transportation in 1868 was about 163,000 (Borrie 119); the official figure for free arrivals in Australia from the United Kingdom up to 1880 was about 1.3 million (Harper 37), or eight times the size of transportation. Not all of these free arrivals remained in Australia, and the scale of return migration from Australia to Europe is only now being fully recognised (see Richards 'Return Migration'), but if those making the voyage out were not necessarily going to remain in Australia, they were not necessarily going to return to Europe either, and the figure of 1.3 million does indicate the sheer volume of passengers who, on the whole, were prepared to make the extraordinarily long and arduous journey to Australia as potential emigrants.

Introduction

Emigration to Australia was part of a mass migration from Europe which was without precedent in human history. The Irish potato famine of the late 1840s accelerated what was already a growing migration from Ireland, forcing hundreds of thousands of starving men and women to seize the opportunity to flee their native lands, most of them finding a refuge of sorts in the United States. Thereafter, further dislocation of the poor through population growth, changes in rural society, industrialisation, religious persecution, and war contributed to the mass emigration of tens of millions of people from all over Europe. Dudley Baines, in the best survey of this migration from Europe, estimates that up to 60 million people left Europe in the period 1815 to 1930 (Baines 7–8). Mass migration might well have passed Australia by had not the discovery of gold in Victoria in 1851, coupled with colonial and British government schemes for assisted migration, attracted a significant proportion at the right moment; had there been no immigration after 1840, relying on only natural growth Australia's population a century later in 1940 could have been as small as one million, a seventh of its actual size (Baines 64). As it was, passenger arrivals between 1815 and 1930 were in the order of 3.5 million, and if the majority of these were British and Irish, there was also significant immigration from other European countries; in the nineteenth century Australia benefited from each of the European migrant populations, attracting in particular Germans, Scandinavians, and Italians.

Of the 1.3 million people who made the long voyage out from ports in the United Kingdom before 1880, most were conveyed by sailing ship. Steam power operated much earlier on the Atlantic crossing from Europe to North America, ousting sail as the main carrier by the mid-1860s, but the available technology did not allow the steam 'auxiliaries' to make the much longer voyage to Australia without frequent coaling stops and a heavy reliance on sail. Although the SS *Great Britain* made thirty-two trips to Australia between 1852 and 1876, the 1850s and 1860s were the years of the celebrated clipper ships. Only a minority of emigrants travelled on the most famous of these, ships such as the *Lightning*, the *Red Jacket*, and the *Marco Polo*, and many would have travelled on much slower types of sailing ship, an often voiced source of complaint by those who sailed on them: 'When I come home I will take care it shall be in a steamer, or at least in a clipper, not in such a tub as this, that can not beat to windward, more than an old water cask' (Edwin Pegler 7 Aug. 1852). But if to sail on a famous ship was the luck of only the few, the publicity surrounding the record-breaking runs of the fastest clippers was an indication of how strongly emigration to Australia had caught the public's attention. It was not until the late 1870s and the development of vastly more efficient engines that steam replaced sail on the Australian run.

Prior to the 1850s it was common for ships sailing to Australia to stop en route for water and provisions, and many passengers were thankful for the break made at Cape Town. But for most of those travelling out by sail during the period of mass migration, the voyage was made non-stop. In the 1870s and with the increase in the use of steamships, not only was the voyage reduced to a series of hops from one coaling station to another, ships could take advantage of the far shorter route via the Suez Canal which had been opened in 1869. In the later years of the nineteenth century, the experience of making the voyage by steamer became quite different from the experience of those who went by sail, as one passenger by sail noted: 'Three months at sea . . . welded us into a community. The passengers did not spend their time counting the days to the next port, as passengers on a steamer do. They settled down to a daily round' (in Woolcock 88). But the rush for gold after its discovery in 1851 meant that, from the early 1850s, sailing ships to Australia made the voyage not only without a stop but usually entirely out of sight of land. Ships from Britain sailed south for the Canary Islands and the Cape Verde Islands off the west coast of Africa, and then sought the northeast trade winds to take them across the Atlantic in the direction of Brazil, passing through the equator and the notorious calms of the doldrums on the way. Once in the latitude of Rio de Janeiro, they swung southeast in search of westerly winds that would carry them in a huge arc, the so-called Great Circle, down towards the icebergs of the Antarctic and then back up to Australia, passing several hundred miles south of the Cape of Good Hope. The clipper ships could make the voyage out in sixty or seventy days, but some of the older ships, lacking their speed, took twice as long, and the average time an emigrant in a sailing ship of the period spent at sea was about one hundred days. After three months out of sight of land, emigrants were immensely grateful to the continent of Australia just for being there. As Andrew Hamilton put it in 1852: 'Right glad to have the prospect of soon setting foot again on "terra firma" after 90 days confinement on board the "Birmingham", and never having had the satisfaction of seeing land from [the] time we lost sight of the Welsh coast till we got the first glimpse of this far-off world' (9 Oct.).

The cheapest way of travelling to Australia in the nineteenth century

Introduction

was by steerage, at least as a fare-paying passenger; a few single men
either stowed away or worked their passage out as members of the crew.
Possibly less than one in ten emigrants were able to afford the relative
luxury of travelling in a first, second, or even an intermediate class
cabin; in the twelve years from 1843 to 1854, the annual reports of the
Colonial Land and Emigration Commissioners (CLEC) show that only 6
per cent of passengers travelled cabin class, though the figure had risen
to 18 per cent for the years 1876–86. Fares varied during the period of
free migration, most dramatically in the gold rush of the 1850s when
the steerage rate rose from £10 in 1851 to as high as £26 before falling
to £23 in 1853 (*Annual Report of the CLEC* 1854), but as a guideline, a
first-class cabin cost something like three times more than a steerage
passage, say £45 as against £15. With a wage level in England and Wales
of around 10 shillings (£0.50) per week for an agricultural labourer in
the mid-nineteenth century, it is surprising that so many managed to
find even the minimum fare.

Of course, many emigrants had what in effect were free passages, and
one estimate suggests that 45 per cent of free arrivals in Australia before
1900 were assisted (Borrie 121). However, assisted emigrants usually
still had to make some contribution; depending on the scheme under
which they travelled, they might have to pay for their fare to the
emigration depot, supply themselves with the regulation outfit for the
voyage, and contribute towards the cost of their bedding and utensils on
board ship. Their total contribution might in this way equal or even
exceed the fare to America (Richards 'British Poverty and Australian
Immigration' 13). As was intended, this was enough to prevent at least
some of the poorest potential emigrants from travelling; Catherine
Burke, for example, tried to arrange for her brother and sister to join
her in Sydney, but her mother had to write to say they were unable to
travel for want of the fare from Ireland to England: 'Your Kindness was
Intended to Have your Brother Thomas & Sister Margret out to you But
oh alas they were Not able to go as far as England for they had Not any
cost to Bring them there' (letter 28 Nov. 1853; in Fitzpatrick 'Over the
Foaming Billows' 142). Official discouragement of the very poor meant
that those who did get to Australia were arguably more entrepreneurial
than those who remained at home, either because they were already
better off or because they could get to Australia despite their poverty, as
David Fitzpatrick has suggested ('Over the Foaming Billows' 145). This
can be further supported by the numbers who arrived in Australia
unassisted. After the discovery of gold in 1851, the majority of

immigrants arriving in Australia from Europe were no longer those assisted emigrants carefully selected for their potential as wage-earners or childbearers, but those prepared to speculate, or able to persuade others to speculate, on their fortune. One estimate suggests that two out of three immigrants in the 1850s were self-financing (Richards 'Annals of the Australian Immigrant' 16).

Emigrants from outside the United Kingdom were largely excluded from British government schemes for assisted passages, though some colonial schemes were aimed at attracting other nationals. In 1861, almost a tenth of immigrants to Australia were from outside the United Kingdom (Williams 188), and the two main groups in the nineteenth century were the Chinese and the Germans. The Chinese began arriving in Australia in the late 1840s as indentured agricultural labourers, but the discovery of gold led to a much larger number travelling from China; China was closer to Australia than Europe and steamships operated relatively cheaply out of European trading posts like Hong Kong and Guangzhou (Canton) (Williams 194). By the end of the 1850s there were around 40,000 Chinese in Australia, accounting for twenty per cent of the male population of Victoria in 1859 (Rickard 39); but because it was almost exclusively male the Chinese population was not sustainable, and as the gold became harder to retrieve and colonial legislation was introduced to discriminate against the Chinese, some returned to China and the number fell.

German emigrants first arrived in 1836, Lutherans emigrating to South Australia to avoid religious persecution in Prussia. 1848, the year of widespread political disturbance in Europe, saw many Germans of mainly Wendish origins follow, and coupled with those who came in search of gold, the German population of Australia grew from just over 5,000 in 1851 to nearly 27,000 in 1861 (Williams 189). After 1861, Queensland had a scheme to recruit farmers from Germany and this was enough to keep the numbers of German-born in Australia fairly constant until the end of the century when emigration from Germany ceased (Williams 199).

Once the extent of the cultural diversity of immigration into Australia in the nineteenth century is grasped it becomes problematic to talk in terms of the typical immigrant. Even among emigrants from the United Kingdom there was a sometimes-forgotten cultural diversity, and because of the homogenising power of greater mobility and the media in the twentieth century, differences within the United Kingdom were far greater in the nineteenth century than they are today: 'We have several Companies of Singers on board but cannot amalgamate on account of our several dialects English Welsh Scotch Irish & German' (William Thompson 12 July 1857). There was no typical emigrant. Some emigrants travelled in cabins, some travelled in steerage; some were assisted, some were self-financing; some came from the United Kingdom, others came from mainland Europe and Asia; some were men, some were women. Yet it is all too easy to overlook this diversity because a number of factors have combined to silence certain voices and give undue prominence to the voices of others; and one of the most frustrating barriers for any researcher interested in looking at the diversity of immigration is the class, sex, and ethnic bias of the archives.

The comparatively small number of diaries in the archives is both a cause and an effect of bias. The National Library of Australia in Canberra (the archive I know best) has copies of around 100 diaries of the voyage out relating to nineteenth-century emigration by sail. It is clear from the accounts themselves that diary writing was a widespread custom: for those literate enough it was part of the experience of emigrating, and several cases have been recorded by Marsha Donaldson of diaries being written on board ship on behalf of less literate passengers; Alfred Craymer, for example, helped write one for Mary Anne Smith, as he recorded in his own diary: '[The boatswain] asked me to do it so far, so with his aid and Watters I set to work and concocted the most absurd thing I ever saw, one or two remarks in it were to the effect that . . . we had seen several large fish called albatross . . . and several birds called porpoises, these and other absurdities formed her interesting diary which she probably has sent home' (in Marsha Donaldson 92). Given this imperative to keep a diary, if almost 1.3 million emigrants left the United Kingdom for Australia under sail, the National Library's figure of 100 diaries seems modest indeed. Of course the collections of the National Library are relatively modern compared with those of the major State Libraries of New South Wales, South Australia, and Victoria, and a certain lack of depth or even representativeness can be expected. Yet the entries in the two volumes of Nicholson's *Log of Logs* suggest that the collections in the state libraries are not vastly stronger, the Mitchell, the Mortlock, and the La Trobe libraries having about 125, 100, and 160 diaries repectively. In addition, the National Library's Historic Records Search, made at the time of the Australian Bicentenary in 1988, located only 105 shipboard diaries still in private hands. If we include diaries known to be held in Britain and those that have been published, the total number of known diaries still hovers only around 850. Some diaries have slipped through the net, two or three in private hands have recently been mentioned to me, but unless there are thousands in various drawers and attics that have not been brought to light by the Historic Records Search (as some researchers still optimistically believe), then we have diaries for only seven in every ten thousand emigrants under sail, which in any estimate must be only a tiny proportion of the diaries which were once written.

The main reason for the loss of diaries will have been the material deterioration of the paper, and many of the diaries still in existence are in a fragile condition. Notebooks in the nineteenth century were not designed to last a century and a half. Yet this deterioration of the diaries would presumably have affected all diaries, and it is clearly not the sole reason for the class, gender, and ethnic bias in the archive collections. We can guess (though it is no more than a guess) that over nine out of ten emigrants travelled steerage, and yet the accounts of the voyage left in the national and state archives are predominantly by those affluent enough to travel out by cabin. Of the 100 diaries of the voyage out by sail in the National Library that I have read, only 29 were written by steerage passengers; the figures for cabin diaries are 43 first class, 9 second class, and 5 intermediate cabin. Again, although detailed lists are not available for the other archives, it is clear that most of the diaries were written by cabin passengers, and if we apply the ratio found in the National Library, there may well be less than 300 steerage diaries in the Australian archives as a whole.

This bias in favour of middle-class accounts is the result of a number of overlapping factors, the low number of diaries surviving being only one. Most obviously working people were less literate because as children of working parents they were not provided with the degree of schooling given by middle-class parents to their children; the income was not available in working-class households to send sons away to school or to provide daughters with governesses, while the pressure in low-income households was for the children to take paid work at the earliest possible age. Yet figures for literacy among assisted passengers of the 1850s show a surprisingly high proportion who were literate: 81 per cent of the Scots, 72 per cent of the English and Welsh, and 49 per cent of the Irish could both read and write (Jupp 765). This does not mean all had the degree of literacy required to keep a sustained account like a diary, and where it is possible to identify the occupation of the diarist, steerage diaries by males seem to have been written mostly by, to use the contemporary term, 'mechanicals,' skilled workers like blacksmiths, carpenters, plumbers, or bootmakers who had undergone an apprenticeship and were more likely to be fully literate. Such working men comprised about 19 per cent of adult males entering Australia from the United Kingdom between 1854 and 1876, and if they were not such a large group as either the agricultural labourers (26 per cent) or general labourers (37 per cent), groups that may have been less literate overall than the skilled mechanicals, the mechanicals were a larger group than those in middle-class occupations (13 per cent) (figures based on Sherington 76). This finding is at odds with David Vincent's finding that of the 142 working-class autobiographies he examined, only a quarter of the autobiographers had served apprentice-ships, but both reinforce my argument that, although conditions in steerage accommodation were not conducive to diary-writing, in abso-lute terms working-class emigrants as a whole would have written more diaries than middle-class emigrants.

The greater loss of working-class diaries can be explained, though again only partly, by the mobility of the emigrants once they arrived. Immigrants characteristically moved several times during their lives in Australia, and the journey to Australia can be regarded as only one (and probably not the first) of a series of moves (Jupp 386); even skilled workers, the artisans, had probably made many moves in their home country in search of work before emigrating (Vincent 69). Such mobility meant there was a greater chance of a diary being mislaid, and it might easily have been dropped from a bullock dray or left in a tent on the gold fields. The survival of many diaries of whatever type depended on chance. Mary Maclean's diary of 1864 was found accidentally by Mr Steven Cross in 1960 in a writing desk in a derelict cottage in New South Wales. Henry Curr's diary was sent back by mail to his brother-in-law but went down with the *Royal Charter* off the north Wales coast in 1859 (459 passengers and a fortune in gold were also lost); the diary was salvaged along with some other mail, partially copied in various hands, the original lost, and the incomplete copy posted back to a descendant in Western Australia in 1955. The diary of William Reay written in 1877 returned probably by mail to England, crossed the Atlantic to Canada in the possession of one family member, went south to the United States in the possession of another, and finally returned to Australia where it is now deposited in the National Library. These last two examples suggest, however, that it was not only the living condi-tions of the immigrant diarists themselves that determined whether or not a diary might survive; the conditions of the family to which copies of the diaries were customarily sent was equally important. The factors which led to emigration probably also displaced many of the households left behind, and diaries are more likely to be retained by generations of descendants who are relatively static. Working-class households in the nineteenth century were in general more mobile than middle-class households, and the loss of working-class diaries would have been proportionately greater.

This bias against steerage diaries also involves the archives themselves which, at least until recently, may well have seen less value in steerage diaries; not only were the diarists as individuals lost to history, they were simply less literate. The vocabulary, the syntax, and the range of expression is, generally speaking, more restricted than diaries kept by cabin passengers, and we are only now coming to realise the value of the voices that have been written-out of history. If diaries kept by working people are different from those kept by the middle classes, the difference reflects a different attitude to, and a different function of, the diary. Steerage diaries seem less literary because their flowing and unbroken syntax is an attempt to capture a conversational speaking voice rather than to construct a sophisticated alternative.

The gender bias of the archives is probably more acute than the class bias and my own experience is that women's diaries account for only 14 per cent. This imbalance is harder to explain than the class imbalance of the archives. Some of the factors applying to the lack of steerage diaries apply here, and women as a group have been written-out of emigration history until fairly recently; unless they belonged to women like Caroline Chisholm or Maria Rye who initiated emigration schemes, women's voices were rarely acknowledged by the agents of emigration. Yet this deafness itself would not have prevented women writing diaries home to family and friends. Women do not seem to have been markedly more illiterate than men in the mid-nineteenth century (Schofield), and I find it hard to explain satisfactorily the scale of the gender imbalance. David Vincent has noted a similar absence of women's voices in working-class autobiographies written during the first half of the nineteenth century, an absence he accounts for partly by a lack of self-confidence among women and partly by the position of women within the working-class household: 'The husband was the head of the family and as such thought to be responsible for communicating its history to future generations' (9). Perhaps the same applied at sea, and there is some evidence that, while women wrote letters, it was the men

who saw themselves as chroniclers for future generations and persevered with diaries. Jane Cannan noted in a letter that her husband
David 'has been writing something like a journal at the rate of a page
every few days – but I have written nothing yet and so kept to my
intention of writing once a month' (2 June 1853). And according to
Charles Bolton, his wife Mary had been 'looking over my diary to call up
the events of the voyage to fill her letters with' (17 May 1872).

The situation with regard to diaries kept by women steerage passengers is therefore doubly acute. Official figures place the balance of male
to female emigrants to Australia for the thirty years 1843 to 1872 at ten
males for every eight females, the actual number of females being
335,723 (*Annual Reports of the CLEC*). Most of these would have
travelled out by steerage as assisted passengers. But in the National
Library of Australia there are only two diaries by women travelling
steerage, the diary of Annie Gratton, who was evidently an educated
woman travelling out alone in 1858 to join her fiancé, and the diary of
Elizabeth Allbon, a working women who sailed in 1879 with her husband and four children. Although there are proportionately more diaries by women travelling out in cabin accommodation, the experiences
and voices of women travelling steerage have been almost totally lost to
us today.

The other main bias of the archives is the bias towards British
emigrants. In 1871, 6.3 per cent of the Australian population (over
100,000 people) were migrants from outside the United Kingdom
(Williams 188), yet their accounts of the voyage are proportionately
nowhere near this. Chinese immigration can perhaps be justifiably
treated separately because of the radically different culture and because
Chinese immigrants did not travel in the same ships as European
migrants (for a fictional Chinese immigrant's diary see Brian Castro's
Birds of Passage). But accounts in European languages other than
English are hard to locate. The National Library of Australia has a diary
for a voyage in 1863 written by an anonymous French visitor on the SS
Great Britain, and the Mitchell Library, Sydney, has a shipboard diary
in German for 1839, the diary of Wilhelm Kirchner on the *Mary*. A
survey in the 1970s revealed only three other shipboard diaries in
German (Fletcher 37), and although Nicholson lists four more, sur-
prisingly there are none in the John Oxley Library, Brisbane, despite
German migration being centred in Queensland in the second half of
the nineteenth century. Accounts in European languages other than
English have clearly not found their way into the official archives in the

numbers we might have expected. Even the English-speaking Irish have been denied a true representation, their effacement being reinforced by the tendency of commentators to use the terms British and Britain as though they included the Irish and Ireland. Some 400,000 migrants, one quarter of all assisted immigrants arriving in Australia during the nineteenth century, were Irish (Richards 'British Poverty and Australian Immigration' 2), and yet in the National Library I found only a handful of diaries by Irish emigrants, and all of them copies of diaries held in the Public Record Office in Northern Ireland.

The situation that results is all too familiar. The archives are dominated by the accounts of affluent Englishmen mainly of the middle classes who travelled to Australia in first-class accommodation. The political and cultural dominance of this privileged social group, even if the individuals concerned were not the most influential members of their social group, has understandably led to its dominance of history and historical sources. One way of allowing other voices to be heard is to concentrate solely on those previously marginalised, as in David Fitzpatrick's forthcoming study of letters by Irish migrants, *Oceans of Consolation*, or my own forthcoming collection of steerage diaries, *No Privacy for Writing*. This is not without its problems since we are dealing with what is by definition a small sample; if the voices of marginalised groups have in the past been suppressed, those that by chance remain have to stand as representative for the many. The range is lost and the conclusions more tentative. The collections of women's writings by Lucy Frost and by Patricia Clarke and Dale Spender are still dominated by socially privileged women of the middle classes.

It may well be that the problems of the archives are being compounded by the way we read the material they contain. The other way of trying to counter the bias of the archives, and the one adopted in this study, is to try to read diaries by the socially dominant group against the grain. This covers more of the available diaries than the preceding option, but the assumption that because there are more diaries by male cabin passengers their experience holds for all emigrants is countered by readings that expose the partiality of their accounts. This type of re-reading is easier to state than to enact, but it involves looking at what the diaries say and relating what the diaries say to their function at any particular moment. For example, when a cabin passenger records the name of those at the captain's table, this is not merely for information but a way of reinforcing social divisions; a similar strategy is not available to steerage passengers since the size of their social group on board ship is much larger. Again there are problems, and it is difficult to keep halting the development of an argument to remind the reader that what is being argued may not apply to all social groups; and it is perhaps harder to keep reminding oneself of it, particularly where a pattern can be discerned in a number of diaries, yet none of them are by women and/or steerage passengers. There are gaps in the evidence that it is not always possible to fill. The best we can do in such circumstances is to keep our ears open and hope that someone who is being excluded will speak up and make her or himself heard; in such cases, I have adopted a policy of positive discrimination and included them.

A note on quotations from the diaries

The diaries in the archives exist as manuscripts or typescripts. All were originally written by hand but not all copies are the originals. Descendants of the diarists have occasionally made handwritten copies where the original is perhaps held by a relative; the manuscript of Annie Gratton's diary is a copy made forty years later in 1898 by Charles Wilson, her 'eldest surviving son'. Sometimes descendants make a transcription in typescript rather than in manuscript. Researchers like myself are extremely pleased to find copies of these transcripts deposited in the archives, both because they are more legible and can be scanned quickly for relevance, and because archivists are more willing to photocopy loose leaves than bound volumes. In other cases, the typescript may be a draft made by a professional researcher for publication, as in the diary of Jessie Campbell deposited in the National Maritime Museum in London by Basil Greenhill; and when such diaries are published, the published versions also find their way into the archives.

The range of forms these diaries take makes it impossible to guarantee the accuracy of a large proportion of the diaries as they exist today. Transcribers may misread a word or phrase (in one memorable case, a passenger was said to have 'read something of German Philosophy and met a physical writer'); common enough is the omission of a line as the eye moves down the page. Transcribers may decide (how dare they) to turn a rich dialect into standard English; or if they are professional editors, they may adjust spelling and grammar to conventional usage under pressure from their publishers. Where practicable, I have checked quotations taken from transcripts with the source document. However, given that many of the 'original' diaries are themselves copies made by the diarist either to send home or to keep, there seems to be no point in becoming overly obsessed with the accuracy of the copy being dealt with. The only guarantee I make is that the quotations as they appear here have been rigorously checked against their source whether in manuscript or typescript.

Standardising the quotations would have made them easier to read but at the loss of the voice of the diarist. Since many of the diarists were unused to writing prose of any length, they often tried to reproduce the spoken voice using a phonetic spelling and unpunctuated syntax, and it is this spoken voice that too often is edited away. Alternatively, to have peppered the diaries with the correct word or phrase in brackets seemed a similarly unwarranted interference, patronising to both diarist and reader. In any case, where a word is not spelt conventionally, it may nonetheless have had currency in that form among a particular community. 'Has' for 'as' is reasonably common in nineteenth-century diaries of working-class emigrants originating from the London area: 'Got up and had our breakfast   made a very good one has it had to carry us till night (G. Annison 20 May 1853); 'what a beautiful sight I had has the sun went down' (Thomas Davies 22 July 1854). Its reverse, 'as' for 'has,' is also occasionally used: 'no light as been seen' (J.P. Ricou 23 June 1872). Of course, no typed transcription can reproduce a manuscript, and there are features of the diaries that are inevitably lost when they are typed out: diarists sometimes use the edges of the pages as punctuation, a new line beginning a new train of thought; and the widespread use of an intermediate form between a lower case and a capital letter is impossible to reproduce. Every transcription is an interpretation.

I have, however, made two main concessions to readability. First, I have not attempted to reproduce the long 's' that looks similar to an 'f' and was used for the first 's' of a double 's'; judging from the diaries, this was standard usage until the mid-nineteenth century and continued at least until its end. To replace it with an 'f' as in 'pafsenger' looks silly. Second, I have adopted the practice used by Lucy Frost of placing additional spaces where the diarist might have used a punctuation mark. Full stops and commas are rarely used, some diarists preferring a liberal sprinkling of dashes, others omitting all forms of punctuation except capital letters for substantives. The use of additional spaces is a minimal intervention in the text and considerably increases readability. No additional interventions are necessary where my source is a modernised transcript.

Introduction

I have also occasionally made interventions in square brackets within the quotations. This will usually be where the word is not easy to guess (say, 'shemees' for chemise) or where I am uncertain of a word, though I sometimes insert what I think has been left out by the slip of a pen. The context should make plain my reasons for intervening. On the whole, though, I have preferred not to intervene, leaving the diary as I found it and trusting to the intelligence and indulgence of my reader.

Chapter 1

Writing a diary

'I have written this journal more for the sake of occupying my mind than with the anticipation that it will afford any gratification or amusement to my friends'

When Edwin Francis, an eighteen-year-old shoemaker from the west of England, sailed on board the *Clara Symes* from Bristol on 16 October 1852, he took with him a notebook, intending to write up every day the events of the long voyage to Australia. Edwin Francis had never been to sea before and like the majority of the million or so emigrants who left for Australia by sail in the nineteenth century, he was soon struck down by seasickness in the choppy waters of the Bay of Biscay: 'I wished my self back in old England again It was my first experance of Sea life.' For several days he lay on a damp bed in wet clothes unable to eat, and it was almost a week before his appetite returned sufficiently for him to take his first food, some half-cooked rice: 'It was very acceptable.' By 23 October, a week after setting sail, he felt well enough to keep his diary, and he began carefully to write-up the first few days of the voyage. Then, after only three entries, the diary abruptly ends.

Very few incomplete diaries of the voyage out exist today, presumably because the diarists themselves felt them not worth retaining; the book could be broken up and the pages used for letters. But Edwin Francis held on to his diary for another sixty-two years, and in January 1915, three months after his eightieth birthday, he resumed his account of the voyage out. In a hand shaky with age, Edwin starts by explaining why his sea diary had been left unfinished: 'I intended to have entered the events of each day of our voyage but I found it impossible There was no privacy for writing.' Having shared his quarters with fifteen other single young men, he had evidently been derided for trying to write a diary: 'several of them were very unruly & disagreble I atempted to write but them come & look at what you were doeing.' First seasickness prevented him writing, then his shipmates.

In his continuation of the diary, Edwin Francis does not mention why, after more than sixty years, he has taken out his old book and written up the voyage. But the very act of preserving his diary through all the disruptions of his early life in Australia, through his life under canvas in Melbourne, his bootmaking businesses in Sydney, and his years on the New England goldfields, is evidence of the importance he attached to the book. Possibly there was some sentimental attachment to the book itself as an object brought with him from 'old England', but the desire to write in it and complete the account of the voyage out is the same that prompted him to begin it in the first place: a desire to give a durable form to the defining experience of an emigrant, the journey from the old life to the new. While the interruption of the diary after only three days is testimony to the difficulties under which diaries of the voyage out were kept, its completion sixty-two years later is testimony to the power and endurance of the emigrant's need to put the voyage into writing.

*

For a significant number of the emigrants their diary must have represented the longest piece of prose they wrote in their lives. In an age before telephones, many of the diarists would have been used to writing letters or notes to friends and family as a matter of routine, and individual entries of the diary, written from day to day, are comparable in length to a short letter. But even discounting obstacles such as the rolling and pitching of the ship, the dimness of the lanterns below deck, and the unruly behaviour of one's companions, great commitment would have been needed to sustain a diary over a voyage lasting three or more months. Once the routine of life at sea had been established and the strangeness of the environment had worn off, it was not easy to generate something new to write about every day for each of the hundred days of an average voyage. Fifteen-year-old Arthur Clarke, travelling out with his mother and brother in 1868, speaks for many of the emigrant diarists: 'There was nothing in particular to write about either yesterday or the day before, as, indeed, there is not today' (17 Oct. 1868).

Even the short diaries are around five thousand words long, and the lengthier diaries are well over twenty thousand words and run to two or three hundred pages. These are substantial books. Indeed, the materiality of these diaries as books is a central factor in explaining why so many emigrants kept them. Diaries as a form of writing have the great disadvantage of being potentially open-ended, and few who start one know exactly where it will end. Not many people live such well-ordered lives that their diary follows a complete narrative. More often, diaries begin and end unpredictably. But for the emigrant diarist, the voyage can be seen as a single event that can be neatly recorded between two covers. There had to be the desire to write the diary, there had to be some content to write about, but what was so attractive to emigrants was that, like all good stories, a journey has a beginning and an end. Emigrant diarists were writing the book of the voyage.

The books in which they kept their diaries varied considerably. The diaries are mostly written in blank notebooks, but these range from imposing, vellum-covered tomes to slim and inexpensive school exercise books. Emigrants used pocketbooks, memorandum books, account books, and order books. The pre-printed Letts diaries, first printed in 1812, were not widely used among emigrants, probably because the practised diarist might write entries of varying length, but also because of the comparatively high price: few emigrants of whatever social status had cash to spare. Moreover, in the case of yearly diaries, if the voyage extended into a new year, a second volume would have been needed. Very few of the diaries take up more than a single volume. Exceptions are those accounts usually kept by highly literate men and women who have had a lifetime's habit of diary-keeping and whose record of the voyage out may span two or more in a sequence of diaries; Oswald Bloxsome's illustrated account of his voyage in 1838 filled two volumes. More often the handwriting in a diary will get progressively smaller as the diarist begins to realise that the voyage may not fit a single volume. The 132-page notebook that S. E. Roberts took with him in 1848 would have seemed long enough for his diary, but the voyage lasted for 146 days, fifty days longer than Roberts may have expected, and his diary is squeezed into the last available space, the final entry extending in tiny writing from the back cover onto the front inside cover. The anonymous male diarist on the *Calphurnia* in 1853 is one of the few who clearly ran out of space, probably because he used his diary also as a commonplace book, and he had to continue in a separate notebook; as the second is a different type of book to the first, it is likely he too thought one notebook would be enough and that he had to purchase another on board ship.

On the whole, diaries of the voyage out are just that, a single volume dealing only with the voyage out. The volume typically opens with the sailing of the ship and ends with disembarkation in Australia, rarely extending beyond a few days on land. On arrival, diarists either began a new diary or gave up keeping one altogether; the lack of diaries covering the first few months in Australia suggests that most gave up, possibly in favour of writing letters as letters required less of a daily commitment. Where the diaries do continue for any length of time, it is often because the diarist envisages staying in Australia for only a short period. Thomas Miller made a voyage to Australia at the age of twenty in 1869–70 and kept a diary covering the voyage out, the two months he spent in Australia, and the return voyage. Duncan McDonald made the voyage to visit his daughter and youngest son in 1871 and kept a similar account of his visit. In cases like this, where the diarist is only visiting Australia, the diary is framed by leaving Britain and arriving back. Alf Evans sailed out to Fremantle in 1895 in order to complete a job contract, and his account covers four pocketbooks, the first giving an account of the voyage out, the last an account of the voyage home. For emigrants, however, whose journey, unlike those of the temporary visitors, was probably to be one-way only, the story their diary tells is the shorter one, that of their voyage out.

*

Probably about half of the emigrant diaries that survive in manuscript today are fair copies. Rough diaries were kept during the voyage but it was a widespread custom to transcribe the diary into a new notebook in order to send a copy home. Sometimes the copying was done towards the end of the voyage. Henry Whittingham began nine days before he reached Sydney: 'On Saturday I commenced copying out my Diary, or notes therefrom, for family & friends in England' (9 May 1853). More often, the diary was copied on arrival. Occasionally two versions have survived, as with the 1875 diary of Alfred Charlesworth, and there are three versions of the opening pages of William Forwood's diary of 1857. As these examples show, copies will not always be exact transcriptions, though unless two versions exist side-by-side it is sometimes difficult to decide whether we are dealing with a fair copy or not.

As a rule of thumb, a diary actually written at sea is in uneven handwriting, and the rolling of the ship in a calm sea could make writing almost as difficult as writing in a gale, as David Cannan noted in a letter to his mother: 'I had a mistaken notion that a calm at sea would be pleasant, it is quite the reverse because then the ship rolls most as the sea rolls just like a carpet waves when the wind blows in under it' (6 July 1853). As David goes on to point out, the best conditions for writing were when the ship was running before a moderate wind. The handwriting in these rough diaries reflects the uneven movement of the ship, as diarists themselves frequently noted: 'The ship is rolling much so I cannot guide the pen comfortably' (Robert Saddington 6 Sept. 1853). Other indicators of a rough copy are errors of spelling or grammar crossed through, notes made at the back of the book recording letters sent and money spent, and the change of handwriting from one entry to the next. Fountain pens were not much used before the 1880s, and if the diarist did not use a pencil, he or she would have to try to cope with pen and ink bottle, as William Chambers did in 1879 when he was working his way out as a steward on board the sailing ship *Sobraon*: 'I am compelled to hold the ink in my hand while writing this, for the ship is rolling heavily, so I will now go to bed, but to get sleep is a thing impossible' (16 Nov. 1879).

Fair copies, by contrast, are generally written in an even hand throughout, and often contain references within them that make it clear they have been written at a later date. Hindsight sometimes creeps in, as happened in the copying of John Carter's diary of 1844: 'Tuesday November 19th. A small land bird was caught & another was seen on the ship. When a bird or fish was caught the interest it occasioned was always very great.' The voyage was over when this last sentence was written. In making the copy, the diarist might inadvertently copy a phrase twice or even reverse the order of a couple of daily entries. Henry Whittingham's diary of 1853 records that he first used pen and ink two weeks into the voyage, yet the previous entries are not written in pencil but ink. Despite the passage I quoted above, the steady handwriting in William Chambers's diary suggests that it too is a copy.

Great care and patience was often devoted to the presentation of fair copies. They were given elaborate title pages that imitated the title page of a printed book even to the printer's name. James Espie White's rewritten diary has one of the more self-consciously imitative title pages:

JOURNAL
— or —
A BRIEF NARRATION
of the principal events which occurred on board the
'HENRY FERNIE'
On her voyage to Australia.

Writing a diary

By
J. ESPIE WHITE L.P.
Author of such and such a work, & such another
work. & all the rest of his works
etc. etc etc.

———

In which is added
AN APPENDIX.
Containing no Copious Notes.

———

FIRST AND LAST EDITION.

———

Published at South Yarra, Victoria, Aust.

In addition to title pages, diaries would imitate printed books by having page numbers, contents pages, and indexes. Many contain illustrations, usually in pen and ink but sometimes in watercolours. In the mid-nineteenth century, the written word was held in great esteem by the dominant middle-class culture; the ability to write was regarded as a mark of education, and the possession of books defined the cultured from the uncultured. Prestige was attached to the book as a cultural artifact, and attempts by the diarists to present their diaries as books reflects a desire to give them an appropriate durable form. They were treasured objects intended to be preserved, and to the degree that they now reside in archives, this was an aspiration they achieved. Of course, the range of sophistication of these books varies considerably, depending very largely on the competence of the diarist; but even an ornamented title at the start of the first page is enough to signal the cultural aspirations of the diary.

This desire to write an account of the voyage as a book is not restricted to fair copies, and some of the rough diaries kept at sea have similar aspirations. Though it runs for only three entries, the diary of the eighteen-year-old Edwin Francis has the following ornamented title page:

Journal of Edwin Francis Who was born on the 25th of October 1834 who is now about to Emigrate to Australia in serch of a better home for himself and frends his trade being a Shoemaker in the laides branch Edwin Francis being a son of the late Samuel

Francis of the parish of Stoke Somersetshire and of Ann Francis of
the same parish and County

Going by the Clara Symes
From Bristol on the 17th of
October 1852
May God preserve
Him
From Evil
Amen
Bath Somerset

Even though his diary was a rough copy, the young Edwin Francis had
clearly gone to some effort to design his title page.

Because both fair and rough copies could aspire to the prestige of the
printed book, the division between fair and rough copies is ultimately
not so very important. It is tempting to accord a greater value to those
diaries that it can be shown were actually written at sea, as though this
conferred on them a greater degree of authenticity. The ratio of rough
to fair copies is interesting as an indication of the degree to which
diaries were written up, but this division creates anomalies which
makes it unworkable as a guide to authenticity; some of the fair copies
were actually made at sea, and those that we call rough copies could
have been composed from earlier sets of notes: 'I am keeping my log on
a scrap of waste paper in hopes that more favorable weather will allow
me to make a fair copy into my book' (Thomas Bolivar Blyth 21 Sept.
1846). How fair is a fair copy? In the end, to try to rank emigrants'
diaries according to their authenticity is not only impossible, it is to
miss the point. Fair copies, when they were made, merely attest to what
is implicit in the practice of keeping a rough copy, the desire of the
diarists to present their experience as a cultural artifact, as a book of the
voyage.

*

The diary as a book of the voyage is a useful way of distinguishing diaries
of the voyage out from accounts of the voyage contained in letters. The
differences between emigrant letters and emigrant diaries are not easy
to specify formally as diaries and letters share many overlapping
features, particularly so in the eighteenth and nineteenth centuries
when journal-letters, letters written on different days over a period of
time, were used in personal correspondence. Emigrant letters are

[26]

commonly retrospective, written up after the voyage, whereas the diaries, kept at sea, are written on a daily basis without the advantages of hindsight. However, some letters were written at sea in the hope of passing a ship homeward bound, and emigrants were keen to send news home if conditions made the transfer of mail possible: 'November 4th. – Great letter writing to-day among the passengers, or more correctly speaking, great attempts at it, in consequence of a vessel being seen ahead apparently homeward bound, and the captain having consented to let us have a boat to go on board of her when we got near enough' (N. C. 1849). Unfortunately, there was no guarantee that letters once written would be sent as expected: 'November 5th. – It turns out that all our labour of yesterday was but labour in vain . . . for the vessel which we imagined was homeward bound, now turns out to have been like ourselves very nearly becalmed, and is this morning seen far away, steering the very same course with us.' On other occasions, one or other of the captains involved might refuse to lower a boat to transfer the mail, though as John MacKenzie recorded in his diary in 1841, that did not always prevent emigrants from despatching their letters:

> all that had letters ready tied a piece of coal to them to throw on board the homeward-bound ship. . . . As soon as he [the captain of the homeward-bound ship] uttered the words 'bound for Cork' a volley of coal was fired at his head with letters attached to each piece, this was succeeded by a second & third volley, on different parts of the ship, the sailors running for and aft wondering what the devil was rong & scrambling for the letters all over the deck (5 Nov. 1841)

In the absence of a suitable ship onto which to hurl coal, the letter once begun might be extended periodically over the following weeks until it became more of a journal-letter.

David Cannan began a letter to his mother on 3 July 1853, two months after leaving London. He wrote three sides of paper before concluding with: 'This is enough for one days writing.' On 6 July he wrote another side, and added a further single side on 9 July, 18 July, 11 August, and 15 August, the day that he arrived in Hobson's Bay. Reaching Melbourne the next day, he added a note in cross-hatching across the first sheet. From comments made by his wife, Jane, in a letter dated 2 June, it seems that David was also keeping a diary alongside his letters home:

[27]

My dear Jeanette
I address this letter to you that it may kill two birds with one stone
– and after being read at Ambleside – be sent on to you. David has
been writing something like a journal at the rate of a page every
few days – but I have written nothing yet and so kept to my
intention of writing once a month. Several of our people keep
diaries but I cannot imagine what they put in them.

David's letter to his mother, written on six separate days, works very
much like a diary; it is a periodic account of day-to-day life on board
ship. It is possible that he had sent back a letter earlier in the voyage
and, indeed, had there been a passing ship it is probable he would have
sent back what he had written before reaching Australia; but in its
absence he produces an account that can be read like a diary.

Yet it would be strange to allow the distinction between a letter and
diary to depend on whether or not the writer had the opportunity of
sending the account back on a passing ship. In at least one case, that of
Edward Towle travelling on the SS *Great Britain* in 1852, the reverse
case holds and what a writer describes as a diary or journal is unusually
sent back before the end of the voyage: 'As we are expecting to meet the
mail steamer from the Cape everyone is getting their letters ready and I
shall just conclude my present journal in the hope it may get off by
steamer' (3 Sept. 1852). In fact the steamer did not appear and the
journal was continued as far as the Cape and then sent back. If David
Cannan writes a letter that looks like a diary, then Edward Towle's diary
here accords with the practice of letter-writing, the difference depending on whether or not the account is posted home during the voyage.
But though it would be an interesting case to argue that both Edward
Towle and David Cannan are potentially writing a diary or a letter
depending on whether or not they can send it back before reaching
Australia, such a case disregards the fact that Edward Towle, Jane
Cannan and, presumably, David Cannan are all quite clear that a
distinction between a letter and a diary can be made.

David Cannan's letters certainly do not amount to a book of the
voyage; they are written on loose sheets of flimsy paper, and are only a
partial account of the voyage. This is not to say that all diaries were
written in books, and very occasionally we do find diaries written on
loose sheets; the anonymous female diarist on board the *Orient* in 1863
addressed a longish diary running to sixteen sides to 'My Dear Children'. Neither is it to say that letters were not also kept by their recipients

as treasured objects, nor that emigrants saw them as more ephemeral; Henry Whittingham on board the *Duke of Wellington* in 1853 kept both a diary and a letter-book into which he copied the letters sent home. Other letter-books survive, such as that of H. Harvey who sailed for Melbourne in 1867. But the letters themselves were not written as books, while some of the diaries written on loose sheets were handsewn into covers.

The basis of the distinction made by Jane Cannan between her letter and a diary is an important corollary of the diary as a book of the voyage: 'David has been writing something like a journal at the rate of a page every few days – but I have written nothing yet and so kept to my intention of writing once a month.' Her assumption is that a diary will be kept more or less daily, while her letter, written once a month, will be written less regularly. The fact that David in practice writes a letter to his mother more than once a month does not invalidate the distinction. Moreover, its reverse is reflected in the diaries. Diaries were not always written-up daily, and seasickness or stormy weather could prevent the diarist from putting pen to paper. But the diarists felt an imperative to write regularly and when gaps appeared in the diary, they drew attention to them and gave reasons why they had occurred, as indeed did the anonymous female diarist on the *Orient* whom I mentioned earlier: 'Wed June 3 [1863] I have not been able to write since Monday week, from various reasons, such as, excessive heat the Vessel tossing stormey not well, could scarcely leave my berth, but thanks we have left the Tropics, we are making but slow progress owing to contrary winds.' The assumption is that a diary should be written regularly, and even if the diary is not in practice kept regularly, the assumption that it should be is a second useful way of distinguishing between diaries and letters.

One distinction between diaries and letters that is often made today is that diaries are private and not to be shown to others. The entirely private diary was certainly a potential in the nineteenth century, and the Letts diary for 1855 suggested that the user 'conceal nothing from its pages, nor suffer any other eye than your own to scan them'. This was certainly good advice on board ship and many diarists, such as S. E. Roberts below, carefully guarded their diaries from the eyes of their fellow passengers:

We begin to find out the real characters by this time and there are some for whose honesty I would not give a button, much less for their honour, and when I get to Adelaide shall be as shy of their company as of that of the devil himself. They are – never mind till the end in case this should fall into other hands on board, and be read by other parties, then ah! crickey!! wouldn't there be a row in the ship, and would'nt poor Pill Garlic catch it? (19 July 1848)

Yet, however private they kept their diaries on board ship, many of the emigrant diaries were addressed like letters to specific individuals at home, and with a large proportion of the emigrants being young men and women in their twenties or early thirties, they would most often be writing to a parent. William Chambers's diary of 1879 begins: 'Dear Father, mother, Brothers and Sisters my object in writing this diary is simply to inform you off a few of the many changes I have passed through since we left each other.' In cases like this, a better category could again be the journal-letter, a category encompassing both diaries and letters of a certain type, such as those of David Cannan. To this extent, there is an overlap between the functions of diaries and the functions of letters, and both were used as ways of sending back information about the voyage to those left behind. This is again a salutary reminder that cultural practices rarely divide into clear-cut categories. Yet though some diaries may be almost identical in form to some of the letters, at the time of their writing there was understood to be a general practice of keeping a diary of the voyage out that was different from writing a letter home: 'after breakfast this morning I finished my letter to you all but a line or two to have it ready in case of being able to send it, which we have great hopes of' (Mary Stack 10 Aug. 1837). Diarists mentioned their letters in their diaries; writing a diary was not the same as writing a letter.

*

Some diaries were copied while the ship was still at sea by emigrants anxious to let those at home know of their safe arrival. A month before the end of the voyage, Daniel Matthews records beginning a copy for his sister 'according to my promise before I left', and two weeks later he notes: 'I manage to keep my log close up every day, and am getting along capitally with sister's copy' (17 Mar. 1870). When a ship took one hundred days out and the mail took half that time to return, it could be over six months after saying goodbye before an anxious relative would get news of a safe arrival. William Loraine died on the voyage out in 1877, but his brother, ignorant of William's death, continued to write to him from England asking for assurances of his well-being. Emigrants were therefore concerned to catch the first mail home which until the 1880s generally left only once a month (Bach 148). As his voyage to Sydney lengthened, William Reay thought of those waiting for news at home: 'I suppose we will be 24 Days more yet I hope to do better or the letters will be a long time in getting to England and you will be anxious about us' (19 Nov. 1877). Some emigrants therefore took the opportunity of copying-up their diary on board ship, in the case of Claudius Cairnes, the night before he was due to disembark: 'I must now conclude this Journal   I am writing it over night to have it in time for the mail so I must beg of my kind friends not to be too particular in reading it' (3 Feb. 1861). In cases like this, the diary, posted on arrival, would become in effect the first letter home, a point made by Marjory MacGillivray in 1893 when she wrote that her diary was 'practically to be my letter home' (29 Dec. 1893).

More typically, diaries, if they were copied, were copied after landing. How much later would depend on when the emigrant could find time in which to write. If they had no relative or friend to meet them, emigrants would need to find somewhere to live. The Passenger Act of 1852 permitted emigrants to remain on board ship for at least forty-eight hours after arrival at no extra cost, and particularly in Melbourne during the gold rush of the 1850s, many took the opportunity of saving the high price of accommodation which resulted from a number of emigrant ships arriving at the same time; with a few thousand people suddenly looking for lodgings, the cost of somewhere to stay, be it only a tent, understandably rose. And while the men trudged the streets looking for work and somewhere to live, the women were equally busy sorting and packing belongings. Once they had found somewhere to live, other imperatives would be forced on emigrants. The period following arrival was a period of great physical upheaval after three months of well-regulated life at sea, with homes to be established and money to be earned, and in such circumstances it required great determination to copy out a diary, as John Hedges, a builder from Hampstead, relates:

> Dear Mother, I have scribbled this out for your information I am afraid that you will be hardly able to read some of it as it is written in such a hurry, I have so little time for I do not get home from work until ½ past 7 or 8 and I have to start again at 20 min to five in the morning, and I want to send it by this mail or it will stay here another month. (John Hedges 1859)

[31]

A later emigrant who signed himself simply 'George,' was unable to find the time to copy all of his diary and he had to send it incomplete: 'I can't write any more in detail now or I shall miss the mail. I began this the first week we landed' (31 Mar. 1885). Thomas Severn finished his diary on board ship but missed the mail because he had no time to add a personal note:

> My Dear Papa I send with this my diary, you must not think it unkind of me because I did not write by the 'Sydney' steamer, to announce my safe arrival, but on arriving on shore everything was as dear and uncomfortable that I could not find a place to sit down to writ in, and secondly I had not time for I went to work the day after. (26 Dec. 1852)

Undoubtedly, a number of emigrants, like Andrew Hamilton, were unable even to contemplate making a copy: 'Brawls were an every day occurence [on board ship] but nine tenths were not worth recording, and had I time to re-write the *whole* I should obliterate many that are recorded and greatly shorten other parts but such a thing cannot be thought of' (Oct. 1852).

The period immediately after arrival was also a time of great emotional upheaval, with meetings with relatives and friends not seen for years and a new normality to be established. Almost immediately emigrants had to cast off their identities as emigrants at sea and learn to be immigrants. William Chambers arrived in Melbourne in December 1879 but it was not until eleven months later that he finished copying his diary, the last page being dated 14 November 1880. Susan Meade, who for a time acted as a governess to Governor La Trobe's children, travelled out in 1842 and took at least another six years to copy her journal. Her diary had still not been copied in 1848 when her father wrote to her on the occasion of her marriage: 'What is become of your long promised Journal What a source of pleasure wd. this impart to your mother and myself' (Henry White Meade 1 Aug. 1848). The diary was eventually completed, her watercolour illustrations being signed with her married initials, S. N. Once a certain period had passed and a new identity assumed, it is possible the diarists found it difficult to return to their diaries. Perhaps that is why it took Edwin Francis sixty-two years to return to his.

Many shipboard diaries were addressed to someone to whom a promise had been made, John Hedges addressing his diary to his mother:

My dear Mother, I promised to send you an account of the voyage and I now fulfil my promise, I intended to send to you the original paper but it is on very thick paper in a Pocket Book and I thought it would only be the trouble of writing out a copy for you and here it is, such as it is, a true and faithful copy. I found very little to write about generally, and many times I was on the point of giving it up as useless, but I thought of my Promise and kept it up to the end of the voyage. (1859)

This act of promising to keep a diary seems to have been an important part of emigrant culture, and others also claimed it helped them to continue writing when they were on the point of giving up. John Joseland made his promise to his sister, Mary Anne: 'When at Portsmouth and indeed before leaving Worcester I promised faithfully to keep a Log. If I had known half the circumstances necessarily connected with so long a voyage [I] certainly should not have engaged to do it. I have however to the best of my ability fulfilled my task. I leave it without any comment' (July 1853). James Espie White, addressing his mother in a preface to his diary of 1862, made the same point: 'it was your desire and this I may say was the life buoy of my journal and always kept its head above the water when otherwise it would have sank never again to rise.'

It would be difficult to prove that the promise made a difference to whether or not a diary was actually kept and copied. Susan Meade's promise to send a copy to her mother and father does not seem to have speeded up the copying process of her 'long promised Journal'. There is also some evidence that the failure rate in keeping a diary was quite high, though there may have been a variation between ships. James Espie White noted: 'There were in our cabin five who commenced, besides four who fully intended to have commenced and kept journals but there were only two who stuck to them and I am happy to say that I was one of the number, there being a great number of journals dying through out the ship besides.' Annie Henning claimed an even higher failure rate on her voyage:

I take great credit to myself for being the only person on board who persevered in writing one at all, good, bad or indifferent – numbers began on first leaving Liverpool but most dropped them at St Vincents and the rest shortly after. Perhaps they were wise for there was nothing going on worth noting down, and I should have left off too but for my promise. (26 Oct. 1853)

George, whose surname is unknown, admitted in a letter home he had let his diary lapse, though unusually and somewhat perversely he still copied out what he had written: 'I commenced writing a diary but did not keep it up, the following is as far as I got' (31 Mar. 1885); unfortunately, because he was trying to catch the mail, he failed even to finish the copying and ended with not one, but two incomplete diaries.

*

Diaries addressed to someone specific are most often addressed to a mother; in the absence of a mother, the diary may be addressed to a father or a sister. Occasionally a diary is addressed to a friend or a former employer who perhaps had sponsored the emigration, partly paying for the passage. But even where a diary is addressed to a specific member of the family, the diarist often has in mind a small circle of relations and friends rather than one particular individual. S. E. Roberts, having begun his diary in an impersonal style, finds himself having to specify his readership when writing about the cargo of gunpowder on board: 'I did not mention it in my letter as I knew it would make you very uneasy till you heard that I had arrived safe, which you could not do for 9 months' (15 July 1848). A footnote makes clear the identity of the 'you': 'Dear Mother, this is addressed to you as most of the previous matter is and all the rest shall be, for it can be of no interest to anyone but you, Father and those at home.' The 'those at home' element is important. In 1853 John Joseland, sailing out with his wife, Martha, to join his brother, writes at the end of his diary that he is 'sending it home to my dear and much loved friends especially my dearest Sister Mary Anne for whom it has been particularly written'. He adds, however, that 'I doubt not it will be read by every one of those far distant but near and dearly loved relations and friends who on their perusal will never think to cease and pray for our success.' George Lister in 1879 addressed his brother at the end of his diary: 'When you and Father have read it, Please send it to Bros. at Flimby, and then you can let whoever you like see it.'

Today we tend to think of diaries either as private and introverted, as a record of our thoughts and feelings, or like desk diaries, as records of day-to-day engagements. Emigrants' diaries are more akin to desk diaries and are concerned primarily with the events and arrangements on board ship rather than with the fears and anxieties of the emigrants themselves. It was this that made joint diaries possible, and a diary written on board the *Torrens* in 1893–4, although nominally that of Marjory MacGillivray, was also part written by her husband John: 'Madge is lazy and rebels at the work of writing her diary, she has given such long histories of the events of the past three days it is no wonder that she now shirks the exertion' (6 Dec. 1893). Rarely do the diarists examine their motives for emigrating, and even more rarely do they speak of what they expect to find in Australia, except perhaps to look forward to a reunion with a relative. Once they were at sea, possibly they no longer felt the burden of what by then was an irreversible decision; such a view is taken by Henry Whittingham in a letter offering advice to his brother about to emigrate: 'Remember that your voyage is for your own benefit, taken voluntarily by you. To lament this, is to lament your own act, & to lament what cannot be undone' (21 June 1852). This is not to say that there are no moments of reflection, particularly when the diarists found themselves alone on deck at night:

> as i stood alone that night on the deck after most of the pasengers had gone below i could not help reflecting it was a cruel destiny which had thus compelled us to leave our nativeland our freinds & homes to face we knew not what in a foreign land, for if i could have obtained the commonst nessasarys of life at home i would never have emigrated to have taken a wife & children away from home & kindred   if man may be excursed for being down hearted & sad it is at a time like this – it was late when i went below & with a heavey heart i went to my bunk (Abijou Good 4 Mar. 1863)

But such passages are not common, and diarists more often shy away from introspection, becoming embarrassed at what may be thought to be a self-indulgence. This is not to say the diaries display no emotion; storms or sunsets offer diarists the opportunity to evoke fear or wonder as the occasion demands. But this is different from personal reflection. John Joseland, led one evening into thinking of 'that dear home I have left perhaps for ever', finds himself being led further than he feels he ought to go: 'I must not go on so, or I shall fill my book too soon. I could write it full of my thoughts about Brothers & Sisters all, but this must not be. Dear Martha is quite recovered, but I feel poorly myself; a little bilious' (24 Apr. 1853). Excursions from the everyday are usually curtailed like this with a sudden jolt back into the here and now. Janet

Ronald, addressing her diary to her mother, chooses New Year's Eve to reflect on the step she has taken in sailing out to join her brother: 'This is actually the last day of /57 and little did I anticipate on the 1st, of my present position. What changes indeed may the next year not bring forth. But away with reflections, and proceed with relation' (31 Dec. 1857). She then goes on to talk about the progress of the ship as it draws close to Sydney. 'Away with reflections, and proceed with relation': emphasis is placed on relation rather than reflection, relating the voyage out rather than the internal reflections of the diarist.

The letter that Henry Whittingham wrote to his brother in 1852, the year before he himself emigrated, also contained advice about keeping a diary: 'Your diary must be kept with rigid, puritanic pertinacity. Write in it every day: even, as Cobbett says, though you note but the wind's quarter' (21 June 1852). The reason for keeping a diary is not given, but the mention of the 'rigid, puritanic pertinacity' needed shows Henry Whittingham thought of diary writing as an act of self-discipline. In this he was following the orthodoxy of the time, an orthodoxy that found a more public voice in the emigrant manual of W. H. G. Kingston.

W. H. G. Kingston was a propagandist of British emigration during the 1850s, seeing in it a means by which Britain could simultaneously export its unemployed and, once the colonies had been built up, its industrial products. He was especially interested in emigration (of others, not himself) to Australia, publishing a number of stories and tracts aimed at would-be emigrants. His *Emigrant Voyager's Manual* of 1850 contained what he at least considered sensible suggestions for keeping oneself occupied during the voyage, and it has sections on such diverse entertainments as making sheep nets from coconut fibre and salt cellars from meat bones. His manual also has a section on keeping a diary of the voyage. Kingston saw diary writing in the same way as he saw gymnastic exercises, as a way of promoting healthy habits on board ship: 'Resolve that nothing shall hinder you from this practice, and depend on it you will often find it assist you in keeping to good resolutions and in avoiding bad habits. . . . the journal of the voyage should be written up every day. If the weather is very bad, and you cannot have the ink-bottle out, write it up in pencil' (23). Like most of those proffering advice to emigrants, Kingston believed that working people, for whom his writings were intended, would quickly fall into sinful 'bad habits' if they had nothing with which to occupy themselves. He helpfully included a specimen diary-entry and specific suggestions of what to write: 'Make a point of noting down the observations of the

Chaplain, or religious instructor. Note what trades you learn, and how to occupy yourself. Observe what fish or birds you see, and describe them. Learn all about them and their habits from the books you have on board' (24–5). The diary was to be useful and educative.

While Kingston was encouraging the writing of a diary, he was only doing so against a background of an established custom of keeping a diary of the voyage. He was, in fact, merely trying to encourage the new wave of working-class emigrants of the late 1840s and early 1850s to adopt what was already a widespread practice among middle-class emigrants. The degree to which it was already an established practice suggests it fulfilled functions over and above those of self-discipline and self-improvement prescribed by Kingston; the kind of diary envisaged by Kingston would have made few concessions to the audience the diarists themselves had in mind.

Kingston's guidelines did not markedly influence surviving diaries; indeed, diarists often claimed that they were writing not for self-discipline but for amusement, either for their own amusement or for the amusement of those at home. In a long and highly rhetorical preface to his diary of 1841, William Wills, writing of himself in the third person, claims he pens his diary 'only for the purpose of amusing himself, and not with the idea that others will derive any gratification from the perusal thereof should it at any period fall into their hands'. The disingenuousness of this claim is obvious, even had we not seen that the title page addresses the diary to 'his friend Mr John Brownlow'. Edward Towle makes the same claim: 'I am ashamed to send such a specimen to my friends to read, but I have written this journal more for the sake of occupying my mind than with the anticipation that it will afford any gratification or amusement to my friends' (3 Sept. 1852). The modesty of the claim that the diary is only for self-amusement should be seen alongside the refusal to record fears and anxieties; both were ways in which diaries could be given a tone of self-effacing humility.

Like Claudius Cairnes, Anna Fowler completed her diary on board ship the night before disembarking: 'So endeth my voyage scribblings which have beguiled some of my many sea-spent hours and I hope may afford you some little amusement if you can make it out' (23 Sept. 1866). Anna Fowler is at least prepared to admit that her diary may have been written to amuse others, but she still has to add a self-deprecating 'if you can make it out'. To write about oneself might have been considered conceited, and diarists tried hard to adopt the correct tone towards an audience for which they would not normally be writing.

They cast themselves as reluctant autobiographers. William Hamilton, perhaps because he was a Presbyterian minister and used to making public pronouncements, was able to be a little more forthright: 'The above journal I have written for the amusement & gratification of my father & sisters & now finish it on a very wet & dull day this 17th Nov. 1837.' Nonetheless, the claim that the diary is written for amusement is itself a denial of the importance of diary-writing for emigrants. In nineteenth-century British culture, the status of different kinds of writing was strictly ranked. Religious writing would have appeared at the top with poetry not far below. Further down would be scientific and instructional writing, and still further down would come the novel. Beneath the novel would have come amusing writing.

The other claim made for the diary was that it was written for the information of its audience, and though this still accords diary-writing a status below those genres likely to raise the human spirit, like sermons or lyric poetry, it does nevertheless make it more useful than if it were merely for amusement. By 1842, an account of the voyage to Australia was already a commonplace, but this was no bar on others describing it: 'To describe particularly a voyage which has been so often described may be superfluous but some things acquainted therewith may be of use and interest' (S. T. Haslett 1842). Similarly, in the preface to his 1850 diary, Francis Taylor remarks: 'should the few lines here penned afford any information which may in any way prove useful to any intending Emigrant or intress any old acquaintance or intimate relative the writers purpose is fully answered'. The information contained in diaries was largely practical. Benjamin Key advised, 'if any of our friends come out should recommend them to be very particular were there cabins are situated and also to take care it is not next door to a water closet as our water closet has been stopt and the cabin's near it have had a very unpleasant smell' (1 Oct. 1838); John Sceales advised his audience that 'every person ought to bring a good stock of Candles to sea with and I would recommend wax as the best' (6 Nov. 1838); Thomas Severn noted that 'A saucepan and frying pan will be found very useful,' though bringing cheese is useless as 'Mr Tullidge brought a great quantity and it is almost all spoilt' (23 Oct. 1852); and even when the voyage had been cut to six weeks by steamship and the hardship lessened, the practice of offering advice to future emigrants continued, as in Thomas Coy's suggestion: 'An Indiarubber collar will last you a whole voyage and save a lot of time and expense' (20 Feb. 1885).

It is probable that the information passed back in diaries was occasionally useful but that it did not markedly affect the decision of those who read it to emigrate; the decision to emigrate was based more on conditions in Australia than those on board ship, and Dudley Baines asserts that, 'It is almost certain that of all the sources of information available to prospective emigrants, returned migrants were the most valuable' (Baines 38). However, although part of the strategy of including information about the voyage out may have been to increase the status of the diary by aligning it with instructional writing, many diarists clearly did feel at the time of writing that their advice would be useful, especially when the diarist had in mind a specific relative or friend who was contemplating emigration. Regional newspapers in particular regularly printed letters from local residents who had gone to the colonies in anticipation that the information contained in them would prove useful to intending emigrants. Sometimes the newspapers published diaries of the voyage out, and at least one was published in *The Times*, an anonymous diary kept on board the first voyage to Australia of the SS *Great Britain* in 1852. Diaries were quoted in emigrant handbooks, and they were also occasionally published as books in their own right, the diary thus attaining its ambition to achieve the status of the printed book. The diary of the voyage out kept by 'N. C.' in 1848 was published as a book in the following year and it contains much supposedly useful information: 'I think people should never go to sea without one of those small portable shower-baths, they shew at the Polytechnic, they cost but a few shillings, occupy but little space, and are easily managed, even in a cabin; for a tub with a blanket on the floor, will obviate any inconvenience arising from the splashing of the water' (20 Oct. 1848). This advice is, of course, likely to be of more use to those who could afford to buy a shower-bath and, for that matter, who could afford to buy the book. Claudius Cairnes admits to having gained some useful information by reading a diary such as he himself tries to write: 'I will mention occasionally what our meals consist of as this Diary may meet the eye of some friend or friends of friends who may like to know something about the food on board ship   any other hints I will mention as I got much useful information from a Journal of this kind' (28 Oct. 1860).

Diarists often formed a link in the process of chain migration, and having read the diary of a relative or friend who had preceded them, they sent back their own diary for those who they hoped would follow: 'My Dear Friends should have sent you this much sooner but had contemplated keeping a copy which I have not yet been able to do – I now sent it to Katherine . . . hoping the news it contains may tempt some of you to try South Australia' (Benjamin Key 1838). In cases like this, if the diarists did not want to put-off others following them (though sometimes they did), they had to trace a fine line between painting an attractive picture of the voyage and giving sensible practical information of life at sea that might, inevitably, be discouraging.

Claims that the diary is written for the amusement or the information of others at home are clearly related to the kind of audience the diarist envisaged. The diary would amuse those such as parents not likely to emigrate, while it could also contain advice to unknown readers through whom it might circulate. The evidence is that copies sent back were passed round the family and a small group of friends, and one of the problems of the diarist was to find an appropriate way of addressing such a diverse group. Rachel Henning gives a useful account of the reception at home of the diary kept by her sister Annie on board the SS *Great Britain* in 1853. Rachel was at the time staying with her sister, Etta, and her sister's husband, the Reverend T. W. Boyce in Sussex; the account is contained in a return letter to Annie:

> I was practising when Etta came into the drawing-room with the parcel in her hand. I have never exactly discovered how it came, but there it was! We cut the string in a moment with my old knife, though Mr Boyce suggested we had better untie the knot! And then we saw the delightful collection of letters and the journal! It was just post-time, and I hope you will properly appreciate my self-denial in rushing into the other room, before I had opened a single letter, and stamping and sending off those directed to others.
>
> Then we sat down to read and finished the letters before tea, and after we read the journal aloud. I cannot think why Annie made any excuses for it. It was a capital journal and most interesting to us. It was very good and kind of her to keep it, for I am sure it must be a very difficult thing to do on board ship among so many people. (27 Feb. 1854)

This is a useful dramatisation of the kind of reception envisaged by emigrants who sent diaries home. The diary is eagerly awaited and gratefully received. Especially important is the ceremony of reading the diary aloud. Reading aloud to an audience was not unusual in the nineteenth century, it was after all an era of home entertainment, and where friends and relatives of the diarist were illiterate, a parish priest or similar figure may have read the diary or letter aloud to an interested audience. Yet, though it may have been common practice, it was this reading aloud that made hitting the right note so important and yet so difficult. In the above case, the diary that was read aloud by Rachel Henning and the others after tea still exists; before such an audience, Annie Henning, like many other emigrant diarists, adopts the role of the reluctant autobiographer: 'And so here ends my journal, and a sadly stupid one it is' (26 Oct. 1853). Having only limited control over the audience of the diary, the diarists were forced to adopt a range of tones and move between the amusing and the informational; indeed, different parts of the diary would be directed to different parts of the audience. There would have been far less of a problem in writing the letters that accompanied the journal; emigrants would have known how to address a mother or a sister individually, and as these letters were not for a general audience, much more could have been said.

*

Theoretically there are two types of emigrant diary. There are those diaries addressed to a small family circle at home which were copied and sent back, and there are those which the diarists wrote only for themselves. The problem with this theoretical difference is that it has very little influence on the kinds of diary being written. Not all emigrant diaries are openly addressed to other people, but that does not mean that the diarist was necessarily writing only for her or himself. Sometimes only the occasional use of 'you' suggests the diarist imagined someone else reading the diary, as in Edward Cornell's diary of 1856: 'if I had brought with me a photographic apparatus you should have had some choice scenes' (10 June 1856). To whom this 'you' refers, or whether it refers to one person or a group, is not stated. Similarly, it is unclear to whom the single use of 'you' refers in William Shennan's diary, 'you may know what I am doing' (27 Jan. 1870), and his diary contains no other clear indication that it is being written for anyone other than himself.

An unusually reflective diary like that of Abijou Good travelling out with his wife and children in 1863 may seem to have been written for himself alone, but it includes a list of weekly provisions 'as this may be read by some who are about to emigrate' (11 Apr. 1863). Henry Whittingham's diary of 1853 is unusual not for any 'rigid, puritanic pertinacity' such as he had advised his brother to use, but because, like

[41]

Abijou Good, he is unusually reflective and keen to record his hopes and anxieties after giving up a position which earned him a very reasonable £90 a year in order to emigrate to Sydney: 'I still believe I have taken a wise, & prudent, congenial, step' (2 May 1853). But Henry too thinks of an audience beyond himself: 'These notings are intended for sending home, in extract, to my family, that they may see that I do think and how my thoughts proceed' (1 May 1853). Byron Ronald's diary written in 1853 when he was travelling to join his brother in a business venture in Melbourne does not appear to be written for anyone other than himself, but three of his sisters, Euphemia, Janet, and Helen also made the journey and kept journals, Helen's diary making the point that it was a family custom to address a diary to their mother: 'as the others in their journals no doubt saw exactly the same, I have never attempted to tell you any of these sights' (5 Dec. 1861). The diary of Byron is clearly a copy, being written in a fair hand throughout, and very likely his diary was written for his mother as well. It is extremely difficult to identify from the internal style of any diary of the voyage out that it has been written solely for the diarist alone.

The crux of the matter is not that some diaries were or were not written to be copied and sent home; rather, the emigrant diaries all addressed a similar audience. All diaries need an addressee because all writing makes assumptions about who will read it. The most secret of diaries has to be directed towards an audience, even if it is the god of the seventeenth-century Puritan diarists. The audience may be addressed directly by name, or it may merely be inferred from what the diary assumes the reader to know. William Reay writes in his diary of 1877: 'Tell Ab Ambler I had some trotters to night   let him send some apples which we want much' (26 Oct. 1877). William here assumes his audience will know the identity of Ab Ambler and the nature of the joke; probably, like William Reay himself, Ab Ambler was a butcher. Emigrant diaries were written in order to give the voyage out a communicable form, they were attempts to give a readable form to the literally unsettling experience of emigration. In order to give the voyage out this shape, diarists had to imagine an audience, and that audience was a group of family and friends at home. Nineteenth-century emigrants, being well-schooled in the prevailing belief in the family as the central unit of a Christian society, wrote in such a way that their diaries might be understandable and acceptable when read aloud to a group of family and close acquaintances. It was writing for the hearth.

Seen in this light, the question of whether any particular diary is sent back is therefore not crucial. The diary performed its primary function of giving shape to the voyage as it was being written on board, and if to write it the diarist had to envisage an intimate home audience, that did not mean the diary had to be sent back. The function of the diary to amuse and inform others may come into play in the writing of the diary because it was a corollary to imagining an audience, but it remains a secondary function.

In this the diaries are unlike the letters; for the letters, the act of writing and the act of receiving were equal aspects of a process of communication which also involved the act of mailing. If some diaries were sent back they functioned in a similar manner, but whereas the letters would almost invariably have been posted back, not all the diaries would have been. The pressures on the emigrants once they landed would have prevented many from making a copy, and since one of the purposes of making a copy was to enable the diarist to retain the rough diary, clearly some would have been reluctant to lose their only copy; although he addressed his diary to 'Dear Sir', Will Sayer retained his diary, and it passed on his death to his sister-in-law and then on to her grandchildren. But undoubtedly, though they may have implied an audience at home, many of the diaries were not written to be sent; the diarists wrote them for themselves alone to keep. To say that these are a different kind of diary from those sent back is to make a distinction on the basis of the mechanical act of posting, not the more complex act of writing. Diaries, once written, had performed their main function; whether they were then sent back is a secondary issue.

*

Emigrants wrote their diaries with an eye on the past, with an eye on the future, and with an eye on the present. Emigrants wrote for the past in the sense that they wrote for an audience at home, an audience made up of all the relatives and friends they would often never expect to see again. They made copies of their diaries, carefully transcribing thousands of words into specially purchased books, to remind those back home of themselves, to leave a token of themselves in the old country.

In terms of the future, the voyage out, cast into durable form, could be relived through the diary: Mary Thomas used hers as the basis of a reminiscence written when she was seventy-nine, thirty years after her voyage to South Australia in 1836; Edwin Francis, as I pointed out at the beginning of this chapter, kept his for sixty-two years, returning to it at the age of eighty. Diaries were written for posterity, to be kept by the diarist and by the diarist's descendants. They have gone on being read by family interested in their own identity and where they have come from, and they have gone on being copied, as each of the many transcripts in the archives demonstrates. Such testaments have proved a vital part of the settler history of Australia.

But we should not forget the present of these diaries, the present of the diarists as they wrote them. Emigrants kept diaries, it was expected of them by family and friends, emigrant handbooks told them to, it was as much part of emigration culture as government depots, crossing the line, and plum duff. Yet while the diaries sent back or preserved for the future were finished artifacts of the voyage out, during the voyage they were incomplete, and it is that incompleteness that needs to be imagined when reading the diaries as we find them today. Janet Ronald sent part of hers back during the voyage: 'My dearest Mamma, Yesterday I despatched my journal to you up to 22nd. Oct which I hope you received' (23 Oct. 1857); Edward Towle, quoted earlier, intended to send his back; and the 'journal' of Sophia Taylor for 1851 is in fact a sequence of journal letters addressed to her father that were later copied into a book, probably by her sister. These three diaries as they exist today are reconstructions, as, in this sense, is the diary of Edwin Francis. This is not to say that the diarists did not have an image as they were writing of their diary completed, of what their diary might become; they knew they were writing a book because it was a book they had bought in which to keep their diary. Indeed, it is the image of completeness that the book offered which helped them write a diary, for what better way was there for emigrants to register the progress of the journey than to see the pages of their diary filling?

Emigrant diaries were generated by the precise situation in which the emigrants found themselves, cut off from contact with land, in an unimaginably strange environment, homeless, and with fears for the future, be it risk of disaster at sea tomorrow or what will become of them once they reach their destination. These people were literally unsettled, they were settlers not yet settled. In such circumstances, few would have kept a diary day in and day out for three months or more had they not found a reason daily to do so: to be writing a diary was to be looking towards when the journey would be over. The shipboard diaries of nineteenth-century emigrants to Australia are occasional, they stem from the occasion on which they were written, and whatever function they may have had later once they were finished, emigrants drew comfort every day from finding a quiet corner of the ship and bringing up to date their book of the voyage.

Chapter 2

Making a start

'Owing to seasickness and then to the heavy rolling of the ship, I have not been able to begin this, my journal so-called, until to-day'

> My dear Mama, Having waited five days for seasickness and the novelty of life on board ship to wear off, I begin today, Thursday, my Diary of events. (Helen Ronald 24 Oct. 1861)

Like many diarists, Helen Ronald casts her diary in the form of a journal-letter and her opening is intended first to establish the relationship between herself and her audience, and then formally to open the proceedings: 'I begin today, Thursday, my Diary of events.' She is setting the context of her account and, in this sense, she is using a discursive or non-narrative form of writing. Helen continues discursively for a little longer, admitting, with slight embarrassment, that 'I do not know whether I ought to be pleased about it or not, but I find that I have not felt nearly so miserable at parting from you all as I thought I should.' Helen is caught in a position characteristic of emigrants, trying to allay the concern of those left behind while avoiding giving the impression that they have been forgotten.

Helen Ronald's diary is instructive, not so much because of its discursive introduction, but because it highlights an ambivalence in the very notion of beginning a diary. Helen Ronald senses that her discursive preamble is something of a false start and so she decides to begin again: 'I must begin properly and tell you of everything since Sunday.' Beginning 'properly' here means not only beginning to write the diary, which of course she has already done, but writing from the beginning of the voyage: 'We left the Mersey early in the morning, and in the most calm sea possible reached Holyhead in the evening. The Skerries and the light in Holyhead harbour seen from the distance, are the last glimpses of England we saw.' Helen Ronald makes two assumptions here that are common to the culture she inhabited: the first is that

[46]

journeys are already narrative events, that they have a natural beginning and ending; and the second is that, as a narrative event, a journey
may be fitted into a book. It is the combination of these two assumptions which leads Helen Ronald to begin her diary, so far as she can,
with what she identifies as the beginning of the voyage.

Some emigrants go a little further back in time for the beginning of
their diaries. The account of the preliminary journey, the journey to the
port, acted for these diarists as a kind of prelude to writing the main
journey; one journey-story prefaces another. Emigrants came from all
over the United Kingdom to the major emigration ports of Liverpool,
London, and Plymouth, most of them making the journey by train,
though Irish emigrants were transferred by steamer to Liverpool or
Plymouth, as also were some Scottish emigrants to Liverpool. After
1853, those who would have gone from London were switched by the
emigration commissioners to Southampton, and among the first were
James and Maryann Murray with their two small sons; having made the
relatively short journey from Ramsgate to the newly-opened London
emigration depot belonging to the London & South Western Railway
Company at Nine Elms (Simmons 323), the Murrays were transferred
with fellow emigrants by rail to Southampton, discovering in the
process that lack of attention to detail characteristic of the practice, if
not of the theory, of assisted emigration: 'lost our dinner as we left about
dinner time from nine Elms and arrived too late for it at Southampton'
(James Murray 29 November 1853). Mark Blasdall in 1862 had the more
straightforward journey to make from Nottingham to London, catching
the 11 o'clock train and arriving in London at 6.30 pm, though he
suffered from the February weather in his unheated carriage ('I was
almost starved of the cold on my journey') and had trouble finding his
way across London to Shadwell Basin in the dark; he finally arrived to
discover the dock closed for the night: 'After standing like a fool for some
time I accosted a policeman, asked him to direct me to were I could
obtain lodgings for the night' (16 Feb. 1862). In 1870, William Shennan
had to make a three-day journey south to the Plymouth emigration
depot from near Dumfries in southern Scotland: 'gets a parcel from the
Station Master to take to his Sister in Melbourne opens my box puts it in,
Hark here comes the Train   draws up   boxes put in van   Whistle
blows off she goes' (22 Jan. 1870). Such emigrants with all their
accompanying boxes and bags must have been a familar sight on
stations and in trains the length and breadth of nineteenth-century
Britain.

These diarists, and those like them who wrote of the journey to the port of embarkation, began their diaries with leaving home: 'Left Ramsgate at 8.8 AM For Margate to meet the steamer for London' (James Murray); 'Started from home (Nottingham) by the eleven Oclock train' (Mark Blasdall); 'Left home 21 January for Plymouth' (William Shennan). Possibly leaving home was chosen as the decisive moment because it defined them as emigrants; it was as emigrants that they negotiated Britain's labyrinthine Victorian railway network. But becoming an emigrant was a role to be adopted, just as the role of 'new chum' could be adopted (or resisted) on arrival in Australia; and this role was subservient to an emigration story, many of which were current during the nineteenth century. To see oneself as an emigrant was already to assume that one's experience took the shape of a narrative; emigrants were to a great extent attempting to act out a journey-story that was already written.

Most diarists, however, omitted the preliminary journey. Benjamin Key, sailing in 1838, was one of a number who began with embarkation: 'May 27th On the afternoon of this day we came on board the above nam'd vessel and commenced stowing our things in the cabin for our voyage.' Eleven years later William Harbottle also began with embarkation: 'March 10 1849. Saturday – Embarked this day on board the "Scotia" a fine Vessel 778 Tons burthen, lying at Deptford, as Cabin Passenger to Sydney.' The account of embarkation is as conventional a beginning as leaving home and is employed throughout the period by writers of all social classes and both sexes. George Greaves, travelling steerage, used it in 1867: 'December 13th Friday, came on board, lay in Mersey all day and night'; and travelling a year before her more well-known sister, Rachel, Annie Henning began her diary: 'Thursday, 11 August 1853. Came on board by the steamer at twelve leaving dear Rachel standing on the Floating Pier.'

Yet by far the largest proportion of diaries begin not with leaving home or embarkation but with the actual sailing of the ship. John Fenwick, a young merchant travelling to Melbourne during the gold rush, began: '*1854 – Sunday 14 May* – Ship "Lightning" towed from the Mersey – a tug on each side & one ahead – as we took our departure at noon.' William Bray, a gold-digger leaving only a month after Fenwick, started his diary: 'Monday June 12th 1854 Left Liverpool about 11 oclock to day   fine weather and head wind, sailing on very comfortable at about 8 knots per hour.' Again this convention crosses class and gender boundaries, and Elizabeth Allbon, travelling steerage, starts her diary in the same way: 'Friday March 21st 1879 Weighed anchor at halfpast four   set sail at six O clock.'

We can only guess at the circumstantial factors that determined whether the diary would begin with leaving home, embarkation, or setting sail, but emigrants may have had in mind that their diaries were nominally kept, like Annie Henning's mentioned above, for friends and relations who may have accompanied them to the ship. Rachel Henning, left on the floating pier, would have reported back all that had happened to Annie up until the moment of embarkation; there was no need for Annie to include it. The unidentified male diarist on the *Kate* in 1853 made this point to 'My dear Sir': 'I will commence an attempt to give you all the information I can from the time I last parted with you and your estimable daughter – a time I shall not easily forget – when our good ship began to move from Shadwell basin.' The muddle resulting from getting this wrong, from beginning too early, can be seen in William Greenhalgh's diary: 'Busy arranging the Birth several friends from Bolton, yourself, sister, & Jno Baines visited us' (12 Mar. 1853). The identity of 'yourself' is not stated, but she or he is told what she or he already knows because the diary has started with embarkation and not with setting sail.

So strong was the need to begin the journey-story with leaving home, getting on board ship, or weighing anchor, that even where diaries were not started until some time into the voyage, the diarist still felt it necessary to open the diary with the beginning of the journey. Here a distinction needs to be made between the story time and the time of narration, that is, between the time of the events first recorded in the diary and the day in the journey on which the diarist actually began to write. Helen Ronald's diary with which I began this chapter is again a good example: 'My dear Mama, Having waited five days for seasickness and the novelty of life on board ship to wear off, I begin today, Thursday, my Diary of events.' Yet Helen begins her account not with what occurred on Thursday when she starts to keep her diary but with setting sail from the Mersey on the previous Saturday, and there is a mismatch of five days between the time of the story and the time of the narration.

Helen Ronald was certainly not the only emigrant to be incapacitated by seasickness. Hardly any of the emigrants would have been to sea before, and some who embarked in London were so sick on the voyage down the English Channel that they abandoned the ship when it called at Plymouth and lost their passage money. Many of the early entries in the diaries give graphic descriptions of seasickness:

The wind rising in the afternoon caused a very rude sea which
sickened most of the people I amongst the rest. Its nature no one
can appreciate but by experience, accompanied by the pitching of
the ship the clatter of pans tins etc the rancorous smells and
loathsome sights, makes seasickness truly a most unwelcome
guest. (Richard Skilbeck 26 Apr. 1858)

In conditions where the emigrants were unable to keep down their food,
it is not surprising that many were unable to keep up their diaries: 'I
have not felt to have pluck enough to write during the last few days
having been very queer sometimes, and sick two or three times a day,
and sitting down or stooping jobs does not agree with sea sickness at all'
(John Hedges 29 Sept. 1858). Isabella Turner was struck down before
she could even begin her diary:

Owing to seasickness and then to the heavy rolling of the ship, I
have not been able to begin this, my journal so-called, until
to-day. Nothing of very great importance has as yet occurred, but
I shall try to let all you dear ones at home know a little of what we
have been doing or *not* doing, I should rather say, during the last
few days. (18 Mar. 1868)

However, like Helen Ronald and other diarists who because of
seasickness or some other reason were unable to write their first entry
on the first day at sea, Isabella Turner duly wrote up the missing entries
until she reached the day on which she was writing. The belief once
again is that journeys are naturally shaped like a story, and the diary as
the book of the voyage has to begin at the beginning of the narrative.

*

The belief that a journey is a naturally occurring narrative that merely
needs to be transcribed to fill a book is so generally accepted that it is
hard to challenge. It is relatively easy to show that the beginning and
ending of a yearly diary, for example, is fairly arbitrary, both because
those of us from western cultures do not expect our lives to follow
annual cycles and because other cultures, such as the Chinese, use
different calendars. Yet that does not stop hundreds of thousands of
people (including, it must be admitted, some from Chinese back-
grounds) gathering round Sydney Harbour on New Year's Eve to watch
the fireworks. There is an assumption in such celebrations that time is

not only sequential, but that it comes in segments, punctuated at either end by significant events. This corresponds to a desire to construct meaningful narratives out of the passing of time. The social tagging of births, marriages, and deaths by various ceremonies is testament to the human lifespan itself being understood as a narrative. The journey already appears like a narrative because the concept of the journey is one of those that we use to give meaning to a sequential passage of time. Journeys are not natural narratives if that means they occur beyond our capacity to construct narratives; rather, they are prime examples of our narrative construction of reality.

In this sense, the choice of where to begin the account of the voyage out is paradoxically both limited and arbitrary. It is limited insofar as the voyage out, already constructed as a narrative, allows only certain beginnings – leaving home, embarkation, or setting sail. The story is already written. But these beginnings are also arbitrary since there is nothing intrinsic to them as events that marks them as significant. Chronological time does not stop and start, the even movement of the hands on the clock cannot separate one period from another. The significance of a beginning is conferred on it by the narrative to which it belongs.

Once the journey is seen as a narrative pattern that has been selected by emigrants to give a coherent meaning to their experience then we can begin to understand its function in their specific circumstances. Emigrants had very good ideological reasons for placing such a high value on the journey-story. Journey-stories are exemplary chronological narratives, they depend on a sequential concept of time and a belief that one event moves on to the next in a cumulative manner. Indeed, the notion of sequential time is so important to the diarists that they usually make a note of the time they sailed: John Fenwick left at noon, William Bray left about 11 o'clock, and Elizabeth Allbon set sail at six. Few other types of diary can propose such an accurate beginning. As narratives, journey-stories rely on a concept of time that is both progressive and non-reversible.

This sense of time as progress matched nineteenth-century beliefs in natural, social, and economic evolution, a belief that movement forward through time and space produced a cumulative, positive effect. Peter Brooks has argued that:

The enormous narrative production of the nineteenth century may suggest an anxiety at the loss of providential plots: the

plotting of the individual or social or institutional life story takes
on new urgency when one can no longer look to a sacred
masterplot that organizes and explains the world. (6).

This secularisation of explanatory narratives, Brooks argues, 'may
explain the nineteenth century's obsession with questions of origin,
evolution, progress, genealogy, its foregrounding of the historical
narrative as par excellence the necessary mode of explanation and
understanding' (6–7). Brooks is a little too insistent on the division
between providential and historical plots, and a medieval providential
plot persisted, if much weakened, at a national level in the link between
the nineteenth-century British Empire and a civilising Christian
mission.

But the need to explain the life of the institution or individual in
terms of social or economic progress does lie behind nineteenth-
century narratives, and emigrants could share the belief that movement through time and space led to attainment because they were
overwhelmingly economic migrants; their voyage out was supposed to
lead to a better standard of living. The diaries do not often include the
reasons for emigration, perhaps because they were self-evident; as
Abijou Good put it: 'if i could have obtained the commonst nessasarys of
life at home i would never have emigrated' (4 Mar. 1863). Joshua
Hughes put it more succinctly: 'Many of the passengers regret they ever
left Old England; I don't know why, there was not much to stop for' (17
Apr. 1863). Of course, as Patricia Clarke and Dale Spender point out,
many women made the journey because they had to, because they were
part of the household of a man who had decided to emigrate; they had
no option to remain since they would have been unable to support
themselves financially (xii). Janet Ronald, who emigrated four years
before her sister Helen, probably made the journey to act as housekeeper to her brother Byron until he might marry, and it is possible that
Helen was making the journey to replace her on Janet's marriage. In
cases like this, women who had no voice in whether or not to emigrate
might place more stress on the journey as part of a providential plan,
and second to clergymen, young single women were most likely to
portray their journey in religious terms with themselves journeying
towards a spiritual goal. Nonetheless, as Lucy Frost remarks of Annie
Baxter, a settler in New South Wales in the 1840s, 'from the moment
Annie Baxter arrived in Yesabba, she was as keenly involved as her
husband in the effort to create there a workable cattle station' (97); it is

clear from accounts like this that some women, if only out of necessity, shared the ambitions of their fathers, husbands, or brothers. Certainly for the men, if not for all of the women, the trajectory of the voyage story, the movement from a departure to an arrival, was analogous to a hoped-for improvement in their fortunes. In this their diaries were secular versions of one of the most popular journey-stories in the nineteenth century, John Bunyan's *Pilgrim's Progress* (1678), with themselves as heroes making their way to a secular Celestial City.

*

The voyage was seen as a narrative whether or not it was written down, because all emigrants knew about beginnings, middles, and ends; it was part of a common way of seeing the world, and writing down the journey-story was in this respect merely giving a material form to the latent narrative. But the actual act of beginning to write a diary, be it inscribing the title page or writing the first entry, can also be seen as a kind of ritual that gave to the emigrant experience a sense of a beginning. Thus ritual is articulated by Arthur Manning in the preface to his diary's reader:

> Dear Reader,
>   I am told it is as necessary to have a *beginning* to a book as it is to have an *ending* to the same – and that this beginning, (I am further told) to deserve its epithet 'Preface,' or 'Introduction,' should be such as to enable the reader to form some idea as to what he may expect from the work before him. (4 Nov. 1839)

The very act of writing, here self-consciously removed from a discussion of the voyage itself, complements the need to begin the diary at the beginning of the journey.

Samuel Rawson was one of those who kept a diary before deciding to leave for Australia, and he formally ended it before commencing a diary of the voyage out: '4th – Went on board, we weighed anchor & sailed at noon – Meeting foul weather in the channel, we anchored in Plymouth Sound again on the 8th and finally sailed on the 11th April. The voyage is described in the Log I kept' (4 Apr. 1838). With setting sail, one diary ends and another begins. So momentous is the occasion that Samuel Rawson feels it appropriate to then quote (more or less accurately) four lines from Shakespeare's *Richard II*:

Then British ground farewell sweet land adieu,
My Mother & my Nurse that bears me yet
Where'er I wander, boast of thee I can
Though banished, yet a true born Englishman.

These lines are spoken by Bolingbroke on being banished by King
Richard for suspected treason, and Samuel Rawson sees his own life in a
similarly historic scale: 'Thus ends the first period of my life.' As an
explanatory narrative, *Richard II* is well-chosen since it ends with
Bolingbroke returning to England to supplant King Richard, a myth of
triumphant return cherished by many an emigrant. But in terms of
ritual, it is not so much what is spoken but how it is spoken that is
significant; Bolingbroke's final couplet, falling at the end of a scene, is
what makes the ending seem like an ending. And as Rawson imagines
himself sweeping off a stage, so Robert Saddington, as his ship nears the
coast of Australia, imagines himself writing the final lines of a chapter:
'This seems something like coming to a conclusion of Chapter 1 in the
History of my Voyages and Travels' (11 Oct. 1853). We not only think of
our lives in terms of stories, we think of them in terms of acts in a play
or chapters in a book, a vestige at the level of the individual of those
medieval plots of divine providence mentioned by Brooks.

Samuel Rawson ended his diary with, 'Thus ends the first period of
my life.' John Brown, the emigration agent for South Australia who
himself emigrated in 1836, ended his diary with a similar rhetorical
flourish: 'Farewell to old England, and now for a new Life and a new
Journal' (in Hope 34). The 'new Life' element here is testament to a
sense that he is cutting ties, not only emotional ties to family and
friends but the spatial ties of home, workplace, and locale. But it is the
ending of one diary and the beginning of another that allows the diarist
to think in this way, to make that psychological division between the
past as an old life and the future as a new life. It gives a material form to
what might otherwise be difficult to tell apart, the distinction between
the old and the new; the blank pages of a notebook metaphorically
represent a spatial severance, a new area to be inhabited and a potential
yet to be fulfilled.

Yet what is puzzling about John Brown's remark is that the new is not
usually thought to begin before arrival in Australia. The end of Edward
Lacey's diary of the voyage makes this clear: 'I must bid a hasty farewell
to my fellow passengers, pack up my traps, and prepare to land in this
new country where I have to commence life afresh and where all are

entire strangers' (25 Aug. 1862). James Walker, at the end of a retro-spective account, writes similarly: 'And so, on the 13th February, 1868, my life in the colonies began.' The new life in the new country begins on landing not on embarkation, and that is probably why emigrants, if they continued to keep a diary after arrival, more often did so in a new book. Samuel Rawson began a new diary with his landing in Sydney, and so apparently did Walter Hume: 'I consider that I have arrived in Australia, so that I shall continue my doings and adventures in another book' (20 Jan. 1863). John Brown's 'new life, new journal,' if it applies to the start of the voyage, also applies to the end; both are beginnings of new books.

But if one life ended on departure and another began 'afresh' in the new country on arrival, what world or life did emigrants inhabit during the voyage out? The voyage out seems to exist only as a gap or an interlude, a stage between two worlds but without substance itself. In this sense it is a liminal world. The anthropologist Arnold van Gennep in his seminal work on social passages identified three types of ritual surrounding the kind of life changes emigration involves: preliminal rites (rites of separation), liminal rites (rites of transition), and postliminal rites (rites of incorporation) (11). In terms of emigration to Australia, rites of separation may take the form of those wakes held by the Irish for departing members of their community (MacDonagh 33; O'Farrell, *Irish in Australia* 58); the ceremonial arrival of Neptune on board ship to mark the crossing of the equator is a rite of transition; and the welcoming of the emigrants into the houses of family already in Australia by the provision of a communal meal may be seen as a rite of incorporation. More importantly, the whole of the voyage out is a kind of liminal or threshold stage, a sacred zone into which the emigrant passes for the transitional period, a zone both spatially and temporally isolated from the secular world.

In work that extends van Gennep's, Victor Turner argues that it is in the liminal stage of a passage, that stage between departure and arrival, that narratives which make meaningful the whole passage are generated (156–7). In Turner's understanding of this, the narratives are generated as public ritual, as theatrical event. But writing a diary is itself a kind of ritual, the act of beginning a diary serving as a rite of separation, and emigrants' diaries may be seen as narratives generated in the liminal stage; they arise out of the specific circumstances in which they were written and if, in one respect, they are already written, they nonetheless act, as narratives, as an attempt to give a coherent shape and meaning to the individual experience of emigration. A diary of the voyage out is a particularly powerful manifestation of narrative as a social practice.

This view of the emigrant diary as having a kind of ritual significance in its relationship to the voyage is useful as it allows us to see that, far from being the kind of passive recorder of the voyage it is often held to be, at the time of its writing the diary was actively producing meaning. But one qualification needs to be made here, and it reiterates one made earlier. If the mechanics of beginning and ending diaries are kinds of rituals framing a rite of passage, they are so not because the voyage out was a natural rite of passage but because it was already culturally defined as such. Charlotte MacDonald has drawn attention to the way in which life-cycle stages coincided with emigration in the nineteenth century: 'The age at which most people emigrated was also the age at which it was most common to marry and establish a new family unit' (140). Yet as she points out, the two types of change are not of the same order; a life-cycle change is affected by changes in human physiology, emigration is not. It is tempting to think of ceremonies that mark life-cycle changes as being natural rather than cultural, yet rites of separation and incorporation mark changes in social status and are separable from physiological change; for this reason van Gennep himself distinguishes between social and physiological puberty (3).

Emigration as a rite of passage, then, is not predicated on any prior non-representational change; changes in social status which are involved in emigration are culturally determined. This means that we should also be careful to see the difference between an old life and a new life sceptically. Without rites of separation and incorporation it would be difficult to tell the old from the new; indeed, it is the function of such rites to define that very boundary. Leaving home, embarkation, and setting sail can be seen as marking the end of the old life precisely because the voyage out is already culturally defined as a movement towards a new social status, a new life. In van Gennep's formulation, the liminal zone is constituted by its frame; it is the gap between a rite of separation and a rite of incorporation. In the case of emigration, however, the commonsense proposition which assumes that frames are naturally occurring is reversible: it is the gap which allows beginnings and endings to be defined. The gap in this case is not so much a gap as a journey-story, a cultural narrative of liminality.

*

To argue, as I have been arguing, that the diary of the voyage out is

already written suggests that the act of writing the diary, its performance, was largely passive. At the very most all the diarist needed was a
longer version of the model provided by W. H. G. Kingston's *Emigrant
Voyager's Manual* (1850); as the voyage progressed the emigrant could
merely fill in the gaps:

> *26th July, 1850.* – At — A.M. left Deptford, and went on board the
> — emigrant ship, of — tons, bound for —; —, Captain; —, Esq.
> Surgeon-Superintendent. The Rev. —, Chaplain; Mrs. —,
> Matron. — Emigrants on board. At — A.M. dropped down the
> river; reached Gravesend at — P.M. Remained there — hours.
> (23)

This example certainly suggests that diarists were in one sense performing what was already written. In its choice of embarkation and setting
sail as a beginning, Kingston's model diary follows and subsequently
reinforces the practice of the time. Nineteenth-century emigrant diaries were highly conventional, the more obviously so perhaps after the
1840s when there was a change in the cultural and educational background of those writing diaries. During the 1840s there was a notable
reduction in the range of rhetorical devices employed, and if diaries
prior to the 1840s often used the literary conventions of sensibility,
later emigrant diaries rarely strove for any literary effect. The success of
diaries written during the period of mass migration from Europe was
gauged more by their completion than by any Romantic concept of
originality; performance was all important, the literary quality of the
performance secondary, and the remarkable similarity between the
diaries reflects the functional nature of diary-writing on board ship.

But to say that the diaries were conventional and lacked rhetorical
variation is not to say that writing a diary was easy or that it required no
skill. Diary-writing was a performance, and it was a difficult performance both because of the physical difficulties of writing in an alien
environment and because of the perceptual or cognitive adjustments
each diarist had to make in adapting to that environment. Paul Carter
has suggested that one of the functions of Australian explorers' journals
was the 'psychic' occupation of space: 'they represent . . . an attempt to
constitute experience historically, to understand how the non-
temporal consciousness of space – the phenomenon of space as an
infinity of directions – might be an essential ingredient in the *psychic*
occupation of the new country' (*Living in a New Country* 16).

Emigrants were not explorers, but this notion of 'a non-temporal consciousness of space' can be usefully applied to the emigrant experience if it allows us to look at the way in which emigrant narratives depended on successfully countering spatial disruption and turning 'non-temporal' space into narratable spaces. Journey-stories are by nature difficult to narrate since they necessarily involve a breaking away from the familiar and a narration of the new, and clearly this involves some degree of perceptual adjustment on the part of the traveller.

Moreover, by writing their journey-story in the form of a diary, emigrants, like the explorers, were compounding their difficulties; unlike retrospective forms of writing, the diary is written from within the overall narrative frame. Those emigrants who chose to write a memoir of the journey once it was over, either in the form of a letter home or as a more extended piece for posterity, had the advantage of hindsight and could more easily construct a coherent account. Diarists, on the other hand, not only had to manage the physical act of writing on a ship, they had to try to write about the voyage before they had a secure perspective on it. Their knowledge of previous narratives would have helped them by offering ways of seeing the voyage, but those ways of seeing had still to be adjusted to the circumstances of the individual voyage; two diarists on the same voyage did not perform exactly the same diary.

The beginnings of diaries were particularly hazardous, since emigrants had to have reached a certain accommodation with the voyage before they could even begin a diary, as Edwin Pegler recounts: 'Weather finer, than since leaving Plymouth, the first day I have been able to write in my diary, I tried one day but could not manage it, and the Ship gave a lurch, when down came cold tea from a shelf and spoilt two leaves of the book. Dinner, roast beef & plum pudding' (Edwin Pegler 12 Aug. 1852). The fact that many of the accounts of the beginning of the voyage were written up not at the time but some days into the voyage suggests that the experience of those first few days was less coherent than would seem from the ease with which those first few days are written into the diaries. I have already spoken of the way in which seasickness disrupted the initial diary entries; it either caused gaps in diaries that had been begun in calmer circumstances, or prevented diarists from beginning in the first place, as in the case of Helen Ronald, whom I quote again here: 'My dear Mama, Having waited five days for seasickness and the novelty of life on board ship to wear off,

I begin today, Thursday, my Diary of events' (24 Oct. 1861). But Helen Ronald also mentions being prevented from writing by 'the novelty of life on board ship', and this suggests a problem less with the stomach and more with the mind. Robert Gouger, colonial secretary of the South Australian Colonization Commission, writing 25 years before Helen Ronald, also mentions 'the novelty' of life at sea: *'July 13th 1836* I have now been on board nearly a fortnight almost a sufficient time to become tired of the sea, of watching the sailors at their employment, and of the general novelty of my situation. Partly by way of amusement, and partly to fulfil my promise to my relations & friends in England, I commence a journal of my voyage.' There is something in the 'novelty' of shipboard life for those unaccustomed to it that hinders writing.

The term most often used to describe the initial period at sea is not, however, the benign 'novelty' of Helen Ronald or Robert Gouger but the more malign 'confusion' of Abijou Good:

> we contrived to get tea but sush confusion i had never seen before
> hooting, shouting, curseing, swearing crying prevailed on every
> side   some were rushing to & fro others were standing
> indivouring to quite their wifes & children when some one else
> would run against them perhaps up setting them & their tea
> scalding others & causeing one of the grandst scenes of confusion
> that any man might wish to see   however every thing must
> have an end & so tea had an end but the confusion in no way
> abbated. (Abijou Good 28 Feb. 1863)

It was the unabating nature of this initial confusion that prevented Elizabeth Ankatell from commencing her diary for nineteen days after embarkation: 'December 19th 1865 – Up to the present time I have been unable to write in my journal as I intended – Came on board "The Queen of Australia" on Nov[r] 30th felt very dreary & lonely & unhappy, could do nothing but cry & wish I had not ventured, everything seemed so confused comfortless and wretched.' Not many diarists admitted regretting their decision to emigrate like this, and if they did it was a sentiment that faded as the voyage wore on; perhaps this was because the confusion became less. Solomon Joseph was another who was prevented from writing because of the 'confusion': *'Tuesday, 28th* [1859]. – Everything has been so unsettled that I could not quiet my mind to do anything – even to read; this diary, therefore, from the 18th has not been written day by day but all on this day.' When he does

[59]

commence his diary, significantly in his first sentence he chooses the word 'confusion' to sum up the start of his voyage: 'All bustle and confusion this morning.'

The term 'confusion' is not a surprising choice given the conditions surrounding embarkation. At the height of emigration in the 1850s, figures drawn up by the Colonial Land and Emigration Commissioners show that over 200,000 people were leaving Liverpool every year for North America and Australia, and many emigrants must have been overwhelmed by the sheer volume of this human traffic. In London, the average yearly volume in the 1850s was 27,000, while in the other major emigration ports, Plymouth and Southampton, numbers emigrating in the 1850s averaged between 8,000 and 10,000. In such circumstances, getting on board with boxes and baggage was not easy. In Liverpool and London, ships could be loaded from a dock, but as fire and lights were prohibited while the ships were in dock and as cargo was loaded up to the last minute (MacDonagh 33), passengers were still sent aboard in a mad final rush; and if the ship was moored away from the quayside, then it was necessary for hundreds of people to crowd on board a steamer to be transferred to their ship.

Alfred Withers travelled out to Australia in 1857 on one of the famous clippers of the Black Ball line, the *James Baines*, and his diary gives a particularly lively account of embarkation in the heyday of emigration from Liverpool to Melbourne:

> the scene on the pier no one can realize unless they have
> witnessed it or been passengers themselves in a ship for Australia
> or America.
>
> The immense quantity of luggage, pyramids of boxes, cases and
> baskets, the indescribable quantity of beds and bedding that one
> would think that Heal and Son had been cleared out, water cans,
> pannikins, hookpots, baths, enough to open a warehouse in the
> tin ware line. This immense quantity of luggage belonging to
> each passenger, there to be measured by the [ship]owners'
> servants, all excess over 40 cubic feet having to be paid for by each
> passenger, the steamer is capable of holding about one fourth the
> passengers and their luggage and so everybody is anxious to get to
> the vessel and arrange their cabin. The squeezing, crowding,
> pushing and confusion is fearful. (3 Jan. 1857)

The liveliness of this account comes in part from the way in which the confusion of words in the second sentence mimics the confusion of objects on the pier: 'luggage . . . boxes, cases and baskets, . . . beds and bedding . . . water cans, pannikins, hookpots, baths'. This list, like the diverse articles being taken on board, seems potentially endless, and space, be it the space of the diary or the space of the dockside, loses its outlines. Alfred appears to get control when he comes to 'one would think that Heal and Son had been cleared out', as though the mention of a large furniture store could help contain the grammar of the sentence; but the listing carries on. The sentence is brought to a halt only by the mention of yet another large building, 'a warehouse in the tin ware line'. The syntactical structure of this sentence suggests that the experience on the pier comes close to defeating not only Alfred's ability to give it some order, but his ability to put it into words. In a similar way the third sentence beginning, 'This immense quantity of luggage', ends with the desire of each of the passengers to 'arrange their cabin', and it is this idea that rounds off the passage as a whole. To arrange a cabin is to articulate space, to allow it to become familiar and narratable.

This passage from Alfred Withers's diary shows how the term 'confusion' refers to a spatial confusion and the way in which writing a diary can be employed to help overcome that spatial confusion. The diversity of the space encountered by the emigrant at the docks and on board ship makes it unnarratable; writing that space would result in an infinity of lists, all more or less simultaneous. With the textualisation of that space, that space becomes textually inscribed, it becomes ordered and metaphorically enclosed in the way that Alfred Withers wants to enclose the articles on the pier in a warehouse; there is a connection here between physical containment and the manner in which the experience can be contained by narrative.

A later passage makes the same point in a slightly different way. Alfred Withers finally succeeded in getting his luggage on board a steamer for the *James Baines*, but 'when all was on board I only just knew the wherabouts of my dirty clothes bag and my writing case, everything else belonging to us was lost for a time in the sea of luggage'. A 'sea' of luggage is an apt metaphor; whereas Alfred used images of enclosure in his articulation of space, he uses an image of the unenclosed sea to signify a loss of differentiation between his baggage and everyone else's. If writing is a way in which an emigrant might contain a loss of differentiation, is it purely fortuitous that, when all but two items of his luggage have disappeared, Alfred keeps track of his writing case?

[61]

The desire to arrange a cabin mentioned by Alfred Withers appears, not surprisingly, in a great many of the accounts of embarkation because it was a primary way of re-establishing spatial differentiation; though the 'squeezing, crowding, pushing' was not necessarily any less once the passengers were on board, for those like Alfred Withers who were travelling out in cabin accommodation, the ordering of a cabin was the first chance they had in the general 'confusion' to construct a narratable space. Not all were immediately successful, and Margaret Walpole, the wife of the ship's surgeon, suffered an initial setback: 'As soon as we got on board, Mother, Alice and I took the luggage to the cabin hoping to arrange it a little before we started but it was in such a state of confusion having been packed with medicine stores of all kinds that there was no hope of getting anything in order then' (13 June 1883). John Joseland had more success: 'I immediately set to work and arranged our little cabin so as to insure some degree of comfort' (1 Mar. 1853); and Richard Watt and his companion made the most of a period spent anchored in the Downs prior to sailing by similarly organising their living space: 'it gave us a last opportunity of arranging the bunks to our satisfaction. Our accommodation before looked anything but a place to live in' (9 May 1864).

This notion of space as 'a place to live in' can be examined further by reference to the sociological concept of the domain. Although the physical space of the ship was already marked out by very concrete markers – the poop deck being higher than the main deck, the interior of the ship being divided by bulkheads, and so on – the spaces of the ship were also specific social domains and the values attached to these spaces were derived from the culture of those who occupied them. The domain, as Fiske, Hodge, and Turner define it, 'is not simply a physical location. It is a social space, organised by a set of rules which specify who can be in it and what they can do. It also controls meanings: what meanings can be expressed and how, and how they will be interpreted' (5). The emigrants clearly brought with them a repertoire of domains, of ways of categorising spaces, yet the dynamics of these spaces should not be underestimated. In the same way as emigrants brought with them a knowledge of previous narratives yet still needed actively to perform the diary, so for the emigrant newly-arrived on ship, the cultural meanings attached to the spaces of the ship were more latent than actual; it is only through actual social practice that cultural meanings are articulated, are preserved or contested. The construction of order out of the 'confusion' of embarkation occurred, then, not only through the arranging of physical space but through the successful investment of that physical space with a narratable meaning. In terms of cabin space, that usually meant that the cabin came to acquire the social and cultural connotations of 'home': 'To day we seemed to be getting more at home – began to arrange some of our things' (George Randall 15 June 1868). The occupation of space brought into being an active social space, the domain of home.

Despite his anxiety to arrange his cabin, Alfred Withers found that he had to return to the shore and spend two more nights at a hotel as there was no food yet on the *James Baines* for first-class passengers. It was, therefore, two days after his waiting on the pier for the steamer that he got down to fitting his cabin. Cabin passengers had to provide not only their own bedding and utensils, but most of their cabin fitments as well, and all the beds, baths and pannikins noted by Alfred on the pier were not necessarily being put in the ship's hold; once on board, furniture for use in the cabin had to be screwed as appropriate to floors and bulkheads to prevent it from shifting in bad weather:

> we went by the steamer on board and finally took possession of our floating home for 3 months, the rent having been settled quite in the Colonial style, viz, paid in advance. Here Madge [Alfred's wife] was soon quite at home: she took over the whole management of the arrangements and *made* me do all sorts of things, in two hours our Drawers, boxes and every moveable article became fixtures by screwing them to the floor and bulkheads so that they could not move by the rolling of the ship and everything was made snug for bad weather. (Withers 5 Jan. 1857)

By screwing down all the moveable items, Alfred Withers is attempting to construct a space that is very much a nineteenth-century middle-class concept of the home; it is a domestic, feminine space distinguished from a masculine, public space surrounding and threatening it. This is achieved in two ways. The cabin is made 'home' by the arrangement of personal belongings, chests being fixed to the floor and other articles being hung on the bulkheads. Yet it is also made 'home' by its occupants adopting roles appropriate to the Victorian home, the woman adopting the dominant role of housekeeper, the male accepting the superficially subservient role of handyman. In these ways, the spaces of the ship are being invested with identifiable cultural meanings and the 'snug' cabin marks out the culturally designated space of 'home'. The same procedure is carried out by others in cabin-class accommodation:

> After breakfast I cleared out our cabin and Martha well cleaned it, which occupied her till lunch time. Then I re-arranged our boxes, laid our carpet and made it very much more comfortable and snug than it has been before. (John Joseland 23 Mar. 1853)

> we took possession of the cabin and I unpacked and I put some things in order, while Mr Boyce screwed up the little cupboard in a convenient corner and made things look quite comfortable. (Rachel Henning 15 Feb. 1861)

Here again is the division of activities between male and female and once more the domain that is being articulated is the 'comfortable' and 'snug' domestic space of the Victorian middle-class home.

In the far more cramped steerage accommodation, there was no fixing of cupboards and beds to organise as the accommodation was in effect a simple dormitory with two tiers of bunks lining the sides of the ship. A few personal effects, mainly clothes, were allowed, and these had to be hung from the sides of the bunks in the bags provided, as Fanny Davis, travelling in the single women's accommodation, recorded: 'Each person has two canvas bags given them and are told to put a month's clothes into them as all the boxes are to be put into the hold of the vessel today and only to be taken out once a month to get out another month's clothes and put our dirty ones away' (4 June 1858). Nonetheless, even though they had fewer belongings with them, steerage passengers also seemed to be anxious to order their possessions and settle in. As Fanny Davis goes on to suggest, this ordering was a way of coping with the loss of coherence: 'Nearly all the single women sit down and have a good cry the first thing, and I feel very much inclined to join them; but first ask myself what there is to cry about and as I cannot answer it to my own satisfaction, think it would be very foolish so begin to put things in order in our berths' (5 June 1858). Although evidence from steerage diaries is scarce, this suggests that the desire to construct 'a place to live in' was not confined solely to the cabin passengers. And although steerage passengers would have had difficulty creating a 'snug' area in the fashion of the middle-class home, emigrants of all classes wanted, as Fanny Davis terms it, 'to put things in order'. In the first few days on board, emigrants were intent on turning confusion into order, and they did so primarily by organising their living space.

Not all diaries were commenced late into the voyage, though we can never be certain that the initial entries of a diary were written on the day they record; not all diarists were as honest as Helen Ronald in admitting a number of days had elapsed before she had begun her diary. But enough diarists give reasons for being prevented from writing to suggest that the main obstacle to writing a diary from the moment of embarkation was a loss of coherence or meaning; the environment was too alien to be narratable. To be able to write a diary, emigrants needed to order the space around them, to make it narratable. This ordering of space in turn depended on investing certain spaces with cultural meanings, the kind of differentiation of space required in establishing a 'home' on board ship. In fact, it may well have been specifically this lack of a sense of 'home' which prevented the diary from being written, as Andrew Hamilton's diary suggests: 'Wednesday 28th. Have not been able to write daily several things intervening – for the first week could think of doing nothing with the feeling that I was "from home"   the rest of the time has been occupied in getting our Boxes in order and arrangeing our little Cabin and sundry other Matters' (28 July 1852). Andrew Hamilton here was unable to write regularly until seventeen days into the voyage because he was 'from home'; yet by ordering his boxes and arranging his cabin he has now managed to invest a certain space with the connotations of home and so begin writing. Having articulated his space by his action, the space can now be articulated in his diary, and the voyage has now become narratable. The term invariably used to describe this initial spatial incoherence on board ship is 'confusion', and its obvious meaning is a loss of order; the ship is yet to become ship-shape. But if the loss of spatial differentiation meant the experience was unnarratable, then 'confusion' not only designates a non-linguistic incoherence, its very use indicates that the situation has been brought under control; language once again works. The ritual of commencing a diary therefore not only signifies a rite of separation, it indicates that a space has successfully been articulated from which to write a diary and about which to write a diary. Space has been stabilised.

*

There is something odd here. In order to begin writing a journey-story, the diarist needs first to establish a domain of home; the articulation of a home makes the journey narratable. Yet journeys and homes ought to be mutually exclusive; journeys imply movement, homes imply hearths, the kind of hearths for which the emigrants imagined themselves to be writing. In the case of emigrant diarists, it is surely their lack of a home that defines them as migrants. Paul Carter in *The Road to Botany Bay* has written of the conditions at sea in which emigrants wrote their diaries:

> Ships were houses on the move. They had something of the convenience of home with the advantage of enforced leisure. They enabled one to write the letters one would never have written otherwise. Despite the salt spray, the heaving deck, the stench and the poor rations, they offered marginally superior conditions in which to record one's experience than a campsite in the bush. (141)

As we have seen, ships offered not only something of the convenience of home, but a space that could be invested with the nineteenth-century connotations of home: the cabins, if not necessarily the accommodation of the steerage passengers, were regarded as snug, private, feminine spaces. Carter is not too concerned that the diarists might then not be writing about the transgressive incidents associated with travel, since for Carter, 'what the emigrants wrote about was the experience of travelling and nowhere was that experience brought home to them more clearly than in an environment devoid of external distractions' (141). This may be true, but there is also a good deal in the diaries about other passengers, and the general social interaction of the diarist's immediate circle would not be out of place in a domestic diary:

> We had a fancy dress ball in the evening. We might indeed have imagined ourselves in a ballroom as nearly all wore wreaths & leaves cut out of writing paper & mixed some with flowers & some with colored paper which had a very pretty effect and many had low dresses. Well we all danced until we were hungry and then had to go supperless to bed. (Annie Gratton 9 Aug. 1858)

Domestic diaries and travel diaries ought surely to differ.

British emigrants to Australia were not, generally speaking, wholehearted travellers, and once they were on board and at sea, emigrants seem to have tried as much as possible to envisage themselves back home. Travel implies transgression and 'confusion,' but I have seen only one instance of 'confusion' being used in a positive sense, and this by a single woman at a hotel in Liverpool prior to embarkation: 'on the whole the busey confusion of meeting so many strangers rather pleased me' ('Jemima' 4 July 1853). 'Confusion' was negative, 'home' positive. This reliance on home resulted partly from the fact that the spatial transgression implied in travel can be made narratable only by the creation of recognisable domains. But this conservatism, this need to counter rather than embrace trangression, was accentuated by the particular combination of the physical conditions of travel and the cultural outlook of those travelling: where the conditions required homeless travellers to live on their means of transport for a long period, then they were likely to invest it with their domestic cultural domain.

Yet the stabilisation of space around the concept of home can only be successful to a degree, and its maintenance was necessarily fragile; it was possible only so far to ignore the fact that they were homeless emigrants on the move. The notion of a home on board a ship offers, according to Michel de Certeau, a different articulation of space from that of the journey itself: whereas the journey is concerned with a movement beyond, the home is concerned with walls and boundaries (Certeau 123). The conservatism of the emigrants privileges the home while trying to efface the journey, yet the two remain in a conflicting relationship, as in the following diary entry:

> I had a very busy morning making my two little rooms tidy, I feel
> quite at home in them now and often quite forget I am on the
> sea but I spend a good deal of time wondering what Papa, and
> Agnes, and all of them are doing at home. I would just like to get
> into the garden, and have a good tuck out, on red currants and
> things for a change. (Frances Thornton 7 Aug. 1882)

Frances Thornton here feels 'quite at home' because she has created a recognisable domestic space in her 'two little rooms' (not 'cabins') on board ship, but all the same her mind oscillates between being able to forget she is at sea and remembering her relations 'at home'. To be at home on board ship is to be both at home and on a journey, to be at once static and on the move. The emigrant diary is both a domestic diary and a diary of a journey, and the movement between the two is a movement between two types of narrative model.

This sense of being at home and not being at home is captured by Alfred Withers in a passage I quoted earlier in another context: 'we went by steamer on board and finally took possession of our floating home' (5 Jan. 1857). The phrase 'our floating home' nicely captures the instability of space on board ship, the combination of an enclosed space and the moving vessel. It is not unique to Alfred Withers and is current over twenty years later in the diary of William Chambers, where it is contrasted with a 'native' home: 'every one seems so happy in this our floating home, as we sail so many thousands of miles far away from our native homes' (17 Oct. 1879). Again there is the positive connotation of the notion of 'home': 'every one seems so happy'. But while a diary may continue to be written if the diarist, like Francis Thornton, temporarily forgets she or he is on the move, it cannot continue if the sense of home breaks down. In other words, of the two articulations of space defined by Michel de Certeau, that of the journey and that of home, the articulation of the journey, the movement beyond, depends upon the articulation of an enclosed space in order to be narratable. We return here to Paul Carter's argument that travellers at sea were more aware of the experience of travelling while lacking transgressive incidents to write about: 'nowhere was that experience brought home to them more clearly than in an environment devoid of external distractions' (141). Carter's own phrase, 'brought home', indicates how much narration depends upon 'confusion' being contained; the 'home' as the place from which a diary is written is more or less by definition 'an environment devoid of external distractions'. Loss of spatial differentiation and the transgression of boundaries would bring writing to a halt.

*

Sue Rowley has looked at the representation of women in nineteenth-century narratives of Australian nationalism, narratives that deal with the journeys made by explorers, pioneers, drovers, shearers, and so on. She argues that, since such narratives depend upon points of departure and arrival, this implies 'a spatial differentiation between the points of departure and return, and the terrain of adventure' (69). In the nineteenth century, this differentiation between interior and exterior spaces corresponded to a gender differentiation between feminine and masculine spaces, between domesticity and adventure. Thus: 'The journeying of men is predicated on the existence of a home: a place to set out from, a place to return to. The home is the place of women's waiting' (69).

Much the same applies to the shipboard narratives contained in emigrant diaries, except that these deal with people who have no home to which they might return. The home, and the women who are doing the waiting, are carried on the journey and in such circumstances the spatial differentiation between interior and exterior, the domains of women and the domains of men, is more unstable. If, as Rowley puts it, the journeying of men is predicated on (i.e. made meaningful by) the existence of a home, then we could argue that within the dialectic between domesticity and travel that I outlined earlier, the maintenance of that home at sea is vital for the voyage out to retain a meaning.

The maintenance of home at sea was achieved primarily by the incarceration of women; to use Sue Rowley's phrase, 'The home is the place of women's waiting.' The movement of women within the physical space of the ship was highly restricted and women were subject to various forms of incarceration. Middle-class women travelling in cabin accommodation were restricted to areas devoid of the lower classes, be they passengers or crew, areas such as the poop deck, the dining saloon, or the cabin. According to her husband, Harriet Gouger spent all but two hours a day in her cabin throughout a voyage of almost four months: 'we have found it a most delightful retreat; in proof of which I may truly say, that on average I have not been more than four hours a day out of it, while Harriet has not been more than half that time' (Robert Gouger 17 Sept. 1836). This may be an extreme example, given Robert Gouger's elevated social position as Colonial Secretary, but it demonstrates the underlying assumption that the natural place of middle-class women on board ship was in the home/cabin.

Whatever their social class, women who had children would have found their incarceration below decks reinforced by the responsibility for childcare. Mrs Hinshelwood, travelling steerage with her husband and seven children, found herself looking after her youngest son during an outbreak of measles on board: 'Still a prisoner 'tween decks on little John's account' (6 June 1883). After ten days in the poorly ventilated steerage area, she herself was having to receive treatment from the doctor: 'I am almost suffocated below, as John is still prohibited from going on deck, though getting over the measles nicely. I have been ten days below, and am feeling the effects of it very much' (12 June).

The most severe incarceration, however, was reserved for the single women in steerage. The Passenger Act of 1852 required the single males to be berthed in separate sleeping accommodation, but it became usual practice on board government ships to split the steerage deck into three not two compartments: single males over the age of fourteen (later twelve) were allocated the forward end of the ship below the crew's accommodation in the forecastle, the single and unaccompanied females were allocated the rear section below the cabin accommodation, and the middle section of the ship between these two poles was occupied by the married couples, a centring of arrangements both physically and culturally on an idealised image of a heterosexual family unit. The basis for segregating the single women and single men was overtly moralistic, though there was no equivalent segregation among cabin-class passengers, and while the segregated single men were placed in single hammocks or bunks, the single women had to share bunks; official regulations ignored the existence of lesbian sexuality. Judging from instances cited in the diaries, there was clearly a need to protect single women at sea from sexual harassment or inducement to prostitution by the male passengers or the male crew. William Nichols relates that on his ship, 'the Captain is a marriad man   he formed an acquantance with a single female on board by whome she is with child' (25 June 1849); in this case the captain was subsequently ordered to pay the woman £100. Yet the determination by the emigration authorities to keep the single women 'respectable', that is, excluded from intercourse, sexual or otherwise, with any of the males on board, resulted in their being the most restricted and supervised social group on board.

On many ships a mature married woman was appointed as matron to supervise and regulate the lives of the single females, the only women, as Charlotte MacDonald points out, invested with formal authority on board ship (82). In organising the cleaning, the preparation of food, the school and Bible lessons, and so on, the matron acted not only to protect the women in her charge but 'to encourage habits of orderliness, industry, deference and self-improvement' (MacDonald 83). Yet the degree to which the single women were isolated meant that their supervisor also acted as gaoler, keeping the keys to the compartment, locking them in at night, and generally preventing the women from coming into contact with men: 'this keeps the young women entirley at a distance from the men   I at this time have no idea of whare the galley is and as for the cooks I never to my knowledge saw any of them   I heard that he is a black' (Mary Maclean 2 Jan. 1865). Those who fought the discipline suffered. Up until the 1840s, single women could be placed in irons or have their hair cut off as punishments for disobedience; throughout the nineteenth century, they could be denied the already restricted time they were allowed on deck, to the detriment of their health:

> the whole of the single females owing to the misconduct of a few
> are sent below at eight o clock and their lamp taken away and
> lockd in the dark untill seven the next morning   the Docter
> keeps them very strict, the Docters assistant counts them every
> night after they are in bed like a flock of sheep   they were quite
> pityable during the hot weather many became very sickly
> (William Nichols 27 May 1849).

Not surprisingly, many of the single women reacted against being treated 'like a flock of sheep'. Following a three-day gap in her diary Mary Maclean writes: 'I am sorry to state that we are stictley forbidden to take notes on account of so many writing to the men   it is very hard to suffer this for I have taken an interest in my diary . . . it seems as if thay tried to deprive us of every liberty' (6 Jan. 1865). The battle with the single women is here fought over their right to speak for themselves rather than to be spoken about, to have their voices heard. One weapon women used, therefore, to express their resentment was song. Charlotte MacDonald quotes an incident concerning two of the single women: 'Last evening when the most of the other girls joined together for Divine Service these two in defiance of the Matron struck-up "Slap-bang, here we go again" . . . in a bad voice, completely drowning that of the others' (91). On board the *Montmorency* in 1863, when the single women complained of not being allowed to dance with any of the men, the surgeon sent them below:

> they for revenge made a song up & sung it about him. He listened
> to it along with others & got quite mad when the people cheered
> the song & sent down the purser to find who sang, but he was
> pulled about in every direction while the people on deck shouted,
> 'Doctor the purser is among the women.' (Joshua Hughes 12 May
> 1863)

The next day the surgeon placed the single women on bread and water and 'disrated' the matron. Song is being used by women in both cases to resist and disrupt differentiation between the masculine and the feminine. In the first case, the two women adopt a song that had been popularised by the street organs, they align themselves with the street rather than the home; in the second case, the song successfully resists the surgeon's determination to keep the sexes apart by causing a man to be sent into the female compartment. In both cases, however, it is the women's voice and more especially their fine sense of irony that cuts through the desire for decorum and differentiation.

A more obvious example of resistance to incarceration involving a transgression of gender boundaries through the use of irony was noted by Thomas Davies on the *Lord Raglan* in 1854:

> after tea I went on deck there was rare fun going on 14 or 15 of the Single Girls were dressed up in Sailors clothes with masks on and were going to have a ball mask, I noticed the previous day that there was a bill posted up on the bakehouse relating to a ball masque taking place, and there they were sure enough, they had one or two jiggs till the Doctor and Captain came out, when they were obliged to get below and undress as soon as possible, all was still after. (Thomas Davies 19 Sept. 1854)

Such an incident is rich in meaning, but one main point concerns us here. Their dressing-up in sailors' clothing authorises the women to enter the unsupervised exterior space of the men, even to dance a couple of jigs, while their renewed incarceration is marked by the removal of their male attire. If the nineteenth-century cultural construction of the 'feminine' involved appropriate voice and dress, then the 'bad voices' and sailors' clothes were tactics carefully chosen to disrupt gender differentiation. In this the women who resisted authority were more resourceful than the single men who had less recourse to femininity as a subversive tactic; the sailors could dress up as women within the permitted carnivalesque ceremony of crossing the line, and Thomas Severn records sailors entertaining the passengers dressed as women: 'In the evening three of the sailors draped themselves up in women's drapes, and danced . . . we subscribed a few pence to get them some extra grog' (3 Sept. 1852). But the resistance of the single men was more often merely refusal: 'an order is given that the Single Men are to carry water for to cook the tea but they stoutly refused' (J. P. Ricou 26 May 1872).

Ultimately, this shrewd attack by these single women on gender differentiation was aimed at undermining the domain of the home upon which the very meaning of the voyage out depended. Emigrant diarists of both sexes were keen to contain transgression because the trangression of boundaries, be they physical or cultural, posed a threat to the narratability of the journey; the diary depended on a stabilisation of space and any loss of differentiation threatened the narrative with 'confusion'. If the narratable space was pre-eminently the feminine domain of the middle-class 'home', there was a special need to control the behaviour of women; any transgression of 'the feminine', the nineteenth-century cultural construction of 'femininity', threatened the ability of the emigrant to narrate the voyage as a journey-story. 'Home' operated as a conceptual site that permitted and maintained differentiation, while the differentiation between men and women became paramount for both sexes if 'confusion' was to be avoided and the home maintained.

Yet the diarists were also on a journey and a journey is by definition a transgression of boundaries; indeed, the voyage out had already been defined by the culture in which the diarists wrote as a liminal narrative. Emigrants caught between the old world and the new were therefore in a perilous position, not simply because of the physical threat to their safety, though that was fundamental enough, but because their need to domesticate their experience was at odds with their need to write a trangressive, and hence progressive, narrative. We see here the fallacy of believing that the journey could merely be transcribed into a book of the voyage. If narratives do give coherence to experience, they do so only despite that experience, for if the experience were already coherent, already a simple narrative, there would be no need to write it. The emigrant diary was constantly under threat, and while beginning a diary meant that a narratable space from which to write and about which to write had been created, that space needed to be maintained if the diary was to continue to the end of the voyage; every day the diary required a stable point for that day's entry to be written. The writing of a diary was a performance of the voyage, a constant struggle to contain the threat of a necessary but ultimately unnarratable 'confusion'. Once begun, the diary continued only so long as 'confusion' could be contained.

Chapter 3

Keeping the story running

'Mr Rankine was this day attacked with the Blue Devils'

One of the most monotonous diaries one could ever fear to come across in a manuscript reading room is the diary of the anonymous 'Mr A'. Every day of the 141 days of the voyage has an entry similar to the following:

> Monday 5th March [1838]
> The early part of these 24 hours a moderate breeze from the N.W. which gradually died away till it became calm at the close of the day –
> Fine clear weather during the early part of the day the latter part cloudy.
> The ship's course this day East going from 1 to 6 Knots the distance run being 86 miles.
> Lat obs^d 39.27. S. Long. 68.00 E.

Bryce Moore, in the Editor's Note to *The Voyage Out*, writes that the shipboard diaries in his collection were selected 'for their descriptive qualities and accessibility'. On an accessibility scale of 1 to 10, Mr A's diary barely registers. Here is his entry for Christmas Day, an occasion usually seized upon by diarists as a way of filling a few pages with something new to write about:

> Monday 25th December [1837]
> The early part of these 24 hours light air from the Southward, which towards 10.p.m. gradually died away into a Calm.
> Cloudy Weather with rain –
> At noon a calm with clear weather –
> The ships course East – distance only 14 miles

Lat. obs^d 5.47 No. Long 18.47. W.

This being Christmas day, divine service was performed in the morning – and after dinner we drank to the health of all our friends in England.

Not really the kind of diary an anxious relative might have hoped to receive. The only concession Mr A makes to mark the occasion of Christmas Day is to add a couple of sentences to the end of his standard entry. Far from being included in an anthology, such a diary would probably find its way into Bryce Moore's wastebin.

The reason Mr A's diary is so boring is because he seems merely to have copied into his notebook the day's entry in the ship's log, and log-books are, on the whole, pretty tedious reading. The ship's log had (probably still has) a standard form, recording each day navigational information such as the wind's speed and direction, changes in the setting of the sails, the ship's position calculated from an observation of the sun at noon, and the distance the ship had travelled in the previous 24 hours. The log also recorded less routine information as general remarks at the end of each day's entry, and it is into his diary's equivalent of general remarks that Mr A noted it was Christmas Day.

It was as I read through Mr A's diary (all 141 entries) that I became more fully convinced that a diary had its prime function on board ship, regardless of whether it was addressed to relatives or destined to be kept for posterity; Mr A was clearly not copying out the log for the amusement of friends at home, it could hardly be read aloud to a small group of family and friends without most of them falling asleep, and neither could the distance the ship travelled on Christmas Day be of any possible use to posterity. But as I read Mr A's diary I was also surprised to find that, amid the tedium of position reports and wind directions, a narrative nonetheless was trying to develop. On Sunday 11 February, the routine navigational information was followed by an unusually long comment:

One of the Cabin passengers (M^r. Rankine) who during the voyage had been drinking heavily was this day attacked with the *Blue Devils* & conducted himself in a very riotous manner like a Lunatic   he could not or durst not remain by himself in his Berth – & consequently Captn Smith & myself who slept in the Cabin co^d get no rest.

[75]

Mr Rankine, with his attack of the Blue Devils, is so potent a disruption
that the following day Mr A is forced to extend his daily entry to twice its
routine length in order to give a full account of the impact of Mr
Rankine on shipboard life: 'Mr Rankine (who still continues very ill &
apparently quite out of his mind) having expressed a wish to address the
passengers and ship's company he was indulged' (12 Feb.). After a
reading from the Bible, Mr Rankine gave 'a short History of his previous
life & concluded with an account of the Events which had occurred on
board during the Voyage'. Mr A himself had been ordered out of the
assembly for laughing at the 'mock solemnity' of the proceedings, but
he concludes his entry charitably: 'His mind is evidently disordered but
I hope he will be restored to Health again before the conclusion of the
voyage.'

Mr A's monotonous diary, however, can only tolerate so much
disruption and at this point the diary fights back and for a month
manages to contain Mr Rankine by reducing him to the monotony of a
formula:

> Mr Rankine still continues very unsettled, he refused to speak
> either to Captn Smith or myself because he says we laughed in the
> Hour of the Lord. (13 Feb.)

> Mr Rankine still continues very unsettled. (14 Feb.)

> Divine Service as usual, at which Mr Rankine (who still continues
> in a very unsettled state) did not attend. (18 Feb.)

> Mr Rankine still continues very unsettled in his mind although
> much better than he was at first. (22 Feb.)

> M^r R still continues unsettled in his mind. (25 Feb.)

> Mr Rankine still continues very unsettled in his mind, although
> more tranquil than he was some time ago. (3 Mar.)

We can take it from these entries that Mr Rankine 'continued in a very
unsettled state.' The reduction of Mr Rankine to a formula allows him to
be incorporated into Mr A's log-book as just a routine item like the wind
direction.

Mr Rankine, though, is far too dynamic a character to be contained
by a formula indefinitely: 'Mr Rankine a great deal worse to day: – he
imagines himself the Commander of the Ship & to be possessed of

immense wealth which he is giving away to all around him' (12 Mar.).
Mr Rankine then turns violent, so much so that 'the Captain has been
obliged to use the horsewhip to him in order to subdue him which has
the desired effect' (14 Mar.); Mr Rankine resorts to verbal abuse, 'using
the most horrid oaths, & the most disgusting & filthy language' (15
Mar). Three days later Mr Rankine is placed in a strait waistcoat 'for the
safety of himself and others' (18 Mar.), and as Mr Rankine becomes
physically more and more constrained, so the diary gains on him,
reducing him once again to a standard formula:

> Mr Rankine quite as boisterous as ever, using the most horrid
> threats and imprications to every one on board: – & his language
> the most filthy and disgusting. (21 Mar.)

> Mr Rankine as boisterous & unruly as ever. (22 Mar.)

> Mr Rankine as boisterous as ever kicking at & biting his Keepers &
> making use of the most filthy & disgusting language. (23 Mar.)

Alas, the tale has a melancholy end:

> This morning, Mr Rankine was at his urgent request brought on
> deck for the purpose of getting a little fresh air – at 1.p.m., when
> the Captain & passengers were at lunch in the Cabin he managed
> to send his Keeper forward on some trifling errand & during his
> absence he (M^r R) threw himself overboard. (24 Mar.)

The alarm is given, a boat lowered, and Mr Rankine returned to the
ship, but two hours of attempted resuscitation fails, 'the vital spark
having fled'. The following day the diary gives extended coverage to Mr
Rankine's funeral, and then with a sense of relief the diary returns to its
equilibrium: 'Mr Rankine's funeral although a very melancholy event
has made a very quiet ship' (25 Mar.).

Mr A's diary is instructive in a number of ways and I will be referring
to it periodically as a kind of touchstone throughout this chapter. For
the moment let me merely summarise two of the points I want to
develop. First, in the same way as a battle is fought on board ship
between disruption and the containment of that disruption, between
Mr Rankine with his filthy language and the captain with his horsewhip,
so a battle is fought in the diary between a disruptive narrative and a
narrative equilibrium; the more that the story of Mr Rankine disrupts

the repetitive daily entry, the more the diary tries to reduce that story to a repeatable formula such as 'Mr Rankine as boisterous as ever'. The physical straitjacket is parallelled by a discursive straitjacket. My second point is really a development of the first: the conflict in Mr A's diary is between two antipathetic types of discourse, between a navigational discourse with its desire for typicality, for what can be labelled and measured, and an anecdotal discourse with its desire for the singular, for what exceeds the typical. Narrative development ends with the funeral of Mr Rankine and Mr A's diary reverts to the form of a log and its monumental monotony.

*

Mary Louise Pratt, in an essay on late eighteenth- and early nineteenth-century African explorers' narratives, posits two modes of travel writing, the informational mode and the experiential mode. In the informational mode, explorer-writers aspired to give their account a scientific status: 'Their task . . . was to incorporate a particular reality into a series of interlocking information orders – aesthetic, geographic, mineralogical, botanical, agricultural, economic, ecological, ethnographic, and so on' ('Scratches on the Face' 125). Adopting a stance that tries to efface the speaking self, the narrative portrays the landscape from an objectivist viewpoint: 'Unheroic, unparticularized, without ego, interest, or desire of its own, it seems able to do nothing but gaze from a periphery of its own creation' (124).

In contrast, the second mode of travel writing, the experiential mode, derives its authority less from informational orders or discourses and more from the active participation of the narrator as protagonist. If the first mode is typified by descriptions of landscape devoid of people, the second is typified by heroic adventures amongst the 'natives': 'It narrates the journey as an epic-style series of trials and challenges, of various kinds of encounters – often erotic ones – where indigenous inhabitants occupy the stage alongside the European' (131).

In terms of the informational mode, there are clearly fundamental differences between what might be recorded in a journey overland (as in Pratt's examples) and what might be recorded at sea, not least because of a lack of solid scenery; but it is still possible to find in emigrants' diaries a similar range of rationalist or scientific discourses (or information orders, as Pratt calls them) through which the experience of travelling to Australia may be recorded. Indeed, the pre-eminent form of rationalist discourse found in diaries of the voyage out is the same one that provided the monotonous equilibrium of Mr A's diary, the nautical log. Mr A was not alone in resorting to the ship's log, and C. Brown, for example, makes use of the same discourse in his diary:

> Thursday 6 January 1859 For the past 24 hours we have had a fine steady breeze which toward the latter part freshened considerably. a clear cold dry sky overhead. at 6 PM Great numbers of Birds about the ship. Uncle G shot a large Gull which fell into the sea. At 10 AM set Fore top Gallantsal Lower and Fore Topmast studdingsals and Flying Jib.

This is about half of the daily entry, but apart from the incidental report of Uncle G shooting the gull, it contains little information likely to be of much interest either to those back home or to posterity; the entry is in any case duplicating material found in the ship's log, and the navigational discourse is adopted merely for something to write about – even when the diarist has nothing interesting to report, it is still possible to record the weather, the set of the sails, and the ship's position. In practice, the nautical entry is the basic entry of the sea diary and almost every diary has an entry solely about the weather: 'Wind rather more brisk, weather fine, sea calm but attended with swells that cause us to roll a good deal' (J. W. Reeves 22 Dec. 1856).

More varied than the navigational discourse are the scientific discourses of natural history, such as marine biology and ornithology, and these play a significant part in how the voyage is recorded: 'I saw several dozen black fish   they are about ten to twelve feet long & the head is very much like a whale with a hole in their head for spouting water they came within six yards of the ship' (unnamed male diarist on the *Scottish Admiral* 7 June 1883). As well as marine creatures, various sea birds are spotted, caught, and eaten or stuffed during the voyage, as though the voyage itself were primarily for scientific interest: 'I see I have not described the Cape Pigeon so full as ought to be. Breast and belly white with a very few grey feathers in the breast, back white spotted with black, wings black & white, beak quite black. Web-footed, and black eyes, as also the two other birds [albatross and fulmar petrel]' (S. E. Roberts 14 Sept. 1848). In a footnote to this entry S. E. Roberts adds: 'measures *three* feet from tip to tip'. This careful recording of the bird's wing-span marks the whole description as an informational discourse and the literary model here is that of the popular journals of seventeenth- and eighteenth-century European navigators, pre-eminent among them Captain Cook: 'Saw 2 Pintado Birds the first I have seen this Voyage, they are larger than a Pigeon and chequer'd black and white over their backs and wings, with white bellies, black heads, and the ends of their tails are black' (21 Aug. 1769). It needs to be understood, however, that in the same way as the emigrant's navigational 'log' really only mimicked the ship's log, so this recording of natural history only pretended to a scientific status, if we take scientific status to mean the recording of fish or birds as a way of expanding established institutional knowledge. Against this standard, emigrants only pretended to be on a voyage of discovery, and while they adopted the discourses of the navigators, previous emigrants had themselves seen, measured, and invariably noted the same birds and the same sea creatures:

> We see a lot of flying fishes, also albatrosses. The birds fly very quickly round the ship and we have caught several of them on lines baited with a piece of pork. Some of these birds have a wing spread of 8–10 feet. (Moses Melchior 21 Oct. 1853)

> A great quantity of birds round the ship today, some of the Albatrosses are splendid creatures, white bodies, wings edged black, measuring 12 or 14 feet from tip to tip. (Alfred Withers 11 Feb. 1857)

> Many porpoises trawling about & many Large birds vis Halbertross & Sea gulls & sea pigeons very beautyful
> birds   Caught one which measured 7 ft 6 in from tip to tip of the
> wings   they are not good for eating. (Mr M 10 Oct. 1877)

An emigrant diary could hardly consider itself authentic without a record of the wing-span of an albatross. Needless to say, those who had read it found this a good occasion to quote from Samuel Taylor Coleridge's *The Rime of the Ancient Mariner*, though the custom of catching and killing albatrosses continued on most emigrant ships without the baleful consequences that followed for the ancient mariner.

A third kind of informational discourse which the diaries use is advice for prospective future emigrants. Emigrants frequently included in their diaries information they thought would be of use to subsequent emigrants; here an example is taken from the diary of fourteen-year-old Maria Steley addressed to 'Dear Eleanor':

[80]

The reason I write is when you come out you will know what to
bring. I have told you how we are going on every day. Bring cheese
& pickles. You need not bring coffee for there is plenty. Bring jam.
If anyone comes tell them if they bring ham not to put it in their
box for when they went to their boxes they were spoilt. They had
to fling them overboard. (15 Dec. 1863)

This kind of advice is of the same order as that contained in the manuals
and handbooks produced specifically for the emigrant. With such eye-
catching titles as *Out at Sea or the Emigrant Afloat: Handbook of
Practical Information for Use of Passengers on a Long Sea Voyage*, they
contained practical information on applying for assisted passages,
choosing a ship, and buying the necessary outfits for the voyage: 'As
there is no washing on board, it becomes also necessary to have such a
stock of under-clothing at hand as will serve for the whole voyage' (*The
Emigrant's Manual: Australia* 9). Since many of the writers of these
guides had never made the journey themselves, the accuracy of the
information could not be guaranteed and, weather permitting, regular
washing days were allowed on emigrant ships to Australia:

I find that it is not really necessary to be supplied for a voyage with
such an extra number of shirts, towels and other odd bits of
drapery as I am; because, I find, there are opportunities at sea for
'washing'! – but in the case of ladies in that matter there exists too
much mystery for me to say anything positively, or give you
information thereon, in which they only have an interest
(unnamed male diarist on the *Kate* 4 Aug. 1853)

It would be instructive to know more about how these handbooks
circulated and whether they had any significant influence on their
readers' behaviour. *MacKenzie's Australian Emigrant's Guide* (1852)
cost sixpence, while Chambers's *The Emigrant's Manual: Australia*
(1851) was double that at one shilling, and at these prices the likely
readership was those who travelled out by cabin, though *Out at Sea or
the Emigrant Afloat* was a twopenny pamphlet and ships' libraries
would have made some manuals and handbooks available to those
travelling steerage. The point, however, is that like the discourses of
navigation and natural history, the advice to emigrants in the diaries
was a normalising discourse that placed the experience of the emigrant
in a familiar context. It was necessary to record the wing-span of an

[81]

albatross or to write about cheese and pickles because in these ways the diary brought the experience within the bounds of the rational, the bounds of the known. Diarists were assessing the singular against the typical.

The experiential discourses, however, operate in a different way. According to Mary Louise Pratt, experiential discourses derive their authority less from the rationalism of informational discourses like natural history and more from the active participation of the narrator as protagonist in the episode narrated; whereas the informational discourses tend to efface human intervention, the experiential discourses typically portray the writer in heroic adventures. It is certainly true that the informational discourses I identified above efface human intervention, and the ship's log and natural history are apparently non-authored discourses; who wrote them is less important than the information they contain. However, with regard to the experiential mode, emigrants at sea had only limited opportunities for articulating a sense of personal agency, of doing something as an individual by choice, and the idea of emigrants on a voyage of adventure may not be wholly convincing. In W. H. G. Kingston's story, *The Fortunes of the 'Ranger' and 'Crusader': A Tale of Two Ships* (1872), the passengers on the emigrant ship *Crusader* bound for New Zealand have to survive an outbreak of fever, dismasting in a gale, the ship springing a leak, and finally being wrecked on an island. Few, if any, actual emigrants had to face such a sequence of disasters. However, the model of the voyage out as a journey-story full of heroic adventures was one which they implicitly called upon.

Catching a shark usually provided an exciting disruption of the routine of shipboard life: 'I have this evening resumed my day's journal to notify the fact of capturing a young shark' (William Wills 4 Dec. 1841). As William Harbottle noted: 'An adventure like this is very seasonable, it helps to relieve the routine and monotony of a long voyage' (14 Apr. 1849). Such 'adventures' very rarely involved the emigrants directly, yet they were eagerly grasped by diarists, and by women as much as by men, as something to write about:

> They let a rope over the stern with a piece of pork on the hook. A large shark was soon attracted to the bait. . . . All hands were employed – for the thing was to get a rope round his body before hauling him up to prevent his wriggling himself off the hook. Just at this juncture the boat came alongside again and was able to

help him from below. The confusion on deck was such that we
thought ourselves better downstairs. (Anna Fowler 17 July 1866)

Emigrants had an ambivalent attitude towards such adventures, welcoming them as new material to write about while, as in this example,
attempting to avoid the 'confusion' that disruption produced; Anna
Fowler and her female companion take refuge from the confusion in the
domestic domain of the first-class saloon.

If they were disadvantaged by their lack of agency, emigrants had all
the advantages of being surrounded by potential adventures while still
retaining a protected environment from which to write them up.
Although passengers were occasionally lost overboard, the dangers
surrounding the work of the crew on board a sailing ship meant that the
loss of a member of the crew quite often gave diarists an exciting
incident with which to fill a page or two:

at 6 A M this morning we unfortunately lost William Anderson
one of the Boys overboard while drawing water to wash the decks.
a hen coop was first thrown to him, and a Boat got into the water
as fast as possible and four men into her the ship was wore round
and crossed the spot, but all efforts were fruitless, and it was with
great danger the Boat and men were got on board in safety owing
to the tremendous sea running. What makes it the more
melancholy was that he was hurried to the presence of his *maker*
with an oath in his mouth. An awful lesson to us who remain of
the uncertainty of life which I hope we all profit by. (C. Brown 11
Jan. 1859)

Despite its sententiousness, this was good copy, an exciting incident
with which to fill a diary.

What these adventures promised was an adventure story, that is, an
experiential narrative that, to use Mary Louise Pratt's words, 'narrates
the journey as an epic-style series of trials and challenges' ('Scratches
on the Face' 131). European cultures have a long tradition of journey-
stories which involve a series of adventures, the epic being one among
stories of courtly romance, pilgrimage, exploration, the travels of the
nobility, and the wanderings of the picaro. In terms of specific models,
the most widely-read journey-stories outside of the Bible would probably have been *Pilgrim's Progress* (1678) and *Robinson Crusoe* (1719),
though it seems volumes of Cook's voyages would have been found

alongside them even in working-class households (Vincent 110). The popularity of *Pilgrim's Progress* and *Robinson Crusoe* was in part due to the respectability they gained from their religious content. *Pilgrim's Progress* was recommended in the *First Annual Report of the British Ladies' Female Emigrant Society* (1850) for inclusion in the shipboard library (20) and it remained widely read in Australia into the twentieth century (Lyons 46). Apart from its spiritual message, *Robinson Crusoe* also offered a narrative model of successful colonisation, though quite when emigration became a narrative model in its own right is hard to determine. Novels like Edward Bulwer-Lytton's *The Caxtons, A Family Picture* (1849) or Alexander Harris's *Martin Beck: or, The Story of an Australian Settler* (1849) demonstrate that by the mid-nineteenth century there was a developed and influential narrative model of Australian emigration available to the middle classes, and on reading *Martin Beck*, Henry Whittingham on board the *Duke of Wellington* noted: 'I have learned more *real* information from this *real novel*, than from all other works put together, though probably my former readings have helped me profitably to read this picture of an Australian *Life*' (2 May 1853). Yet even while there may have been narrative models of adventurous journeys to call upon, constructing a consistent narrative of the voyage out in a diary was almost impossible in circumstances which prevented the diarist knowing what would occur the following day: 'although I have no doubt that I shall be able to fill this book tolerably well before I have done with it, yet, *at present*, I cannot imagine what are to be its contents' (Arthur Manning 4 Nov. 1839).

Occasionally a narrative grows fortuitously, as when William Harbottle gave a young girl a copy of Lord Byron's *Childe Harold's Pilgrimage* because she seemed particularly sad at leaving 'her native land'. The girl died a month later, enabling William Harbottle to evoke suitably Byronic sentiments when he recorded it in his diary: 'strange and melancholy it is' (9 Apr. 1849). Byron's poetry and persona provided mid-century middle-class travellers with a particularly influential standard against which they could measure their own feelings (Buzard 115). Although a retrospective narrative could manufacture many such coincidences, for the diary-writer such narrative links between separate diary-entries are rare, and the battle rehearsed in Mr A's diary between what I have now identified as Pratt's informational and experiential orders, between the navigational log and the encounter with Mr Rankine, must always be fought with the advantage on the side of the informational. While the informational order can afford merely to mark time, repeating day after day the same words, the same gesture, the power needed to give impetus to the diary as a progressive narrative has to come from the experiential order; to take the narrative forward, a sequence must be identified and followed. However, the informational discourses do not have a total advantage, as Pratt herself points out: 'this informational kind of writing suffered from one serious defect: it was terribly boring' ('Scratches on the face' 130). If a diary is to avoid boring not only the reader but the writer, once a whale bird, an albatross, or a dolphin is spotted and recorded, once it has been incorporated into the rationalist discourses of the emigrant, some new information must be attached to it to make it worth recording a second or third time; in some way it must exceed its previous description and move towards the experiential mode if monotony is to be avoided. Few diarists would attempt to record the wing-span of an albatross daily.

Catching a shark, which I identified as an experiential adventure, may, of course, be preceded by, or more likely incorporate, a natural history description of a shark: 'He was a "blue shark," his back fins etc. were a blue black, his body white underneath, *10ft. 6ins.* from nose to tail' (Anna Fowler 17 July 1866). But the interweaving of these discourses is part of the battle between them and should not disguise the differences. The description of a shark is a typical description authorised by the rationalist discourse of natural history; name, length, and colour are all part of the apparent objectivity of the description. On the other hand, the adventure of catching a shark is not something that can be weighed and measured; it transgresses the typical routine of life on board ship, 'it helps to relieve the routine and monotony of a long voyage', as William Harbottle put it, and because of its narrative potential catching a shark becomes one of the 'adventures' of the passengers and crew on board W. H. G. Kingston's fictional emigrant ship *Crusader* (96). Amid the repetition of the ship's log, it is this trangression of the typical that constitutes the narrative impetus of the diary.

*

The type of discourse found in emigrant diaries that is the furthest removed from the navigational log is the sailor's yarn: 'This day has been nearly a copy of yesterday, very fine, very hot, and the ship rolling excessively, tho' Mr. Gray the 1st Mate says he has seen the yard-arms dip in the sea. This I regard as a "sailor's yarn" ' (Robert Saddington 18 Aug. 1853). Sailors' yarns are essentially oral travel narratives and the crew of emigrant ships frequently amused the male passengers by telling them about themselves and their adventures:

> In evening, a yarn with a Sailor, who related, with much relish, his adventures – chronicled in his diary – of hunting, debauchery, &c. I was glad however to hear an occasional expression of regret, & proper cognizance of such depraved conduct. When he had finished, I gave him a glass of marsala. (Henry Whittingham 22 Feb. 1853)

If the exchange value of such stories was usually a glass of wine or spirits, the number of yarns being spun by sailors on emigrant ships is hardly surprising. The emigrants in their turn passed on the sailors' yarns through their diaries:

> All greatly amused by a mistake made in the dusk of the evening by the sailor at the helm – an amusing Portugese, who mistook the Captain who was sitting on the Monkey Poop close behind him for one of the passengers, and confidently whispered in his ears 'I say, Our old Woman' (the Skipper's nickname in the forecastle) 'ess dronk' – You might imagine his look and start on discovering his error, by the Captain's angrily exclaiming 'What do you mean, sir?' (William Johnstone 3 Mar. 1842)

But yarns were also generated and exchanged between the passengers:

> As yesterday was calm it was a regular day for trouble, the captain, who held a bottle with powder in his hand, came too close to the fire and the bottle exploded; he himself, two passengers, the carpenter and V. got wounded. . . . As the doctor had had no opportunity to practice on the whole trip, I believe he was quite happy to come into action. It is told that when he was called he exclaimed: 'Hurrah! I'll come!' I can't say whether it is true. (Moses Melchior 17 Nov. 1853)

Being anecdotal, the yarn here clearly forms a contrast to the rationalist, informational discourses. Yarns are themselves more fully narratives and they depend for their effect on the skill of the telling rather than on any scientific proof. And in the sense that yarns are repeatable (as in the examples above) and so become detached in time and space from their origins, they exemplify a different kind of knowledge, what, following Jean-François Lyotard, we might call narrative knowledge rather than scientific knowledge (Lyotard 18–23). Yarns are told for the sake of the telling, not for the accuracy of what is told, and Moses Melchior's admission, 'I can't say whether it is true', is reiterated by Daniel Matthews: 'I was going to bed at 10, but the boatswain's mate kept me until 11, relating sea yarns, which had the merit of being interesting, if not quite true' (12 Feb. 1870).

The absence of verification is also the virtue, if that word is appropriate in this context, of scandal. Scandal is a cousin of the yarn, and it too circulates without origin and apparently without a specific destination:

> Another scandal is afloat this morning that a man was pulled out by the leg from Mrs Peacock's cabin in the night by the carpenter's mate. The man is supposed to be Gordon.
>
> Two or three attempts have been made to get into the Gloucester girl's cabin. The carpenter's mate informed me of this, and I casually mentioned it to Gordon adding that I thought it was an infamous shame. He said 'what's the use of you blabbing a thing of that kind all over the ship; I can tell you something about that girl', and then he began to relate some story about her in relation with the minister in whose family she served; and that it was this minister who was sending her out and not her brother. Whether there is any truth in what he says I am unable to say.
> (Daniel Matthews 24 Feb. 1870)

Tales about Mrs Peacock, Gordon, the Gloucester girl, and the role of the carpenter's mate circulate through the ship until no one is sure where they came from, where they might end up, and what their truth value is. The same can be said of another associated experiential discourse, rumour: 'Rumers were again afloat that we should have to put in at the Cape, or some where else for water, and more provisions' (George Randall 26 July 1868). Travellers' tales are in this way like the travellers themselves, in transit, afloat at sea: 'Another scandal is afloat this morning,' 'Rumers were again afloat.'

The informational discourses in the diaries are written types of discourse which may be verified by empirical observation, measurement, and recourse to other books:

Another of the so-called porpoises caught to-day, upwards of 6 feet in length: – having a work of Natural History at hand, for amusement, I took out the book on deck, to compare the description with the animal, and to my surprise discovered that what the sailors called a porpoise, was really no porpoise at all, but the true Dolphin, (*Delphinus delphis*), a very different animal. (N. C. 4 Dec. 1848)

In contrast, yarns, scandal, and rumour all assume an oral context. They are used primarily for mediating social relationships on board, as a way by which a community may be formed or undermined, though these social relationships, it needs to be stressed, have a masculine bias. 'Yarning' in the examples given earlier occurs solely between men, and scandal almost always degrades female sexuality more than male sexuality: 'I will conclude my description of her [Miss Moore] by saying that she was no better than she should be and from what I saw going on between her and the Capt I did not associate with her on the voyage' (Claudius Cairnes 1 Feb. 1861). And of course, when yarning involves women it becomes the more derogatory 'gossip': 'There is a good deal of gossip carried on even among our small number, Mrs Scott the widey [widow?] with the cat wont speak to her bed companion Miss Hastie the old maid because Miss Hastie spoke familiarly to Miss Brown the flirt' (William Forwood 4 Dec. 1857).

In turn, the use of this type of narrative in emigrant diaries mediates the social relationship between the diarist and her or his audience; William Forward ironically is gossiping to his audience. Again the audience is not a real audience but one imagined by the diarist, yet yarns, scandal, rumours, and gossip nonetheless all require the diarist as narrator to position her or himself *vis-à-vis* the narratives being passed on. Disclaimers such as 'Whether there is any truth in what he says I am unable to say' reveal the attitude of the diarist as narrator to what is being narrated, while the very choice of subject matter reveals what the diarist imagines, with mock reticence, is appropriate for the diary's audience: 'circumstances which have caused me much annoyance came to a climax this day I will give a detail of them in another place' (Claudius Cairnes 11 Jan. 1861). In such ways, the diaries stage through writing an oral storytelling situation.

In the same way as yarns by their nature weave in and out of the shipboard company, so yarns weave in and out of the diaries; they are exchanged between crew and passengers, between the passengers themselves, and between the diarists and their imagined audience. Yarns are always shifting from place to place, from discourse to discourse: 'Another scandal is afloat this morning.' Yarns are surreptitious. Yarns rarely, if ever, extend beyond the individual diary entry and it remains the case that the emigrant diary is more a collection of odds and ends in different and contradictory modes than a consistent narrative of the voyage out. Circumstances and the need to write regularly prevented the linking of more than a handful of diary entries at most into a narrative sequence such as occurred fortuitously with the tale of Mr Rankine.

Rebecca Hogan uses the term 'parataxis' for this aspect of the diary. Parataxis is a grammatical device whereby clauses are placed side-by-side without the use of conjunctions to indicate co-ordination or subordination. Diaries are therefore paratactic because of their formal flexibility: 'Diaries are elastic, inclusive texts, which mix chronicle, historical record, reflection, feelings, descriptions of nature, travel, work accomplished, and portraiture of character rather haphazardly together' (Hogan 100). The elements of the diary, its constitutive discourses, are placed side by side without being linked or organised into a hierarchy, and yarns make full use of this. Yarns have the ability to weave a community together, they have the ability to tear a community apart, but the surreptitious way in which they operate prevents them from providing the diary with any structural coherence.

*

The emigrant diary is made up of informational discourses and experiential narratives, but none of these provide the diary with a sense of coherence, a sense that the parts belong to a broader whole. The paratactic organisation of the diary means that the content of any individual entry will not necessarily link with the content of another. Indeed, even within a single entry there is no necessary coherence. To the degree that the diary is an autobiographical genre, perhaps the diary might alternatively cohere around the life of the writer, and one way of reading a diary would be to say, this is what it was like for Edwin Francis or Helen Ronald to make the voyage out. Such a reading may be adopted by someone interested in the diary as a document of their own family history, but diarists themselves were reluctant autobiographers, they included little of their own thoughts and anxieties, and even less of their own lives prior to emigration. Emigrant diaries were on the whole less concerned with themselves than with recording what was happening around them, either by retailing yarns or by adopting informational discourses (the descriptions of fish or a note of the wind direction) which took their authority not from the diarist but from a presumed objectivity. A diary like Mr A's adopted a mode that is essentially unauthored – a ship's log has no author and it is of secondary importance who kept it. While many of the diarists gave their diaries elaborate title pages, they rarely placed their own names on them and many diaries remain anonymous. A diary is not an autobiography, and what is selected for inclusion every time a diarist adds an entry may, as Rebecca Hogan points out, 'be selected according to a different set of rules or impulses on each occasion' (105); there is no reason to assume that because a diary is written by one person it will be consistent or form a coherent narrative.

The coherence of the diary does not then necessarily reside in the figure of the diarist. But it is clear that the diary must have some kind of coherence simply because of the general assumption among emigrants that it could be contained within the covers of a book. Writing about travel narratives, Peter Bishop finds narrative coherence in the notion of the route:

> Most travel accounts consist of small islands of personal narrative afloat on an ocean of dates and geography. These well-structured stories are often threaded together into a sequence which is entirely dependent on the idea of *route*. The image of the *route* emerges as the key to their apparent coherence and authenticity. Even the personal experiences of the traveller are secondary to the coherence and logic of the route; the route gives the traveller the authority to narrate. (4)

What Bishop calls 'the logic of the route' can be established by the route being socially structured and sanctioned, as in the case of pilgrimages. In such a case, Bishop argues, 'the route is known beforehand. It is already mythic, already a narrative *before* the journey is undertaken. The journey merely activates and actualizes the route and the map' (4).

In terms of emigrants sailing to Australia, the route is certainly already structured and sanctioned, and changes in route over a period of time (stopping at Cape Town, the Great Circle, passing through the Suez Canal) are witness to changes in economic and technological wisdom. When a ship left port, the captain already had an idea of the

route to Australia, and it is this idea of the sanctioned route that allows
Arthur Manning to remark:

> We were rather surprised to see a vessel in this quarter, as we are
> now in what Jack would call 'no man's land,' or rather 'no man's
> water'; being out of the ordinary track of vessels to or from any
> part of the globe; except such as, like ourselves, have been driven
> far to the Westward by the prevalence of Easterly and Southerly
> winds. (14 Dec. 1839)

Should any of the emigrants have had access to an emigrant handbook,
the chances are they would have found a map with the route out marked
on it.

But if the route gives some narrative coherence to the diary, it
certainly does not work quite in the same way as it would for overland
travel, witness the concern at sea for position reports. One of my
favourite contemporary illustrations of the voyage out shows a group of
emigrants below deck peering by the dim light of a safety lantern at a
map spread out on the table; the illustration is called, 'Night – Tracing
the Vessel's Progress' (*Illustrated London News* 20 Jan. 1849). The
ship's position was calculated at noon, weather permitting, by
measuring the height of the sun above the horizon, a procedure
described sometimes more, sometimes less accurately by emigrant
diarists: 'They tell in what longitude or latitude they are by looking
through a thing like taking a portrait but they call the thing a sextant.
They look straight at the sun at 12 o'clock and they tell what time it is by
the sun at 12 o'clock and then they put the clock right every day' (Will
Sayer 4 Aug. 1876). The ship's position was often posted up on a
blackboard or something like it above deck; where there was a more
personal relationship between the captain and the passengers, as in the
first-class saloon, the captain might actually show the passengers the
chart. The position reports once calculated and posted were avidly
recorded in the diaries, either daily as in Mr A's diary or in a tabular
form at the end. From the diaries, it is clear that these position reports
were important in giving the emigrants a sense of where they were.
Without them, the emigrants felt lost:

> they say we are eight days good sailing from the Cape but I cant
> beleive what I hear there is so many different stories   I beleive it
> is the custom on most of the Passenger Ships to mark up every

afternoon where she is and the distance sailed every twentyfour hours but it is not so here so I am Ignorant of where I am. (William Shennan 25 Mar. 1870)

As on this ship, the position reports were sometimes deliberately withheld, though there seems to have been no single reason for the secrecy, and diarists give varying interpretations: 'At sea, a secresy is aped at respecting the position and course of the vessel: some say to prevent mutiny in crew' (Henry Whittingham 27 Apr. 1853). One diarist suggested that the captain would have looked foolish had his calculations proved wrong, while in another case a captain suddenly stopped issuing the position: 'It seems that a Cuddy passenger named Miller has chose to tell the Captain he is running on some rocks. The Captain has accordingly given orders that none of the passengers shall be told the latitude and longitude' (Thomas Severn 24 Oct. 1852).

What fascinates me about the illustration I described above, 'Night – Tracing the Vessel's Progress', is the acceptance by the artist that looking at a chart below deck at night gives emigrants a better sense of where they are than being on deck during the day. There is a similarity here between ships and planes, the chart for the emigrants being equivalent to the computerised displays on Qantas international flights showing the present position of the plane. Most other forms of travel allow the traveller to trace her or his progress by reference to the physical world beyond the mode of transport, and even in a car we need to keep an eye out for road signs. Yet looking out of a ship, like looking out of a plane, was to look merely into an emptiness, and there is a recurring complaint in the diaries that there is nothing to see but 'sky and water':

Nothing worth mentioning except Sky and Water and Water and Sky. (Henry Widdowson 23 Nov. 1825)

You cannot imagine what an object of interest this barren Island became to all of us and presume only those whose eyes have rested on nothing else but sky and water for a whole month can fully appreciate the sight. (Henry Curr 8 Aug. 1856)

it is so very monot[on]ous on a sailing vessel, never seeing anything but sky and water the whole of the way. (Frances Thornton 6 Sept. 1882)

[92]

Occasionally a more varied note is heard: 'nothing but the placid surface of the unbounded ocean to gaze upon – nothing to relieve the dreary sameness of the watery waste' (William Harbottle 22 Apr. 1849); but this is just an elegant variation on an old theme. The underlying cause was the undifferentiated nature of the sea, which for the unpractised eye meant there was no way of gauging progress from one day to the next by looking at it. The sea gives a sense of space, indeed, too much space in some instances, but no sense of place.

In such circumstances, the physicality of the map can substitute for the physical space the ship is traversing to give some sense of spatial coherence to the voyage:

> We have now passed the Cape and the 3rd and last Chart (on which the Captain marks our course) has been begun and we have now no particular object such as the line or Cape to surmount between this and Canterbury. (William Kennaway 11 Sept. 1851).

> We always look at the chart when Capt. A. has worked her up and marked our daily progress. We are now on our third chart. The first took us down to the Line, the second to the Cape, the third to Australia and the fourth will take us to Moreton Bay when the Chart of the Harbour will come into requisition. (Anna Fowler 29 Aug. 1866)

The points mentioned in these accounts, the Line, the Cape, and the coast of Australia were more psychological boundary markers than actual places, and the Cape of Good Hope at the southern tip of Africa was a particularly important indicator of progress, as Richard Watt points out: 'once past the Cape we shall then have before us a very definite object – our destination, Australia, straight ahead, to which all our thoughts must necessarily be directed' (2 July 1864). On the non-stop voyage to Australia, passing the Cape on the map gave a sense of progress, but it was not accompanied by a view of the Cape, as some reasonably, though mistakenly, thought: 'I had a funny idea when I was at home, I thought we would see the Cape, but they only know by what Latitude they are in' (Maria Steley 2 Dec. 1863). There is a mismatch between the chart and the physical environment, and although the route might be drawn on a chart, there was often little chance for the emigrants to describe the difference between where they are today and where they were yesterday. The route was there on the map but there was no image of the route, as Peter Bishop puts it, to activate and actualise. The map provided a sense of position, but, like the sea, it too could provide no sense of place.

This is not to say that nothing was 'actualised' in the diaries and although the emigrants were making the voyage non-stop and therefore not passing through any geographical places, as would be the case in, say, a pilgrimage, a kind of pattern does emerge. There are a certain number of set themes that recur in the diaries, and as these mostly depended on the location of the ship, they occur (when they do occur) in a more or less predictable sequence: seasickness in the Bay of Biscay; sighting Tenerife; flying fishes landing on the deck; the heat of the Doldrums; the dead horse ceremony; the crossing the line ceremony; standing under the sun with no shadow; the Cape pigeons following the ship; the strong winds and the cold of the southern latitudes; passing the Greenwich meridian; spotting the island of St Paul; first sight of land. Anyone writing a fictional account of the voyage out would need to include at least some of these for the sake of authenticity.

Of course, not all emigrants would have known about flying fishes or the dead horse ceremony before they made the voyage out, and on the whole, they wrote as though they were the first person to have ever encountered a Cape pigeon. This posture of ignorance could be due in some cases to the presumed ignorance of their imagined audience, but the diaries also show emigrants depending heavily on the crew to identify birds and fish and to interpret the natural environment for them. On the other hand, some of the emigrants clearly had prior knowledge of what to expect on the voyage; Maria Steley, a fourteen-year-old from Wales, reported in her diary: 'We are into the Trade Winds. They blow us along pretty sharply. I think of what Mr Fudge told us about the Trade Winds & the Tropical Showers. We shall pass through it all by & by' (11 Nov. 1863). Maria does not identify Mr Fudge, but it may well have been an enterprising teacher who took the opportunity of one of his pupils emigrating to teach some geography. Although the evidence of the diaries suggests emigrants generally had a meagre knowledge of the voyage before they embarked (hence the advice about what to bring directed to those at home), more research is needed into the effectiveness of information about the voyage out, its circulation and its accessibility, before the point can be determined.

In either case, however, this sort of pattern does not match up to Peter Bishop's notion of the actualisation of a route. Shipboard diaries are certainly 'small islands of personal narrative afloat on an ocean of dates and geography', but Bishop discounts these as the basis of coherence: 'The personal experiences of the traveller are secondary to the coherence and logic of the route.' This is similar to the position taken by Michel de Certeau in his discussion of what he calls 'spatial stories'. In this essay, de Certeau makes a distinction between the 'map' and the 'itinerary' (118): the itinerary is a representation of space as a discursive narrative, as an active movement through space, whereas the map is a totalisation of space, a kind of god's-eye representation of space without the connective itinerary. It is a difference of perspective, the difference between, say, describing the route through a maze as though we were walking it and describing the layout of the maze from above. Applying these terms to Bishop's argument, the travel narrative or walk through the maze merely actualises a route that may be imagined by looking down on the maze from above; the map authorises the journey. Or as de Certeau himself puts it: 'an element of mapping is the pre-supposition of a certain itinerary' (120).

The travel narrative is therefore not a pure itinerary since it relies on the map: 'stories of journeys and actions are marked out by the "citation" of the places that result from them or authorize them' (Certeau 120). If some foundational narratives authorise the map, other travel narratives are authorised by the pre-existent places along the route, and, once again, what is missing from shipboard diaries is any description of places through which the traveller passes. Although emigrants may have had access to a god's-eye map of the route from the available promotional literature, unless the ship called at a port on the way there were no places on the voyage which emigrants could look forward to seeing. To a great extent, the emigrant voyager was always in the same place, on board ship somewhere at sea, afloat, like Bishop's small islands, on an ocean of dates and position reports.

One of the best descriptions of this lack of a sense of geographical movement occurs in a letter written in October 1856 by Daniel Jones trying to persuade his friend, William Griffith, to follow him from Wales to Australia. In his letter, Daniel offered the following account of his experience of the voyage out:

> I can't for the life of me form a just conception of the real
> immense distance between Victoria and England. You may
> recollect the last sight of land I had was the Stack Point, and the
> next was a portion of Australia. The interval of 74 days between
> was filled with the same daily scene – sea and sky – like an

[95]

immense round dish and domed cover – the sea for dish and sky
for cover. The ship, to the sense of sight, appeared stationary in
the centre of the dish, for there was always the same horizon
before us and around; and let the vessel sail never so fast that
horizon appeared ever just as distant. If one should be taken in a
large ship and stationed in the English Channel just out of sight of
land, there remain for three months, could experience all the
various changes of climate; be visited, when like in the tropics,
with sharks, &c., and when in the cold regions by albatrosses,
&c., and perhaps sight an iceberg or two; then you would have as
much chance of forming an idea of the distance to Australia as I
had. So think of this my lad. You have only got to make up your
mind to get on board ship in England, remain on board for three
months, then hug a kangaree in Australia. (in Lloyd 129–30)

The experiences of the voyage are all here, the heat and the sharks, the
cold and the albatrosses, yet the monotony of the sea and the sky, 'the
same daily scene', means that there is little sense of progress to be
gained from the physical environment: 'The ship, to the sense of sight,
appeared stationary.'

The consequence of this is that for emigrants at sea there is a split
between map and place. The coherence of the diary comes in a large part
from the map, the recording of position reports actualises, if it
actualises anything, the sense of a journey implied in the diary as a book
of the voyage. Emigrants consult maps, refer their readers to maps, and
draw maps in their diaries. But their sense of place comes from elsewhere. If the emigrant at sea does inhabit, as Paul Carter suggests, 'an
environment devoid of external distractions', then spatial investment is
effectively shifted from the places through which the traveller passes to
the ship itself: the external space and the internal space of the ship are
in an inverse relationship. The stopping places cited on the route which
authorise travel narratives turn out to be all the same place, and the
space in which the emigrants invest during the voyage is not that of the
space through which they move, but the space of their own 'floating
homes'. In this sense, the ship itself becomes a town and a landscape, a
place which moves with them and which provides the focus of the diary
of the voyage out: 'It is very interesting watching the working of the
ship. There is constantly some change being made in the sails – & I hope
to get to understand that complicated mass of ropes etc' (Anna Fowler
15 June 1866). This contradicts a point made by Yi-Fu Tuan in his

[96]

discussion of place: 'A great ocean liner is certainly a world, but it is not rooted in location; hence it is not a place' (236). But Yi-Fu's definition of place depends on a strict division between travel and place, a division which the emigrants' 'floating home' disrupts. Emigrants describe their location by describing their mode of transport, and as the once popular, now long-forgotten, W. H. G. Kingston so optimistically counsels in his *Emigrant Voyager's Manual*: 'let me assure you, that if you look about you properly you will every day find something of interest to note down in your journal' (25). The space of the ship is not only the place in which the diary is written, it is the place about which the diarist writes.

*

If emigrants' diaries are primarily concerned with the spaces of the ship rather than with any external places through which the ship passed, diarists needed to be particularly resourceful if they were to keep a diary running daily for the length of the voyage. As Richard Sheraton put it in his retrospective account of the voyage out: 'A diary or log seems to me a very useless way of spending time and paper for it is utterly impossible with the routine on ship-board to find something day by day for 140 days which would render amusement if read over' (29 Jan. 1853). To remain in effect in one place and yet to be able to write of it daily was not easy, as the frequent examples of diary failure make clear:

> Finding it next to impossible to fill up my journal with any thing new every day, I shall only do so once or twice a week in order to note down any thing a little out of the way, and for the sake of keeping the dates, for life on board ship is exceedingly monotonous. (S. E. Roberts 5 July 1848)

> As every day is little different from the one preceeding, I thought it not worth while to write every day. (Byron Ronald 2 July 1853)

The closed company and the routine of shipboard life meant that once the novelty had worn off, there was little left to relate:

> we begin to tire of each other, not that we positively dislike one another, but the stock of anecdotes which each was possessed of, is all told & exhausted – breakfast, dinner & tea arrive in the dull monotonous round day after day – boiled salt beef and boiled salt

pork keep one alive & *thirsty*! (William Wills 7 Dec. 1841)

Another hot day – Very little wind, until the evening, when it
freshened, and carried us along about 9 knots – Beginning to feel
tired of this lazy life, there is scarcely anything for us to do, except
read – We have quiots on board (i.e. ship quiots) but it is too hot
for them now. (J. R. Waight 20 May 1882)

In an environment in which there is 'Nothing worth mentioning except
Sky and Water and Water and Sky', it is not that nothing is happening, it
is rather that there is nothing new happening. To be sure, at one level,
even when there is little to write about, monotony is not really monotony when the voyage has still to be recorded; writing a journal is also a
way of passing the time: 'Most of the passengers betook themselves to
their pet amusements below, some to sleep in their bunks, others to
cards, draughts, dominoes and log writing' (Richard Watt 11 July
1864). Yet a journal with nothing to record is like a ship in the
doldrums, going nowhere, and in the absence of anything to be written
about, all the journal can do is mark time: 'Nothing to write about, days
are so uniform here' (Isabella Turner 15 Apr. 1868).

In his discussion of self-reference in settlers' and emigrants' diaries
in *The Road to Botany Bay*, Paul Carter quotes a similar diary entry:
'Our days now pass away in so monotonous a manner, not even a new
bird or fish breaking the dull routine of time, & the difficulty of finding
employment for such a party as mine is so great, that I can hardly make
out a few notes, without repetition of same uninteresting trifles' (142).
Note here that the requirement is not for birds or fish, but for new birds
and fish – the diarist has become familiar with those he has already
recorded and is unable to generate a narrative from them. There is
nothing to write about. Carter's own conclusion is that the recording of
nothing to record is evidence that the diary itself can progress in the
absence of anything to record: 'the true dialogue the writer conducts is
not with external reality, but with language itself' (142–3). Writing
about having nothing to write about is at least writing.

However, although the type of self-reflexive entry that Carter highlights may demonstrate that the emigrant's diary brought to the diarist's consciousness the experience of travelling, this does not necessarily mean that events were unimportant. There may be an imperative
on the diarist that she or he continue writing in the absence of things to
record, but this does not mean that this is the best sort of entry to give

direction and shape to the journal and through it to the journey. What sort of narrative is it that blandly records, 'Nothing of any note worth remarking' (John Whitings 6 July 1854)? The dialogue that the nine-teenth-century emigrant to Australia entered into was not so much a dialogue with a private self but with an imaginary addressee at home; to whom else is the apologetic tone of these entries that record that there is nothing to record directed? In this imaginary dialogue, something had to be said.

I argued earlier that the nautical entry was the basic entry in the emigrant diary; when all else failed, the emigrants recorded the wind and the weather:

> Nothing occurs of particular importance, the weather which yesterday was bright and clear is today changeable and threatening. (Edward Cornell 29 July 1856)

> There has been nothing to remark the last week, except that the weather has been changeable sometimes wet at others fine. (J. R. Waight 8 July 1882)

The use of 'ditto' by some diarists pushes this to an extreme; when even the weather failed to be 'changeable,' to provide something new, one wrote 'ditto' under an entry recording the previous day's weather:

> [Sept.] 13 Very fair still hot all well
> [Sept.] 14 do – Do –   do –
> [Sept.] 15 do – Do -- 3 ships in sight
> [Sept.] 16 Do – Do – very hot (George Kershaw 1841)

Or again:

> December 7 Steady breeze, hot nights.
> December 8 Ditto, Average 5 knots.
> December 9 Ditto. 20.30 S Lat. 35 West Long.
> December 10 Sun vertical in 22.30 S Lat. We get fruit instead of pudding most days now, but get tired of it – the South American fruits are rather satiating. (J. W. Reeves 1856)

Even the fruit becomes monotonous after the novelty has worn off.

This use of 'ditto' highlights the fact that the basic impulse of the diary is one of repetition, and when all else fails, the diary merely marks time, it repeats the previous entry. The diary is itself a repetitive genre, it builds up its length by repeating the same gesture: as days follow days, so entries follow entries. Each entry is equivalent to the other entries. As Paul Carter puts it:

> The regularity of diaries prevents them from being truly open-ended: they stress repetition, the even flow of time, characterizing any departure from regularity as exceptional. The contingency of being in history, the experience of flying, is suppressed. Even that continually evolving, non-repetitive theme, the weather, is constrained to repeat itself, differences over time being 'averaged out.' The possibility that life is experienced as a series of discontinuities is excluded. (*Living in a New Country* 90)

I agree with Carter that the repetitive nature of the diary means that contingency is suppressed, as in the suppression of Mr Rankine in Mr A's diary, yet this repetition also means that the diary does not so much stress the even flow of time as a time suspended, placing the diarist precisely outside history. As Alan Mayne remarks in his discussion of sea journeys: 'To take passage was to mark time, as well as to exchange worlds' (Mayne 62). Repetition here, though, is as much spatial as temporal; the order of such entries is not important, and one entry is able to take the place of another. The repetitive diary, like the emigrant on board ship, remains in the same place.

Repetition, therefore, does not constitute a temporal narrative: 'Just a repetition of yesterday – sea still stormy, sometimes coming over the under deck' (Isabella Turner 17 Mar. 1868); 'The voyage begins to be very tedious and the days are dreadfully alike' (Richard Watt 2 July 1864). Such repetition constitutes instead the equilibrium underlying the narrative of the voyage out. Tzvetan Todorov has theorised narrative in this way:

> The minimal complete plot consists in the passage from one equilibrium to another. An 'ideal' narrative begins with a stable situation which is disturbed by some power or force. There results a state of disequilibrium; by the action of a force directed in the opposite direction, the equilibrium is re-established; the second equilibrium is similar to the first, but the two are never identical. (111)

In broad terms, Todorov's ideal narrative scheme can be applied to emigrant diaries by arguing that the beginnings and ends of the diaries comprise the stable points within which the disruptive narrative of the voyage out takes place. Here the stable situation might actually coincide with the physically stable situation of being on land and it would be replaced at the end of the diary by the emigrant being once again on land: 'Between three and four in the morning we were wakened by the anchor chains running out, we had arrived outside the dock, between five and six the tug arrived and by eight o'clock 26 Jany. we were once more able to step on land' (Marjory MacGillivray 25 Jan. 1895). Stepping on land re-establishes a physical balance, and in this respect, a sea voyage is almost an archetypal narrative, with the notion of 'passage,' as used by Todorov, being a sea passage from one equilibrium to another. The metaphor of being 'at sea' to indicate a confused state of mind can then be applied to the unstable middle of the narrative: 'You must indeed be very bemused [?] with me with regards care [?] to spelling as well as sense for as they say I am all at sea my head seems all in a whirl while reading writing playing a game organising attention to any thing or attempting to' (Harry Woolley 5 Dec. 1850).

However, once the voyage is under way, a different, if temporary, order is established on board ship, both in terms of physical space (the allocation of berths and the arrangement of the cabin) and in terms of social space (the establishment of cultural domains such as 'home'). The confusion of embarkation is overcome precisely by the establishment of a new balance or equilibrium on the 'floating home', a domestication or familiarisation of the novelty of shipboard life. Thomas Mort in 1837 put it like this: 'I am becoming so accustomed to sights which upon leaving home I should have considered extraordinary, that they fail to attract my attention as they did' (24 Oct. 1837). Twenty-five years later, an unnamed French passenger on the SS *Great Britain* made much the same point: 'La vie est bien monotone à bord maintenant que nous avons épuisé la nouveauté de la situation' ['Life is indeed monotonous on board now that we have exhausted the novelty of the situation'] (5 Mar. 1863). The diary successfully contained the confusion and novelty, but at the cost of reducing contingency to repetition. In her discussion of women's diaries of the American Midwest, Elizabeth Hampsten sugests that repetition and sameness in diary entries may act as 'strategies for controlling disturbances and asserting normality' ('Tell Me All You Know' 57). The re-establishment of a 'home' on board ship marks it as a site of permanence and stability, even if the domestic site is itself a site lacking progressive narratives. Rachel Bowlby pointed out in a recent paper on domestication how the endless circularity of domestic routine is summed up in the phrase, 'A woman's work is never done.'

The problem for the diarist is, of course, that there is nothing new to write about, that writing about shipboard life has exhausted the topics available to the diarist. To use Mary Louise Pratt's terms, the shipboard reality has been incorporated into the available informational orders. Of course, repeating the same diary entry day after day gives an accurate representation of the experience of domesticity, but unless the diarist is prepared to be as monumentally tedious as Mr A and merely give a weather report day after day (and some others *are* prepared to be as monumentally tedious as Mr A), then the diary will slide towards silence and a sense of failure that has implications for the way in which the voyage out is experienced. The logic of the nineteenth-century progressive narrative, the logic that an end will assuredly follow from a beginning, promises future stability both in terms of an ending to the voyage and in terms of a resolution to the factors which gave rise to the decision to emigrate. By writing a diary, many of the emigrants are giving this promise a material form, and so long as they can keep the diary continuing, their destination will seem to be guaranteed. By keeping the story going during the voyage, emigrants are implicitly expecting a resolution to their discomfort and a happy outcome to their passage.

Some diarists do allow their diaries to fall silent for a while: 'This past week has been devoid of interest that I have thought it not worth while to write up my diary' (Thomas Miller 16 Jan. 1870); but a diary is distinguished from a letter by the need to write in it regularly, and diarists on the whole feel compelled to keep the diary running: 'I have been confined to my berth since the 29th by illness, and as I could not observe what was going on around me, I have filled up the space with an account of our festivities' (Mrs Hinshelwood 4 July 1883). Pages must be filled, space must be covered, and a diary that ceases to progress as a narrative allows no sense of progress, no sense that the voyage is moving towards its endpoint. The journey and the diary become analogous: 'if you get through this journal as well as we have got through our voyage to this place you will succeed much better than I expect' (Edward Towle 22 Sept. 1852). By writing a diary, emigrants give their voyage a sense of progression, the end of their diaries corresponding to the end of the journey.

The diarist is therefore caught between opposing demands. On the one hand, there is the need to establish a narrative equilibrium by creating a sense of home and by reducing the environment to rationalist informational discourses; it is this containment of the 'confusion' that makes the voyage knowable and narratable. On the other hand, there is a need for that space to be continually transgressed if the voyage is not to be brought to a halt by the lack of incident, the lack of an experiential narrative. If a diary is paratactic it is also spasmodic, alternating between stasis and transgression. This desire for transgression is felt most keenly when the stasis is at its strongest: 'I wish some stirring scene would take place to stir my torpid imagination, for really the day dawns and night arrives with its intervening mealtimes all in such mechanical order and with so great a sameness that the mind is paralyzed' (William Wills 8 Dec. 1841). Yet the desire for transgression, for that 'stirring scene', cannot be wholehearted because of the threat it poses to the equilibrium that is the basis of a progressive narrative; as Todorov argues, narrative tends towards equilibrium and reversal of transgression: 'by the action of a force directed in the opposite direction, the equilibrium is re-established.' This desire for equilibrium in emigrant diaries exists both as a desire to reach the destination, and a desire to maintain the 'home' side of the 'floating home' paradox.

The notion of the floating home contains, as I argued in Chapter 2, an uneasy alliance between interior and exterior, between an incarceration by the mode of travel and a movement beyond spatial boundaries implied by travel. To the extent that the cultural space of the ship as 'home' is the privileged norm, the main disruptive narrative force is the transgression of the interior by the exterior. As William Harbottle bound for Sydney succinctly put it: 'it is said there are only two things to relieve the monotony at sea "Sometimes we see a ship, sometimes we ship a sea" ' (12 Apr. 1849). Both of these involve a sudden shift of attention from the space of the ship to its exterior. Except for the possibility of pirates off the coast of Africa in the early years of the nineteenth century, seeing another ship was usually pleasurable: 'The most pleasant circumstance that can happen during a long voyage is to speak another ship. It seems as if you had discovered a new world' (Thomas Bolivar Blyth 16 Oct. 1846). Shipping a sea, however, was potentially more threatening:

> Of all the nights we have had yet, last night was the worst. The
> wind rose to a perfect hurricane; they fastened down the hatches

but that did not prevent the water making its way down to us. . . .
All at once there arose a cry that we were sinking and, of course,
that added to the general confusion and many were on their knees
praying who had perhaps never thought on the name of God
before, and the Matron was as much frightened as the rest. (Fanny
Davis 14 June 1858)

If many diarists on embarking postponed starting a diary until order
had been established and social space defined, then storms at sea
threatened to recreate that initial spatial 'confusion' when the space
lost differentiation, a loss signified linguistically by the potentially
infinite list:

We have passed the worst night since we left England. About 12
o'clock a very heavy cross sea commenced rolling which caused
the ship to lurch fearfully. We were awoke by the noise of boxes
casks etc., getting adrift and rolling from one side to another as if
determined to break down our partitions. Then again the
breaking of bottles in the cabin, the crockery in the pantry, the
upsetting of water pails, basins etc, etc. I got up and found the
greatest confusion. Some of the passengers were in a dreadful
state, their luggage and all pell mell over the place. (John
Joseland 24 May 1853)

With the 'breaking of the bottles in the cabin, the crockery in the
pantry, the upsetting of water pails, basins etc, etc,' the spatial
differentiation that is a prerequisite for writing disappears. In passages
like this the 'etc, etc' signifies precisely a loss of signification:

Many of the sails set today are taken in again – wind increasing to
a gale – every now & then away goes a batch of crockery with a
crash, and a lot of tins & pails with a rattle. . . . Awoke at
midnight, rather a fearful night than otherwise. Bottles, cans &c,
&c, rolling to & fro on the cabin floor in grand confusion. (John
Fenwick 13 June 1854)

The 'confusion' is such that there is a collapse of that differentiation
needed if space is to be narratable; '&c, &c' indicates not so much
unnamed objects as that which cannot be named and represented.
Storms therefore not only produced the degree of 'confusion' that made

life on board both unpleasant and terrifying, they prevented the writing of a diary:

> Since the last date the wind has been so high and the motion so great that it has been impossible for me to write. (John Joseland 9 June 1853)

> I have not been able to write any of my diary since last Saturday for it has been one continued hurricane. (Fanny Davis 9 Sept. 1858)

Storms made all too evident the 'floating' side of the 'floating home', the way that the home of the migrant was a place in transit, a place that was always unstable and always subject to that instability being revealed. Storms provided an incident to write about, yet in their disordering of space they prevented writing. If too much repetition leads to the almost silence of 'ditto', then too much transgression threatens the space from which the diary is written. Too much 'confusion' of the spatial order leads ultimately to a loss of differentiation and the silencing of the diary.

The diary is therefore caught between two silences, the silence of 'nothing to report' and the silence of 'unable to write'; too much order or too much confusion suffocate diary writing. In one circumstance a calm may be associated with those moments when the diary marks time, when it has nothing to record: 'Monotonous in the extreme. Besides suffering again from calm we have had no occurrence of importance' (Richard Watt 27 May 1864). With not even a wind to record for its audience, the diary slides towards silence. In the same diary but in other circumstances, however, a calm can function as a relief from the confusion of between-decks life in a storm, when writing is impossible: 'we have had the good fortune to have almost a calm, running about five knots on the average through the day, and giving us good opportunity to take down and replace with new gear all the wreck and havoc of the tempest' (Richard Watt 8 Aug. 1864). The calm after the storm gives time not just for the crew to repair storm damage but for the diarist to catch up on the storm: 'I must mention here several accidents which occurred last night' (Richard Watt 8 Aug. 1864). By this time, spatial differentiation has been restored and the storm can be narrated.

Ultimately, therefore, what makes emigrants' diaries difficult to write is what makes them possible. Written in a spatial and temporal gap with a tendency towards repetition and silence, they struggle to give shape and order to the voyage. Yet it is precisely the fragility of the order on board ship, the confusion into which any temporary social order is likely to be thrown at any moment, that guarantees new narratives. For the diarist faced by monotony and a blank page, the consolation must be that anything may happen. And if she or he is not lucky enough to have a Mr Rankine with an attack of the blue devils on board, at the very least, the vagaries of the weather and its effects on board a sailing ship ensure that any decline into narrative equilibrium will always be temporary.

Chapter 4

Passenger sketches and social identity

'A journal is incomplete without this description'

In my pursuit of emigrants' diaries, I often find myself travelling the path of the genealogists. Many of the Australian immigration lists still remain (the British lists prior to 1890 were destroyed by the Board of Trade in 1900), but the official lists are rather spare in the information they provide. In any case, the immigration lists are too easily accessed (genealogists are nothing if not obsessive in their searches), so for the true genealogist the passenger lists found in the diaries are the real strata of immigration, the point at which the digging becomes strenuous, the outcome more uncertain. Sometimes the result will be tantalisingly minimal, as in the list of those in Francis Taylor's mess:

Francis Taylor	Agriculturalist	Herefordshire
Caleb Broadbent	Miller	Yorkshire
Donald Campbell	do	Scotland
Henry Dickens	do	Northamptonshire
Robert Davy		
Charles Davy brothers	do	Norfolk (21 Feb. 1850)

Whether the other messes contained a similar number of millers or whether they had all congregated in this mess is not revealed; and it is likely, as Marsha Donaldson has shown, that some of the names in lists like this are incorrectly spelt (102). In many cases, though, the diarist has taken the trouble to include not merely a list but a series of character sketches, as in the diary of a Mr Barton sailing first class from London to Adelaide on the *Irene* in 1853:

And now that I am able to wield a pen without splashing the paper or my neighbours I will give a slight sketch of my fellow-

[107]

passengers, bipeds and quadrupeds. – With the exception of some
ducks and fowls upon whose Fatherland I will not presume to
decide the former are almost all from the land o' cakes [Scotland].
A Mr Arnold, a builder, with a family of several Daughters one son
and a cousin, Mr Hill, all from Aberdeen; Mr Dubois with an
enormous wife, 2 boys and a baby; Mr Miller the surgeon, who is a
great lion on account of his having been wrecked on the coast of
Brazil in the 'Sir Howell Buxton'; a tallowy individual answering
to the unusual name of Brown, and myself from the passengers. –
The crew are all Scotch excepting the Black cook and a boy from
Bremen, who is always being sent up aloft, why I cannot tell. I had
omitted among the passengers Mr & Mrs Parker, a new married
couple of which the inferior moiety owns several ships in the
Aust. coasting trade and is a very larky fellow. – He tells strange
yarns about Australia and would dishearten any one less sanguine
than myself. – We carry besides, two dogs, some hectic looking
sheep and some small pigs, who will be porkers before we cross
the line, if we go on at this rate. (3 Sept. 1853)

Rich findings for a genealogist. In entries like this, a more suitable
analogy than that of archaeological strata would be the snapshot, and
the character sketches that are a part of the convention of voyage diaries
become a sort of photographic trigger for the memory:

The variety of character in the passengers – a journal is
incomplete without this description. Although this will fall short
of the character of a journal, and I am a poor judge of character,
and a worse delineator, I shall just transcribe their impression on
my mind, by which I may at a future time realise the assembly in
the cuddy of the 'Amelia Thompson'. (Rev. John Jennings Smith
27 June 1839)

The Reverend Smith called the resulting study his 'little camera
obscura of our party', and a few diarists, such as John Sceales, drew
portraits of their fellow passengers.

If family historians respect these little camera obscuras, then so
ought the cultural historians, though they seem to have made little use
of them, partly, I suspect, because of the time expended in searching the
archives, and partly because as data they are too insignificant: it would
be difficult to generate a theory of immigration from a group of maybe a

dozen passengers on one particular voyage. Yet immigration historians are showing a growing interest in individual case histories, and there is an untapped potential here for investigating not only the diarist's motives for emigrating (though diarists are generally reticent in recording their own motives) but those of a whole cross-section of emigrants. For example, the character sketches made by Edward Cornell on board the *Red Jacket* in 1856 record that in the second-class accommodation there were almost as many women as men (eight to ten), and apart from the two newly married wives of returning gold-diggers, there were three matriarchal groups, one travelling out to join a husband, one rumoured to be leaving a husband in the workhouse, and one unspecified. Although many married women emigrated to Australia as part of a patriarchal structure, it would be interesting to know how many married women travelled alone.

My own interest, however, is in the social function of these lists as they were written on board. Not all those found in diaries were written at sea, and sometimes they form part of a discursive introduction to a fair copy of a diary along with a description of the ship; sometimes they form an appendix along with a daily listing of the ship's position. In these cases, the listing performs what is always its ostensible function, that of recording the details of the voyage for posterity. But where we can guess that the character sketches were written at sea, then they were generally written during the first month at sea, and most likely during the first few days. There was a certain point in a voyage when the diarist felt it possible to write such a description, and this depended not surprisingly on how quickly the diarist felt she or he had come to know their fellow passengers: 'I am not in a position yet to say anything of our fellow passengers for hitherto they have nearly all been stowed away below out of the weather' (Alfred Withers 9 Jan. 1857). Mr A appears to have had a similar difficulty: 'We had on board besides myself and Family [blank] Cabin & [blank] steerage passengers: – whose characters I will endeavour to delineate in the course of this Journal: – but I will not do this hastily lest I should fall into mistakes' (15 Nov. 1837). Not only did Mr A never insert the number of passengers travelling cabin and steerage, unfortunately (especially since it might have relieved the tedium of his diary), Mr A failed to give the promised character sketches. Yet in a sense, the gaps in his diary are present in nearly all diaries, except they go unmarked. Unless there were only a few passengers on board, it would have been impossible to write sketches beyond, say, twenty passengers. On ships carrying two, four, or six hundred passengers, there would always be gaps in the diarist's knowledge of the other passengers.

These gaps are instructive. Diarists could, after a little time on board, attempt a listing or even a description of those passengers within their immediate social circle. The Reverend Smith includes only those in the cuddy (the first-class saloon), Edward Cornell restricts himself to second class, while Francis Taylor, travelling steerage, lists only those in his mess. Such gaps suggest that there were some very well-defined social groups on board ship, and that there was almost no social interaction with individuals beyond these groups. It is the relationship between these groups and the role of the diary in constituting them that is my concern in the present chapter.

*

When a British emigrant sailed to Australia in the nineteenth century, the space she or he occupied on board ship was not just a physical space marked out by decks and bulkheads, it was a social space that aligned the passenger with a certain passenger class. The division of space between the passengers was made primarily according to what passengers could afford to pay, and to the degree that wealth and class status coincided in the Victorian period, the best accommodation was usually occupied by men and women from the wealthier middle classes, the men being merchants, builders, doctors, clergymen, and such like. In a society in which the dominant groups were so obsessed by class differentiation, all differences in accommodation carried with them social connotations, and when a passenger bought a ticket, that ticket determined the broad social class to which the passenger would be aligned for the duration of the voyage. The force of the system can be seen in the case of stowaways who, having no tickets, fell outside the system of social classification and became scapegoats: 'They are cuffed by all the officers and kicked about by the men, they are neither sailors nor passengers, belong to no class on board, they are all young fellows and can bear anything, certainly, but poor devils how they must wish for a quiet passage' (Alfred Withers 7 Jan. 1857).

Those who paid the cheapest fares or who had assisted passages travelled in steerage (third-class) accommodation and occupied the lower decks of the ship, the decks on or immediately above the waterline. The meaning of travelling steerage changed with the increase in emigration, and prior to the late 1840s the high cost of any passage to Australia meant that, excepting those travelling as assisted emigrants, steerage passengers might have their own cabin, be one of no more than a dozen steerage passengers, and be persons with some capital; most of the early steerage diaries were kept by members of the middle classes. As emigrant ships looked to carry cargo, primarily Australian wool, in the place of emigrants for the voyage home, the steerage deck was usually a converted cargo space and by the time of mass migration the fittings were both temporary and minimal:

> This is a splendid merchant vessel engaged for the trip,
> consequently the berths were temporarily fitted up between
> decks, to be taken down when we reach Rockhampton, as they
> intend going to the East Indies for merchandise and may not
> come home for two years. (Mrs Hinshelwood 18 June 1883)

Mrs Hinshelwood was travelling to Queensland and Queensland's immigration agents preferred married emigrants to be housed in enclosed cabins (Woolcock 90), but generally steerage accommodation was just a communal dormitory, with two tiers of bunks lining the sides of the deck and a dining table running along the centre-line of the ship between them. Mrs Hinshelwood might have been less enthusiastic about her accommodation had she suffered the lack of privacy felt by Elizabeth Allbon travelling steerage to Sydney just four years earlier: 'Doctor came down at twelve Oclock to see if any one was sick   we wished we had not come   our bunks are all fitted up between decks not private at all side by side & just a curtain hung in front' (23 Mar. 1979). As might be guessed, the majority of steerage passengers from the 1850s forward came from the poorest sectors of society, and they were in particular agricultural and general labourers, displaced rural craftsmen, the families of these, and female domestic servants.

To the rear of the ship and on the deck above the steerage passengers travelled the cabin passengers, passengers who could afford and were provided with more substantial private accommodation in cabins. These rarely referred to themselves as 'emigrants', a term reserved for those who had assisted passages and inevitably applied by association to all steerage passengers; those who travelled by cabin were socially superior 'passengers' and had the distinction of having their names listed in the newspapers on arrival. As one emigrant manual counselled: 'Coming in the cabin is, in short, considered to be a species of guarantee for "respectability" ' (*The Emigrant's Manual: Australia* 9). The ratio of steerage to cabin passengers on any particular ship varied depending on the size of the ship and the commercial factors operating at the time of sailing, and there is little research we can look to here, but my own guess is that as few as one in ten emigrants travelled by cabin; the figure for immigration to Queensland, which had particular problems attracting immigrants with capital, was one in twenty travelling cabin-class (Woolcock 33).

Cabin class, however, could itself be sub-divided and where ships provided a relatively large number of cabins then cabin accommodation was usually graded, again according to cost, into first and second class, though on some ships there was occasionally an additional 'intermediate' class of cabin accommodation situated amidships, either in a deck-house or below the deck on the same level as the steerage passengers; intermediate passengers were 'intermediate' as they had cabins but were organised into messes like steerage passengers. Cabin classes differed mainly in the size of cabin, the area of deckspace allotted to them, and the quality of the food. Although it should not be over-emphasised, it is true to say that cabin passengers with fresher and more varied food, and with lighter and more airy accommodation stood a better chance of remaining healthy and free from infectious diseases than the steerage passengers in the poorly-lit and poorly-ventilated lower areas of the ship.

Because cabin passengers occupied decks above the steerage passengers, it was not only more healthy but socially more prestigious to be higher in the ship than lower; the vertical plane of the decks corresponded to differences of social class. There was therefore a direct correlation between spatial organisation and a social hierarchy, and it is hard to escape the point that Don Charlwood makes:

> Products of their time as they were, it probably did not surprise
> the emigrants that life on board ship mirrored the class structure
> of Britain. The masses below deck represented the masses at
> home. At the other extreme, the captain's table was the seaborne
> equivalent of a manor house, the captain its squire. (105)

The captain, of course, presided over the table in the first-class passengers' saloon. Charlwood's analogy usefully relates the spatial and the social organisation of the ship but I think it needs to be qualified. Charlwood adds his own qualification:

> And yet, this was a spurious image. On shore the captain might

not have amounted to much socially at all and those who shared
his table might not have been particularly elevated themselves –
the aristocracy was rarely represented on the run to Australia; the
upper classes infrequently. But a hierarchy had to be established;
the passengers' habits of life demanded it. There must be some to
look up to, others to look down upon. (105)

The social classes to be found on board an emigrant ship did not cover
the spectrum to be found in Britain; emigrants went to Australia
primarily in search of improved standards of living, and few passengers
would be drawn from the landed sectors of British society. The divisions
between the various cabin classes, and the division between the cabin
classes as a whole and the steerage passengers, though they may be
analogous to the social hierarchy of Britain, are therefore not the same.
Yet Charlwood's suggestion that the shipboard social hierarchy exists
mainly out of habit and his implication that, although the captain was
not literally a squire, he mimicked the social role played by a squire
because it was expected of him, needs to be taken further. Such a view
may have been the view of those who regulated space on board ship but
it underplays the distinctive and continual social dynamics of life on
board ship and its material basis.

First, the captain's table was not merely a social nicety, a substitute
for real social relationships, it had itself a material function as a site for
displaying power relationships. The captain may not have been socially
elevated through birth, but his power was no less a power than the
squire's for all that. To be sure, he was himself subject to the various
Passenger Acts and other emigration regulations, and his power
devolved in some cases to the ship's surgeon who was given overall
responsibility for the discipline as well as the welfare of the passengers.
Only in extreme circumstances could a captain be successfully challenged, and in the sole instance I have seen, Henry Dodds relates how
on board the *Frances* in 1853 the captain, habitually drunk, was locked
in his cabin after threatening his chief officer first with a revolver and
then with a bayonet. So unprecedented was this removal of the captain
from command that the passengers felt it necessary to sign a
declaration taking full responsibility for the captain's arrest. But
challenging the captain's authority would rarely have been seriously
contemplated, and William Harbottle gives the prevailing view of the
captain's powers: 'he reigns King on board – and maintains his
authority as such – a Czar was never more absolute' (17 Mar. 1849).

Before telegraph and radio links, once a ship left port it was totally isolated from direct contact with any authority higher than that of the captain.

Don Charlwood's view that shipboard society was an unconscious 'habit' is also complicated by the active resistance to the social order by the passengers themselves. To be fair to Charlwood, he does go on to argue that 'there was among cabin class a sifting to be done: claims to degrees of respectability to be staked, a pecking order established' (105). Yet I think this view that differences in social class on board ship could be resolved by consensus underestimates both the continual play of this 'sifting' and the degree to which British society itself was in a state of flux. British society during the nineteenth century was far from static; rapid industrialisation and urbanisation were transforming the traditional social structure of Britain, for the first time bringing into being an industrial working class as well as redefining the older middle and upper classes. Charlwood's sifting was a commonplace in Britain itself, as one of Rachel Henning's non-Australian letters makes clear:

> We went to an awfully stupid evening at the Hollins's Monday night. Mr Hollins is the incumbent of St Clement's. They had invited a number of rather underbred young people to meet us, and the only entertainment of the evening was music, each young lady singing rather worse than her predecessor. I hardly ever heard such inferior performances. Mr Boyce was so disgusted he said he would not go out any more, and I am sure I hope he will not, for I hate that sort of party. (6 Jan. 1858)

Some cabin passengers no doubt did feel that life on board ship ought to mirror the idealised rural hierarchy expected at home, one of them Rachel Henning herself on her first voyage to Australia: 'There are very few ladies among them at all, and hardly any in the real sense of the word' (Henning 10 Aug. 1854). However, if shipboard life did reflect the social structure of Britain, it did so through the resistance to and negotiation of social relationships which characterises class difference in times of rapid social change. As in Britain, wealth and perceived social status did not always coincide: 'Mus. belongs to second class, but considers himself first rate, and in his opinion it is a mistake he came 2nd Class. Consequently he is not well liked, neither in 2nd nor 1st' (Moses Melchior 1853). Conversely, where tickets for all accommodation were open to anyone who could afford them, there were those who were perceived to be below the social class in which they were travelling: '[Hogan] ought to have been in the Steerage – we tried to induce him to change but without success' (Solomon Joseph 18 June 1859). Although the assumption behind both of these quotations is that there should be a correlation between social and passenger class, it is clear that class on board ship, as in Britain at the time, was not socially homogeneous.

The spatial relationships between the passengers may have been mapped out in advance by the ship's rules in order to reassure potential cabin passengers that their social privileges would be maintained, but in practice boundaries between social classes were often contested. Even the highest spatial privilege on board, the right to sit at the captain's table, was on occasion challenged:

> Some of the second-class passengers are very troublesome. The first day one of them with his wife took their seats at the captain's table, and refused to show their tickets, alleging that they were first-class passengers. However, the purser enforced the appearance of the ticket and the steward expelled them. (Rachel Henning 10 Aug. 1854)

Social relationships and the power that legitimates them are not fixed habits but are, as in this case, dynamic material practices that point to underlying anxieties and aspirations about social status, both on the part of the guilty couple and the writer herself: the couple here aspire to a higher status than that to which they are aligned according to the ticket they hold, while Rachel Henning is highly conscious that any successful breaching of class boundaries will undermine her own position.

Moreover, on a later voyage Rachel is concerned not just about the spatial relationships between passenger classes but even about the spatial configuration of those who sit at the captain's table: 'The captain sits at the top of the dining-table, next the mast. Mrs Bronchordt sits next him at his right, and next her I sit; then a Mr Brand, a Scotchman; the pretty German and her husband sit opposite, and the "commercials" down the same side' (17 Feb. 1861). We are back to one of those lists of passengers beloved by genealogists, and quite a few of them, like that of Rachel Henning, take the form of a seating plan. Clearly such lists are not innocent as they participate in demarcating social space: Rachel Henning, the daughter of a country clergyman, is quite precise in her occupation of a more socially prestigious space than the 'commercials', the middle-class merchants, who also travel first class; the rural middle-classes take precedence over the commercial middle-classes.

The case, then, is that the social hierarchy on board ship is, as Charlwood notes, modelled on a comforting image of class difference; differences of passenger class corresponded to differences of social class. And these in turn, it might be noted, corresponded with religious differences: 'the services . . . in fine weather are held on deck, but in foul, the English service is in the first cabin, Catholics in the steerage and Presbyterian in the second cabin' (James Walker 1868?). Yet this is an abstract model, which, though supported by rules, regulations, and religious practices, nevertheless guarantees neither class cohesion within passenger class nor class segregation across spatial boundaries. Indeed, the attempt to demarcate class differences by the precise regulation of space on board ship is the very motor that provokes resistance to social boundaries. A passenger may have perceived her or himself to be socially equivalent to those sitting at the captain's table, but the right to sit there depended on the type of ticket one had. Although the captain did have some discretion in such matters, in most cases it was strictly no ticket, no seat. Social class at sea thus depended primarily on a strict spatial exclusion, but it was a spatial exclusion which, in a period of social change, itself provoked contestation and required a constant policing if class distinctions were to be maintained.

*

Given the correlation between accommodation space and a hierarchy of social status, the exclusivity emigrants bought with a ticket rested primarily on their power to expel from their physical space emigrants of a lower passenger status: second-cabin passengers were not allowed in the first-cabin passengers' saloon, intermediate passengers were excluded from both first and second-class areas, and steerage passengers were kept out of all cabin-class accommodation. An emigrant travelling in cabin accommodation could spend three months at sea without meeting an emigrant travelling steerage. On the other hand, the same cabin passenger could, if she or he so desired, visit the quarters of the less 'respectable' emigrants. First-class (saloon) passengers could enter the space of the second-cabin passengers uninvited: 'After dinner one of the ladies of the Saloon came and held Church etc. in our cabin, much to the disgust of many passengers. There are a lot of Humbugs on board' (Joseph Sams 27 Sept. 1874). All classes of cabin passengers might go below decks into the steerage accommodation: 'I went below and distributed a few tracts this afternoon, they were gratefully received by most. It was pleasing to see so many carefully reading their Bible, a matter which is by no means easy below Deck for want of good light, by far the greater number however were playing at cards or dominoes' (Edward Cornell 24 May 1856). Only the seamen were more restricted than steerage passengers as they were prohibited from all passenger accommodation, though they did have two methods of retaining their self-respect: any passengers caught climbing the rigging were tied to it and released only on payment of a bottle of rum or brandy, a practice known as 'paying one's footing'; and occasionally the crew would bundle a pig or a sheep down among the cabins at night, no doubt as a kind of proxy invasion of the prohibited space:

> the sailors threw a sheep down into our cabin last night which
> [woke?] the greater number of the sleepers by its continued
> bleating   it was very amusing to see a big fat steward trying to
> carry it upstairs in his arms, many of the passengers caught up
> the sheep's cry for from every quarter of the cabin you could hear
> the 'Ma, Ma' during the greater part of the night and there are all
> the Gentlemen bleating to amuse themselves today. (Unnamed
> male diarist on board the SS *Great Britain* 28 Nov. 1863)

On another ship, the sailors even managed to invade the single women's accommodation by proxy: 'About 11 o'clock the sailors dressed some clothes up like a man that is on board & flung it down the hatchway to us. We put it into the bed of that young woman who is not right. She pulled him about & believed it was the man. They are up to all manner of things to have a bit of fun' (Maria Steley 20 Jan. 1864). But unlike the sailors, steerage passengers could charge no one their footing, and with no legitimate power of exclusion they were accorded the lowest social status. At sea, exclusivity, wealth, and élitism were closely linked.

If the captain's table was one site of class anxiety, the question of access to the poop deck provides most examples of the way in which spatial exclusion provoked resistance to the social order on board ship. The poop deck was the highest deck to the rear of the ship and those who had access to the poop had a psychological advantage over those on whom they looked down, as a guard captain on a convict ship noted in his diary: 'At 10 o'clock paraded to see Mr Mountjoy flogged – I put half a dozen men on the poop where they looked rather formidable' (J. D.

Sailing to Australia

Forbes 9 April 1827). The poop was the focal point of the ship's command structure; beneath it, like the first-class passengers, the captain had his accommodation and actually on it, to the rear, was the ship's wheel and the ship's compass. Whoever had command of the movement of the ship, be he the captain or the officer of the watch, could be found on the poop deck.

As far as the passengers were concerned, the poop as the apex of the ship's command structure added a further plane to the social dimensions of the ship. While passengers on the upper decks were accorded more social prestige than those on the lower decks, it was also a social advantage to be further to the rear of the ship than to the front, and the most prestigious cabins were the state cabins in the stern. In cultural terms, it was proximity to the captain which seems to have counted, though it needs again to be remembered that social privilege had a material base; the first-class accommodation immediately below the poop was also the driest on the ship: 'I feel very sorry for the people on the main deck (2nd cabin people I mean). They cannot come out in this weather owing to the water covering the deck, indeed sometimes they have to keep their door shut for fear of the water getting inside. It must be so uncomfortable for them' (Isabella Turner 30 April 1868).

Given the rarity of its social air, the poop deck was absolutely forbidden to steerage passengers: 'some of them had mounted on the Poop, from whence they were most unceremoniously expelled by the Captain, who commanded them never to have the impudence to shew their faces there again' (William Johnstone 7 Nov. 1841). Those from a lower class are once again expelled. This particular episode occurs on the first day at sea when the passengers might be forgiven for their 'impudence' and for not knowing their place. This was once again part of the 'confusion' of the first few days at sea when spatial order had not yet been established. Yet it is precisely through the expulsion of some passengers from certain physical spaces that class status on board ship was in practice demarcated and borders maintained.

Interestingly, there are no instances in the journals of steerage passengers trying in any organised way to dispute the rights to the poop deck, and this suggests that the dynamics of social identity are contained within steerage rather than operating across steerage and other passenger classes, a point I will take up later. In the case of cabin-class passengers, by contrast, a sense of social identity is more obviously defined by disputing spatial boundaries with a differing passenger class:

it is all the fault of the Doctor his wanting the 2nd Cabin
passengers to be allowed on the poop   it has caused a great deal
of ill feeling and if granted by the captain it will cause more – and
end no doubt in complaint in the colony   his reason is that by
so doing it will prevent sickness but if he understood his business
and looked after them and saw them all turned up on deck while
their place was cleaned and that they were all washed and properly
clean in their person there would be no fear of disease   it is
certainly very injust towards the cabin passengers – I would
strongly advise any persons of respectability if emigrating to
Australia to do so in a merchant ship and not in an imigrant one.
(John Whitings 25 May 1854)

Where there was more than one class of cabin passenger then the
question of who had rights to the poop deck became less clear. The
dividing line between the poop and the main deck, the line between
cabin and steerage passengers, remained, but the line between the
different categories of cabin passenger was in this case open to some
negotiation.

Given that the power of exclusion ultimately resided with the
captain, the captain himself could make limited concessions to suit the
occasion either through granting access to the poop on special occasions – 'The captain has given us permission to walk on the poop as that
is the only dry place on the ship' (J. R. Waight 14 June 1882) – or by
granting unlimited access to a section of the second-class passengers
only, in this case the women:

Only Saloon [i.e. first-class] passengers are allowed on the poop –
a promenade 90 feet long by 35 feet for 50 people – a much less
space is left for 500 of the others! My wife and the other females of
ours were invited up by the Captain when they please. The rest of
the deck is a dense crowd of men, women & children – ropes,
luggage & confusion of all sorts – some read, one knits, others
smoke, & most are idle. (John Fenwick 15 May 1854)

First-class passengers were understandably unhappy when the exclusivity of the poop was relaxed:

it is not agreeable to find the best and most convenient seats on
the benches and hen-coops pre-occupied, young men smoking

their pipes, swarms of noisy children squalling and running about playing, and no possibility whatever of holding any conversation that you would wish not to be overheard. . . . it may not be very liberal in these democratic times to say so, but on a long voyage it is a serious inconvenience. (N. C. 19 Nov. 1848)

The exclusion of one set of cabin passengers from the poop deck is a perennial theme in the diaries:

some of the 1st cabin passengers, fancying that they had not a sufficient monopoly of the poop laid in some complaints to that effect that the space which ought to be as they imagined solely devoted to their use was constantly sacriliged, so to speak, by a *class* of passengers which caused an annoyance to that aristocratic society. To gratify these complainants the Capt. ordered a large spar to be placed across the centre of the poop the 1st class to have the use of the stern the 2nd class the other department, thus shortening the promenade by one half and causing it instead of being an accommodation to one to be useless to both (it was certainly short enough originally). This piece of arbitrary power drew forth the indignation of the 2nd cabin passengers in the shape of a letter in which they expressed their opinions of the transaction in as plain language as possible. (Robert Corkhill 31 May 1855)

The solution proposed here, of dividing the poop deck crosswise so that second and first-cabin passengers both have space on the poop deck, is ingenious but nonetheless this compromise still maintains spatial privilege – social space now becomes relative to the fore and aft axis of social prestige rather than to the vertical axis, and the first-class passengers maintain their social differentiation.

On board another ship, the poop was divided not crosswise but lengthwise: 'Today was posted on the mizzenmast the following: "Chief cabin passengers weather side of poop; second, leeward side." "Caste" it seems is an institution on board the *Young Australia*' (Richard Watt 16 May 1864). Social prestige here becomes relative to the direction of the wind and the first-class passengers are given first option on the fresh air, important in the tropics though in strong wind the weather side would also be significantly higher than the leeward side. In neither case, though, does the partition of the poop deck lessen the resentment at exclusion. Of course, the opposition to segregation here comes not from any democratic principle, there is no suggestion that all passengers should share the exclusive rights to the poop deck. Its basis is a desire for social elevation and a feeling that the passenger is not being accorded the status she or he feels they ought to have. In talking in terms of 'caste' rather than in terms of class, Richard Watt is trying to deny that divisions between the middle-classes are themselves class-differences and he is affirming a perceived solidarity with other middle-class passengers travelling first class; it is a strategy based on class aspirations. This is made explicit when he and several of his fellow second-cabin passengers present a petition to the captain complaining of the way they are being treated by the ship's officers: 'We came on board under the impression that we should be treated as gentlemen which treatment we claim as our right' (20 June 1864). The division between the various cabin classes is viewed differently from the division between cabin and steerage passengers, which is taken for granted. Such incidents as these demonstrate anxiety among cabin-class passengers about class status and the way in which their class aspirations are translated into an occupation of physical space.

Even intermediate cabin passengers felt riled at their exclusion from the poop, some deciding to retaliate by putting up notices excluding first and second-class passengers from their space:

> A few days ago two notices had been stuck up excluding all
> passengers except those belonging to the 1st & 2nd Cabins from
> the Poop of the ship. I thought it a piece of downright humbug,
> and said so. Found on enquiry it was usual on board Passenger
> Ships. Thought it would be a good opportunity to put up Notices
> . . . excluding 1st & 2nd Cabin passengers from our part of the
> ship. (George Randall 19 June 1868)

This is fairly minimal resistance, but in at least one case excluded intermediate passengers took access to the poop deck (or, in this case, to its equivalent) into their own hands:

> the day before the captain arrived on board the following notice
> was posted at the head of our stairs: *The passengers in the
> Intermediate Cabins are not allowed abaft the Capstan.* This
> produced an altercation between Mr Thomas and some others
> with the mate. . . . He said it was usual with all passengers who

[121]

were not in the state cabins [the first-class cabins], and he should insist on the order being obeyed, which they flatly told him they would not – and to show that it was disregarded we went to any part of the deck, the same as before, without being interfered with by anyone. (Mary Thomas 1 July 1836).

Here spatial exclusion is successfully challenged and there is no indication that the captain enforced the order when he came on board. Although the space of the ship may be demarcated by the rules of the ship as set out by the captain, such incidents show clearly how the policing of spatial areas has to be seen as a dynamic process. Though Charlwood may be correct and it would have come as no surprise to the emigrants to find themselves spatially segregated according to social divisions, this spatial segregation is not a passive 'mirror' of an idealised and cohesive British society, but an active process. The division of space on board ship works primarily on the basis of exclusion, of excluding differing groups from certain areas of the ship, and this in turn provokes a rivalry which provides a focus for the affirmation and maintenance of social identity. What Greg Dening has said about William Bligh's *Bounty* can be applied in part to all emigrant ships: 'The Ship is much more an outsider's image, part of other conversations. The Ship, for the insider – in all its spaces, in all its relationships, in all its theatre – was always being re-made, was always in process' (27).

*

At the beginning of this chapter I pointed out how the lists and sketches of passengers that many diarists included in their diaries were usually restricted to the class to which the diarist belonged: a diarist travelling first class would describe other passengers travelling first class, a diarist travelling second class would describe others travelling second class, and so on. So when, for example, Isabella Turner writes that 'I must tell you a little about the people here before going any further' (9 Mar. 1868), what she in effect means is that she is going to write about passengers travelling first class like herself: 'There are but four cabin passengers besides ourselves – Mrs. Rae and her daughter, a girl of about twelve, Miss Smith and a Mr. Style, a young gentleman somewhat between twenty-five and twenty-seven.' A fairly detailed description of each follows. The sketch of her own social circle takes precedence over a description of the second class: 'Of the second-class passengers I may say something again, not just now, though.' Then when they are introduced they remain unnamed as befits their lower social status: 'I must tell you a little of the second-class passengers. Well, there is an Englishman and his wife, a Frenchwoman, and their three children' (27 Mar. 1868).

The strategies adopted by Isabella Turner and other diarists who included passenger lists and sketches are not so surprising since emigrants clearly wrote about the people they met daily, and those they had no contact with they said little about: 'Of the first class passengers I can say nothing. Some from the distance seem very seedy but that matters not they are there so I suppose can dress how they like' (Joseph Sams 24 Sept. 1874). Yet against a background of anxiety about class status, these lists have a particular significance. There was very clearly a great deal of competition for space on board emigrant ships, and competition for space was usually coded in terms of social status. Emigrants were not only worried about the social position they could secure in Australia, but their social position on board ship. In these circumstances the lists and sketches of those travelling in the same passenger class as the diarist have a material function in defining and maintaining social class on board ship; they map a social circle around the organising focus of the diarist, drawing some passengers into its sphere and marginalising those not travelling in the same class as the diarist. In effect, the lists are of dramatis personae, the key players in the diarist's account of the voyage, and the active restriction of physical movement on board ship is paralleled by restricting the dramatis personae of the diary to those travelling in the same class as the diarist.

There is a direct correlation between diary-writing and social segregation on the emigrant ship, and the diary as a practice for mapping a social space colludes with the regulations that divide the space of the ship among differing passenger classes. The diary becomes another material practice that dynamically polices the social boundaries, which is why the lists are so often found in the first three or four diary entries; the 'confusion' on board ship during the initial days at sea may be a spatial confusion, but it is a spatial confusion with clear social connotations. As space becomes unnarratable, so the fear grows that social boundaries are becoming eroded, and writing a diary is intended to reassure the diarist and those at home that social distinctions have been preserved. Suzanne L. Bunkers has written of women diarists of the American Midwest: 'For these women, the diary or journal became a place to write about relationships with others, thereby validating themselves as members of communities' (198). But if the emigrant diarists were validating themselves as members of communities, they were also in the same act validating the communities. We can see therefore why it was so important for Mr A to write: 'We had on board besides myself and Family [blank] Cabin & [blank] steerage passengers' (15 Nov. 1837); even though he was ignorant of the precise numbers of passengers, in his first diary entry he is at least making a gesture of marking out the two passenger classes. We can say, therefore, that the act of listing and describing other passengers in the diary works also to describe, in the geometrical sense of marking out, the social circles of the ship.

The issue which needs now to be addressed, however, is the extent to which this account of the diary is appropriate to the social and spatial experience of those passengers travelling steerage. So far I have been discussing mainly lists and sketches that corresponded to passenger classes, and the account of competition for space I gave earlier was an account of competition between cabin classes. But steerage passengers also included lists in their diaries: 'in our mess William & Ann Reay & Francis and Meggy Curry John W Bond and youngwoman they call Haynes and all of us is sick' (William Reay 31 Aug. 1877). If the diary colludes with the demarcation of space and the exclusivity of social status in terms of those middle-class emigrants travelling in the various cabin classes, we need also to consider its function in terms of those travelling both communally and at the bottom of the shipboard hier- archy in steerage.

The social exclusivity of those travelling steerage was imposed rather than necessarily desired – there were few material benefits in relation to cabin passengers in travelling steerage. Accommodation was less airy, less spacious, and less dry. Though steerage passengers might psycho- logically resent threats to their social identity as a class of passengers, they had no social privileges to defend, and questions of gender apart, cabin passengers had free access to the steerage accommodation: 'Mrs Macdonald and I went down to the steerage and women and girls berths for the first time. Quite delighted with the cleanliness of them' (Jessie Campbell 7 Nov. 1840). Those in the between decks area had no rights to exclude others.

More especially, though, any sense of cohesion around a particular passenger class was undermined by the sub-division of steerage passen- gers into messes. With the numbers of steerage passengers on emigrant ships running into hundreds, the mess system was part of the manage- ment of large numbers of working-class emigrants, a system of management carried over from the convict ships (Charlwood 196). One of the initial tasks of the purser or the surgeon was to divide the steerage into small groups, although in at least one case it was a passenger from the second-class cabins who carried out the task: 'Today I got the people into Messes – the purser had made three attempts & failed. People now have their flour, &c, and feel contented' (John Fenwick 19 May 1854). Clearly, keeping the steerage passengers contented was seen as an important priority for those in authority, though the strategy of the mess as a system of social organisation also worked to keep the steerage passengers not only contented but busy:

> all the morning is taken up by the regular work of the day, such as cleaning, getting food, prepairing it and taking it to the galley to be cooked, and fetching away again, then in the Afternoon there is the water to fetch and filter which takes some considerable time, then comes tea, after which there is no chance to do anything except stand on deck and look at the stars etc. for there is not light enough to do anything by downstairs. (John Hedges 30 Oct. 1858)

As Helen Woolcock points out, the authorities feared a breakdown of social order would result from such a gathering of working men and women with nothing to do: 'The Queensland authorities, recognizing the potential for good or evil of the hours of leisure at sea, applied the maxim quoted by one schoolmaster: "When men have nothing to do, they are sure soon to do something worse"' (Woolcock 105). Or as it appears in other places: 'For Satan finds some mischief still, For idle hands to do' (*MacKenzie's Australian Emigrant's Guide* 6). In so far as the workplace was a domain which regulated the behaviour of workpeople, it was felt by those not subjected to the workplace that its absence on board ship would lead to steerage passengers adopting alternative, less orderly social identities; leisure, of course, was by definition solely the prerogative of the leisured classes. The assumption that working people needed regulating if disorder was to be avoided was clearly articulated by one particular ship's surgeon whose task it was to carry out the regulations: 'I have to use the greatest strictness, amounting to what seems a severity, but I am obliged to do so, in order to preserve order' (Henry Lightoller 12 July 1878).

In first and second-class cabin accommodation, male (and occasionally female) stewards organised the provision of meals, leaving the passengers themselves free from most domestic tasks, as they may well have been in Britain. In the steerage accommodation, domestic servants were not supplied and it was the function of the mess captain to collect the provisions from the purser, take them to the cook, and then to collect the food when ready to eat:

> We are divided into messes, with a captain over each mess which includes 10 adults. This sometimes means four parents and twelve children [i.e. counting children as half a statute adult]. Tom is captain of our mess, comprised of ourselves and an English family with five children. The two men take week about to seek in provisions, and it is a constant run, especially on Saturday, when we get two days' provisions. (Mrs Hinshelwood 11 July 1883).

Where the mess comprised both male and female passengers, the women, in line with social convention, carried out the actual preparation of the food and other domestic tasks: 'We wash our dishes, while the husbands sweep our floors' (Mrs Hinshelwood 29 May 1883). Messes which comprised only males therefore faced certain difficulties: 'if there is no female in it, then some of the men tuck up their sleeves and set to work – some of them do well, but it is laughable to see some of the compounds of suet, potatoes, pork, flour & raisins, thick & thin, sent to the Galley to be baked' (John Fenwick 31 May 1854). I wonder whether the writer of this entry, John Fenwick, would have managed any more successfully. But whatever the composition of the mess, the welfare of its members was linked. At each stage in the provision of meals, food might be lost either through the purser or cook defrauding the passengers of their rations, or, as in the following case, through mismanagement by the mess captain, and in such circumstances all members of the mess suffered equally:

> Monday 6th September [1875]. I made a blunder today in not attending at the butcher's shop for my pork so we had only Peasoup and Preserved Potatoes for dinner.

> Friday 24th September. Today I am messman again and miss my beef having to go for a loaf and there was such a crush at the store I had to wait till after 10 o'clock and then the butcher had shut up, rather a bad beginning for mess. (in Ball 84)

Don Charlwood argues that the mess system, for all the hard work it entailed, promoted group co-operation: 'Most steerage men took their turn at being mess captain, and so received rations for all. This was a position of trust. Even if a man and his family were not by nature trustworthy, they dared not take extra food for themselves, for soon it would be the turn of one of their shipmates to be captain' (215). Charlwood sees the voyage out as teaching a lesson in co-operation which prepared emigrants for life in Australia: 'Thus the voyage played its part in shaping the Australian ethos.' Yet in his search for shipboard consensus, Charlwood overlooks cases in which messes were internally divided:

> I will now tell you about our mess   we have agread better than any mess in the ship we have not had A miss word all the time while the next mess to we have A row every meal and some times two they will fall out how they shall cook the meat or meals and then as soon as they have eaten it they will begin hoo wash up is it and they have had blows several times   thear one north country man one welsh man one west and one as been at work near alton tows [Alton Towers] and them two chaps from hednesford and Alfred Joins he is the cakey dofey half baked slopey cakey headed fool I hever seed   they will find falt with one another twang especly the Durham mans language   it is A very rong thing to mak game of another twang it will cause A row sooner than any thing else (Will Sayer 22 Aug. 1876)

Although the editors of Will Sayer's diary standardised Will's English, thankfully they also included a reproduction of this particular entry, and Will's Staffordshire dialect gives some idea of one of the many varieties of English that were being spoken on board emigrant ships and which could lead to members of a mess falling out. Yet if the mess promoted group co-operation despite internal dissension, it did so in an environment of rivalry between messes: 'You know we are divided in messes of 8 and we have nothing to do with the others. We have a table to ourselves so we don't have to borrow anything from the other messes but I can tell you we are all teetotallers' (Will Sayer 7 Aug. 1876).

It is possible to see the mess system as organising the steerage passengers into groups equivalent to cabin classes, yet if in terms of psychology messes may have given the emigrant a sense of social identity within a small and easily determined group, the mess could not coincide with an entire class of passengers as it might in the various

[127]

cabin classes. The organisation of the cabin passengers into different classes was fundamentally different from the organisation of steerage passengers into messes. Unlike the relationship between the different classes of cabin accommodation, the relationship between messes was not organised hierarchically; all messes had the same type of accommodation, the same rations, the same access to the ship's space. This meant that the organisation of steerage passengers was fundamentally unstable since messes could and did break up and reform in different configurations without the loss of any differential status; the new messes had the same privileges as those from which they had been formed: 'Our mess which has existed hithertoo in confusion and disorder breaks up, myself and Dr. Cassel remove to the next table' (Stephen Brennand 20 Sept. 1883).

Of course there were comparable movements within passenger classes, as Mr Barton, travelling first class, makes clear: 'Cabin divided into factions; discontent being excited by a move on the part of the childless passengers to get an end of the table to themselves; out of sight, heaving, and smell of the younger branches and their progenitors. We have established a separate teapot, knife-tray, and cruet-stand' (Mr Barton 9 Sept. 1853). Yet passenger class was based on the notion that all in the same class ate at the same dining table, and cabin passengers could not have removed themselves from the first to the second-class table (or vice versa) so easily as steerage passengers could move from one mess to another. Moreover, if all messes ate together, then neither could the mess coincide with a regulated passenger class division within the ship. This is not to say that there were not the same social tensions that existed in and between the cabin classes, nor that messes could not secure for themselves particular places at the dining table or on the decks. It would be wrong to see steerage passengers operating outside any form of competitive social dynamics. But when steerage passengers identified themselves with a particular mess, the identification was not also one of class, and the possibility of class definition through rivalry for space with passengers from another class was severely restricted.

This also means that the social space described by the diary did not coincide with boundaries of class status. There are certainly lists or sketches of other passengers to be found in steerage diaries, and diarists could still list members of their immediate social grouping, but these lists did not reinforce class divisions. I have already quoted the mess lists of Francis Taylor and William Reay; the following is Fanny Davis's description of the other single women travelling in her mess:

> In my Mess I have of course myself and Miss Wellington, two
> sisters likewise from Cornwall who are going out to be married,
> and one more Cornish girl who is going out to be married to a
> man she has never seen. She has been recommended by friends.
> And one little married woman with no children going out to her
> husband, and a young girl who is going out to her mother and
> stepfather who she has never seen. I hope they will all be
> agreeable and then we shall get along nicely. (5 June 1858)

As in the case of the diaries of those travelling cabin class, the diary
describes the social circle. Yet the social circle described is that of the
mess, not that of a specific passenger class.

Indeed, rather than operate to police the boundaries of a class
identity, the steerage diary is typically socially divisive within the
steerage class. When steerage passengers embarked on government
chartered ships they were generally given berths next to friends and
people from their own locality (Woolcock 101); this made sense in ships
which, even if they carried only British emigrants, carried emigrants
from what were still distinctively separate cultural communities:

> one mess of eight young men mutually agree to disolve
> partnership a portion of them possessing too much Scotch Blood
> in them for the remainder they being pure bred English, Scotch
> Oatmeal Cakes and such like things being unnatural to an
> English appetite, being their favorite luxuries – and as these dry
> husky ingredients of which these Cakes are composed require too
> much help from the Sugar, Butter, Treacle, &c, the English think
> they had better Balance ac[com]pts and disolve partnership
> before their books become more unsettled. (Francis Taylor 7 Apr.
> 1850)

By taking care that Scots were not put in the same mess as the
English, or that Irish Catholics and Cornish Methodists were kept
apart, emigrant officials made it more likely that members of a mess
would get on with each other. But the wider implication is that the
steerage accommodation was divided into sections by region or
nationality: 'First the English go on board, then the Scotch; after them
the Irish' (Fanny Davis 5 June 1858). This gave the passengers a sense of

identity through association with those who belonged to the same language community and ate the same food, but the beyond of the mess, the beyond of the inclusive social group with which the diary dealt, was unlike the beyond of the cabin classes in that it was defined as foreign rather than as a different social class:

> in the morning to our no small chagrin, found myself *lousey* . . .
> we have not the slightest doubt that they came from our close
> neighbours the Irish who occupy ¾ of the side of the vessel at our
> left, we likewise found that they had travelled further than us, as
> our neighbours on the other side found a few on their bodys when
> they examined themselves. (John Hedges 9 Oct. 1858)

The division between us and them is seen here in terms of nationality rather than in terms of social class; the discourse normalises 'Englishness' as the point from which others are viewed and in consequence both displaces and subordinates 'Irishness.' Similarly, on Robert Corkhill's ship, the Irish steerage passengers in the forward part were 'characterised by the name of Sebastapool' while German steerage passengers aft 'received the designation of Sodom' (Robert Corkhill 31 May 1855). The division of steerage passengers into nationalities worked against social cohesion around the notion of a social class, and the space with which a steerage diary dealt was a divided space (Sebastapool, Sodom), not one pertaining to a specific passenger class. Passengers saw themselves first and foremost as English, Irish, or German, or first and foremost from the West Country, the North of England, or London; only then, if at all, did they see themselves as steerage passengers.

In these conditions, competition within steerage strengthened the separate cultural identities and further undermined any possibility of class identity:

> our London dancing does not amuse the Cornish or Devon people
> much, for most all the Emigrants consists, of those two
> countries, the principal of them are miners, the lower order of
> them we have on board, sneers and laughs at seeing the Polka
> danced, but of course we took no notice, as we guessed that they
> had never seen it danced before, so we computed it to their
> ignorance, I even heard one young woman say to another (they
> call that dancing I should like to take them by the heads and drop

them overboard) a very nice thing for a young woman to say because she did not admire the Polka (Thomas Davies 15 July 1854)

Among men the competition could be more violent, with fights between, for example, the Irish and Cornish, or Irish and English (J. P. Ricou 6 May 1872). But be it through dancing or fighting, the issue in steerage was national rather than class identity.

Yet if steerage passengers saw themselves as groups of differing nationalities, it was also how they were regarded by the cabin-class passengers. If those travelling by cabin distanced themselves from other cabin passengers in terms of class, in their descriptions of steerage passengers they also distanced themselves in terms of nationality:

> There are at least 80 people from Jersey & Guernsey; they speak (besides English) a lingo I can make nothing of. The majority of them are bound to the Diggins. There are too, numbers of Welsh and Cornish people – 3 or 4 Frenchmen. The rest are made up of English, Scotch, with a sprinkling of Irish. (John Fenwick 16 May 1854)

The cabin-class descriptions of the steerage passengers tend to see them less as a particular class of passenger, less still as named individuals, but as a collection of differing national groups. Of course, not all cabin passengers came from the same region or country, but nationality was not such a large determinant of social groupings as it was in steerage. A French or German cabin passenger was primarily an individual belonging to an inclusive, if predominantly British, cabin class: 'I had a row with a Frenchman about a caricature' (Thomas Miller 7 May 1870). This example is also a good reminder that there was rarely total harmony even within cabin classes: 'Discontent is rife and I take a malicious pleasure in anticipating the progress of events' (Mr Barton 25 Sept. 1853). Discontent could evidently find a physical expression: 'there was a fight among the chief cabin passengers this afternoon which ended in several being well bruised' (G. Annison 13 Mar. 1853). Yet though there may have been conflict within the first or second cabins, there was still a possibility, as the lists show, of seeing passenger class as an entity. This was not the case in steerage, and the fragmented description which follows could not be mistaken for a description of cabin passengers:

[131]

in one of the corners will be about two dozen singing, in another a
lot talking scandal about everybody. . . . In another place will be a
lot of Scotch girls dancing with one of them imitating the
bagpipes and not one of them with either shoes or stockings on;
then the Irish will be squatting down under the boats talking over
everybody's business but their own and vowing eternal hatred to
the English. (Fanny Davis 23 July 1858).

Fanny Davis was quite able to write a full description of her mess, but
her description of the unaccompanied women travelling steerage,
though it was written by one of their number, might equally have been
written by a member of the cabin classes. Passengers were not seen as
individuals but as national groups, a description totally unlike that of
cabin classes. And once again, the space which these passengers
inhabited was viewed not as socially inclusive but as a fragmented
space: 'in one of the corners . . . in another. . . . In another place . . .
under the boats.' Having no need to invest in a common social identity
since they had no privileges to maintain, steerage passengers invested
in a socially and spatially divisive nationalism.

The space steerage passengers wrote about was more diffuse than
that of cabin passengers, and although the mess may have provided an
inclusive group equivalent to a cabin class, the fact that it did not
correspond to an exclusive physical space meant that there was no class
focus for the diary. And since there was no socially inclusive spatial
border to police, there was no promotion of class identity through the
kind of contest for space that occurred between other classes of passenger. Steerage passengers on the whole saw their fellow passengers not
as part of a group to which they themselves belonged but as members of
opposing regional or national groupings, a finding which bears out the
argument made by Gertrude Himmelfarb that a sense of working-class
unity does not appear in Britain before the latter part of the nineteenth
century (288–304).

The only image of unity found in steerage diaries is not that of a
passenger class but that of the 'village', and this is an image found
exclusively in steerage diaries. If ships were 'houses on the move', for
many of the emigrants they were also villages or towns on the move: 'It
reminds me of a little village; as you look night or morning down the
long 'tween decks it is as if people were peeping out of their little
cottages. On some mornings when certain days bring round their extra
duties we have all the bustle of a little town' (Sophia Taylor 22 Aug.

1851). In the same way as the cabin diarists created a domain of the home, so steerage passengers here articulated a more inclusive social space that would mitigate the spatial fragmentation. Like the 'home', the 'village' and 'town' gave an impression of spatial stability and allowed emigrants to construct an image of themselves as if on land. Moreover, it is notable that whenever the words 'village' or 'town' are used of the shipboard 'community', they have positive connotations and generally signify a community in harmony: 'The evening is now the pleasantest part of the day altho quite dark at seven o'clock. We stay on Deck until nine o'clock, it is very amusing to see how some of them enjoy it. I am reminded of a Country village feast all appear so happy & never think of danger' (Annie Gratton 3 July 1858). This image of the happy village erases the experience of the voyage: 'It is like being in a village. The time flies along while we are chatting, looking at this one and passing remarks about another' (Anna Cook 14 Dec. 1883; in Frost 21). Even when the sea is rough the 'village' manages to domes-ticate the transgression of shipboard space: 'the waves washed over the bulwarks . . . and run down the main hatchway into the Marriad peoples appartment which causes a little sport throughout the Village' (William Nichols 29 Apr. 1849). The sense of well-being contained in the use of 'village' imagery indicates that there was at sea already some nostalgia for an idealised image of the home country. This was a pastoral image, and Sophia Taylor's 'people peeping out of their little cottages' quoted above were in full accord with the 'village green' of the unnamed male diarist on the *Ganges*, a village green complete with 'the children playing in all directions' (5 Aug. 1863).

Yet this retreat into a pastoral nostalgia could only be locally successful in providing an image of unity and it could certainly not provide the basis of contesting space with the cabin passengers. Because of the way in which steerage passengers were organised into messes, working people saw their fellow passengers in precisely the same way as they themselves were seen by the cabin-class passengers, not as a class but as a collection of differing groups. The diaries of the cabin-class passengers give a sense of belonging to a particular class of passenger, a reflection of the much more cohesive sense of class among the middle classes, but in steerage diaries, despite the flights into pastoral harmony, the diarist remains isolated within the passenger class to which she or he belongs. In circumstances where national rivalries were more important than class identity, and where other cultural practices such as dancing and singing reinforced regional or national identities, the steerage passenger perhaps had less need of the diary as a means of mapping social identity; it would certainly have been harder to write in the more spatially fragmented conditions in which steerage passengers travelled. Although the lists found in steerage diaries may be as helpful (or unhelpful) to the genealogist as those found in cabin diaries, the function of the list during the voyage differed according to whether the diarist was travelling cabin or steerage. For cabin passengers, the list policed a social identity based on class; for steerage passengers, it undermined any chance of creating a social identity based on class.

Chapter 5

Narrators and personas

'I have made a Pudding for the first time in my Life!'

Emigrant diarists were preoccupied not with what lay outside the ship, but with what lay within. Outside was the unchanging blue scenery; inside was a more varied space but also a more controllable world. This world had to be learned, had to be organised, and as the luggage was stowed and hooks nailed up, so the diary played its part in the articulation of a domestic space. If they had one, the first space to be described by passengers was their cabin:

> I then went down to inspect my Cabin. The dimensions of which are as follows 6 feet x 6 feet height 7½ feet it is lit by a small window in the side and a dead light in the ceiling   it is fitted with berths for two but I am the sole tenant (except for the odd cockroach of which I find there are plenty on board[)] my cabin has a wash-hand stand in the corner a good door with lock & china handle. (Claudius Cairnes 16 October 1860)

The cabin is described right down to the china handle on the door, and once the cabin has been traversed by the diary, the diary moves outwards to organise the saloon:

> [my cabin] opens off the saloon Cabin which is about 14 feet square with a sky-light which admits air & light   the furniture consists of a Mahogany Table with a settee round it a sideboard swing lamp the Captain's arm chair and a mirror, the cabin is painted a light green color my berth is the same.

Writing about space helps the diarists to create a space in which they are comfortable, a space which they can know through narrating it. The same happens in steerage diaries, and though they had no cabin, steerage passengers nonetheless contrived to describe their sleeping accommodation:

> In the place where we sleep there are 104 young men. The beds are placed in rows of two from the ground. The number of my bed is 95 and *David's* is 93, the top beds are the best. The mess is 39, which is the last. We have to be in bed by 10 o'clock and up at 7, which is the rule of the ship. (Samuel Shaw 6 Feb. 1877)

The cabins and the steerage bunks permit different kinds of descriptions, and the spatial differentiation of the cabin description is more detailed than that of the steerage accommodation, compare the china door handle with the simple number of the beds. Steerage space was far more uniform, more repetitious, and less adaptable to an expression of individuality. Indeed, the way in which space and the occupation of that space is officially regulated can be gauged by the numerals; there are no less than five numbers in the passage from Samuel Shaw's diary: he gives the number of men in the compartment, the number of his and his friend's berths, and the times of rising and getting to bed. Steerage passengers not only occupied a more flexible space, their occupation of it was more regulated than that of the cabin passengers.

Nevertheless, both the description of the cabin and the description of the bunks are part of a general normalising discourse that almost obsessively describes the practical details of life on board ship. Probably the most frequent description is of shipboard food, and while archaeologists dig up middens to discover what past generations ate, the diaries offer cultural historians plenty of evidence of both official and unofficial rations:

> The meals that we get on board are only just moderate. Water, not too much, only just enough to quench your thirst. Bread, occasionally, three times a week. Biscuits, as many as you can eat and as hard as you could wish. Butter, twice a week as salt as you like, at least a great deal saltier than you do like, but nevertheless it is always eaten a long while before the next distributing day comes round. Salt pork and plum dough three times a week, also preserved potatoes, peas soup, preserved carrots, mustard, pepper, salt, &c. You get tea, black nasty stuff; sugar, very brown but still good; and molasses, as black as coal. (Arthur Clarke 29 Aug. 1868)

Sometimes the description of food is simply a copy of the official 'dietary' or scale of provisions, a listing in pounds and ounces of the various food stuffs allowed each passenger every week during the voyage: '3lbs Biscuit, 1lbs Beef, 1lbs Pork, ½lbs Bacon, 1½lbs Preserved Meat, 1½lbs Preserved Fish or Soup' and so on (J. R. Waight 14 June 1882). Of course there is again a contrast between different classes of passenger, and as cabin accommodation is more varied than that in steerage, so the food provided cabin passengers is more varied:

The first bell rings at half-past eight, dinner at half-past two o'clock, and tea about 6 p.m. I cannot say I care for the way of taking meals here, but I suppose the captain and the others do, which is all right. It seems such a lot of eating. Fancy, for breakfast, fried steak, stew and curried meat of some sort, with a dish of rice every morning. Of course, the dishes are sometimes varied, but there are always three. Then at dinner, always soup, two kinds at least of meat, vegetables of course, two kinds of pudding, always some kind of pastry, and cheese. On Sunday we had fruit and wine besides. When tea comes on there is meat again; two kinds of cold meat. I never took it for tea, nor do I now for breakfast. I have taken a bite once or twice. We have nice new rolls every morning for breakfast which we both enjoy very much. Oh, if you just tasted what horrible tea we get! (Isabella Turner 10 Mar. 1868)

Arthur Clarke would probably not have complained of Isabella Turner's menu. Yet the point still remains that all classes of passenger were obsessed by recording every detail of the voyage, even to the extent of noting daily what they had to eat:

Tuesday 31st – Gale of wind same course. Provisions gruel twice beef & potatoes.

Wen June 1st – Gale of wind same course Prov. gruel twice fish beef & potatoes.

Th 2d – Gale & sea worse than the Bay. Prov. gruel twice salt beef & pot. (Thomas Trotter 1836)

For Thomas Trotter, recording what he has to eat is as essential as recording the weather.

These are not isolated examples, and a great many of the diaries have equivalent passages in which the diarists describe in some detail their accommodation or what they had to eat. The diaries are crammed with practical information about the voyage, and no doubt some of the diarists hoped this information would prove useful for future intending emigrants: 'I will mention occasionally what our meals consist of as this Diary may meet the eye of some friend or friends of friends who may like to know something about the food on board ship' (Claudius Cairnes 28 Oct. 1860). But the same information is found in diaries by travellers rather than emigrants, or in diaries not written to be sent back, and the recording of practical information, as Thomas Trotter's diary exemplifies, appears to be some kind of reflex on the part of the diarists. Shipboard diaries seem to compel their writers to include details of everyday life at sea.

I argued in Chapter 2 that the domain of 'home' was centrally important to the immigrant diarist as a stabilised space, it allowed space to be differentiated and the voyage to become narratable. In Chapter 4, I considered the listing of the diarist's social circle and the way in which such lists functioned to define group identity on board ship. Looked at from another perspective, however, the description of marking out a home on board or the character sketches of fellow passengers are similar products of the diarist's obsession with recording everyday details of the shipboard environment. The list of food and the list of passengers are much the same.

From this perspective, we can begin to see how the diary is intent on fixing the voyage by defining what is normal. Aspects of the voyage are identified and then fixed in the diary: this is what we ate, this is who we met, this is where we slept. The voyage is broken into components, it becomes, as it must always become if it is to be narratable, differentiated. The obsession with detail is part of the larger impulse in the diaries to arrest transgression and reduce the voyage to a normality that can be narrated. The alien is flattened out, transformed into what can be known about the journey.

Writing of explorers' narratives, Mary Louise Pratt has argued that descriptions of a typical day constitute a normalised discourse, one which 'bleaches out irregularity, uncertainty, instability, violence' ('Scratches' 128). Pratt instances Livingstone's *Narrative of an Expedition to the Zambesi* (1866), pointing out how life in camp is seen from the point of view of an all-seeing, effaced European narrator who defines the perimeters of what is seen. This notion of an effaced narrator is one I have already used in Chapter 3 when I was looking at the diary in terms of Pratt's informational orders, and I will be pursuing it more fully a little later in this chapter. But Pratt's point about normalising discourses can be applied to the kinds of descriptions I am dealing with here: descriptions of fellow passengers, sleeping accommodation, or food are all this type of generalising, normalising discourse. Indeed, the sketch of a typical day in Livingstone's narrative which Pratt instances is paralleled by similar passages in emigrant diaries. Annie Gratton writes here of the domestic routine in the single women's accommodation:

> We have to get up early, each one folding up their bedclothes & roll up the mattrass sweep out her own Berth. Then we take it in turns for cleaning out the Cabin, Wednesdays & Saturdays it is scoured & the rest of the week swept & rubbed with a stone & with sand, all done before breakfast at 8 o'clock. (Annie Gratton 12 June 1858)

By recording the morning routine of tidying and cleaning her quarters, Annie Gratton establishes a norm that, to use Mary Louise Pratt's phrase, 'bleaches out' the particularity of the individual situation.

What remains in Annie Gratton's diary is a description of a routine prescribed by the agents of emigration, and we can see how, by adopting a normalising discourse, emigrant diaries collude with the regulation of social activity on board ship. As Helen Woolcock points out, the emigrant ship was one of the most controlled of the regulated environments of the Victorian period (105), and once on board ship emigrants would have found that almost all of their activities were organised for them. There were restrictions on their movements within the ship, on what they could eat, and how they could pass the days, and for the duration of the voyage emigrants were in effect incarcerated in a space controlled by the captain, the surgeon, and in the case of single women, the matron:

> we are expected to wash up our tin ware & sweep up our floor take our beds on deck twice a week to give them a blow   we take our turn at watching for 4 hours which Came to my turn 4 times during the Jurney   the single Woman are Cabin Passengers with use of the Poop & every Comfort with a Matern & under Matern with 3 Constables Selected from Maried Men to wait upon

them for which they get £3, the Jurney we visit our girls once a Week but see them every day in fine weather. the single Men are by them selves in the for part with use of Forcastle for receratian Married People go where they like except Cabin (Mr M 23 Aug. 1877)

Whatever the personal predilection of the diarist, in order to describe and make familiar the environment, the diarists found themselves necessarily colluding in the regulation of their own lives. If they tried to bleach out uncertainty and instability through describing the typical, they did so by describing typicality in terms of the highly regulated life on board ship. The desire to make the voyage narratable is overlaid by shipboard regulations, with the result that the diary was in effect reinforcing official regulations. The typical day became the regulation day.

*

For cabin as opposed to steerage passengers, the regulation day was one in which there was little opportunity to articulate a sense of personal agency. The days were punctuated by eating and drinking, the time in between being spent in largely passive occupations. For women travelling cabin class, the available activities were the most restricted, being largely reading, writing, and sewing. For men travelling cabin class, and especially single men, appropriate activities were to some extent enlarged to include more physical activities such as playing games, climbing the rigging, and killing the wildlife, though the day was still largely seen in terms of a domestic routine, as in John Fenwick's description:

> In the second cabin our ablutions are all performed below, & at ½ p.7, one half being seated (this occupies the whole table), the stewards bring a tall pint mug of Tea or coffee. The Biscuits are placed on the table, each one taking what they require. Shortly after 8, nearly every male & many of the females, find their way on deck, some to take their pipe, others to see what is going on & get the fresh air. From this time until noon is generally an idle time; many read; many do nothing but look over the side; some roll about and sleep or bask on the ropes, &c; a good many amuse themselves with games such as Cards, dominoes, drafts, tric trac, &c, &c. . . . After our dinner at ½ p.12 or 1 – reading, writing,

smoking, playing, lazying, &c, go on until 5½ when our Tea is
brought down – this is only Tea & Biscuits. Some have had messes
of their own prepared to help it out. In the afternoon we can get
bread, cakes, &c, baked. After Tea more pipes are lighted; some
remain below & play games; very few read – the light is so bad;
many sit and walk about on deck, & now & then a group sing
songs by turns and joins in the chorus. One or two sing a song
very well; but the bulk would shine more by listening. By 10
o'clock nearly every one is in bed; some few hang about the deck &
cabin. At 10 punctually all the lanterns between decks are put out
– one only being left burning near the main Hatchway; this being
close to our room, we have always some light, the only drawback
being that often a few sit at it & play or laugh until past midnight.
(John Fenwick 31 May 1854)

John Fenwick has all but written himself out of this entry as he
conforms to the set pattern, and the highly-regulated social practices
that the diary reports are once again duplicated by the diary itself as a
normalising social practice. Small wonder that, once the day has been
normalised and the activities described, diarists complain of having
nothing to write about. The diarist has been caught by the typical, has
invested heavily in maintaining a normality which the diary has helped
to bring into being.

Steerage passengers, by contrast, had less time for 'lazying', as John
Fenwick puts it, as they had to prepare their own food and were kept
relatively busy with all the other tasks that were handled by stewards for
the cabin-class passengers. Mrs Hinshelwood here describes the
steerage passengers' day:

We rise before six, get the children bathed and ready for school,
and our bed folded up on hinges by half-past seven; breakfast at
eight. We wash our dishes, while the husbands sweep our floors,
and we are all expected on deck by nine o'clock for the day. We
have a free library, and read and chat till one – dinner time. Tea
about five, then comes time for getting ready for bed our little
ones, who are all very merry. The first mate scrambles sweets
among them, has put up a swing, and seems to enjoy their
company. We generally bed about nine, as it gets chilly on deck.
(Mrs Hinshelwood 29 May 1883)

[141]

Because they were kept busier than cabin passengers, steerage passengers might be expected to have had more of a sense of individual agency, to have been able to construct more of a sense of who they were from all that activity. Yet even in Mrs Hinshelwood's description there is no establishment of individual agency. It is true that steerage passengers are more active than cabin passengers, having to fold up their beds, wash dishes, and sweep floors, but the degree of compulsion in these activities takes away agency; steerage passengers were not free to decide whether or not to clean or fetch water, they were the most regulated of the passengers on emigrant ships. In addition, the kinds of tasks which kept them busy were communal, and the passage above, like the two previous passages, notably has no instance of the first-person singular 'I', instead signalling the loss of individual agency by the use of the collective 'we'. What is missing is any sense of what Mrs Hinshelwood herself may have chosen to undertake on her own initiative, and once again the description of the typical day, in steerage as much in cabin class, bleaches out the individual diarist. Despite the amount of work expected of the steerage passengers, once a 'normal' day had been established there was not much left to say: 'there seems nothing to write about except our little ailments' (John Hedges 25 Nov. 1858). The regulations excluded significant independent action on the part of the emigrants, and in resorting to a typicality based on the regulations, emigrant diarists in effect wrote a sense of themselves as individuals out of their diaries.

*

In their diaries emigrants think, see, and speak, they describe events, but only rarely do they initiate what they regard as significant actions – in most cases they are acted upon by the ship or the agents of emigration. Even where they are not trying to establish the typical, they remain acted upon rather than actors in their own drama. Examples are not hard to find, and here is one chosen almost at random from diaries lying to hand:

> It commenced raining in a truly grand style about 12 o'clock last night and did not cease till 6 this morning. The sailors caught sufficient water to fill the remaining empty casks. We now have more on board than there was when the ship left London! So there is no fear of being short of water. Captain tells us this will probably be the last storm of any extent, which I sincerely hope

will prove the case, for the dampness of the atmosphere does not agree with dear Martha at all. Till now she has been unusually well, but today her health is very bad. The Doctor has examined her and given her some medicine which, I trust, will speedily have the desired effect. We are making very little progress, having such light breezes but we expect to be in 'the Trades' again soon, which will take us 2000 miles. (John Joseland 19 April 1853)

Syntactically, there are very few active constructions in this entry, that is, sentences that have a subject-verb-object structure. The instances here are: 'The sailors caught sufficient water'; 'Captain tells us'; 'The Doctor has examined her and given her some medicine'; and 'We are making very little progress.' In the first, second, and third of these, the subjects are all agents of emigration rather than emigrants themselves (the doctor, though possibly also an emigrant, acts here as an agent of the shipping company), while in the second and third action sentences the emigrants are actually the passive objects acted upon. Only in the fourth instance, 'We are making very little progress,' do the emigrants stand as the subject of the verb, but quite apart from the fact that this sentence expresses a negative, it does not represent any directed action. Looking at this passage from another viewpoint, there are only two uses of the first-person pronoun, 'I sincerely hope' and 'I trust', both of which are modality indicators expressing the diarist's attitude rather than any action.

One more example, this time from a steerage diary, will serve to reinforce the point:

Very cold and dismal still   first mate been round this morning to all the bunks with his pocket full of pins gave all the women handfull each   they were very acceptable   children were disappointed were all after him thought twas sweets   he generally carries some with him   six weeks to day since we left Plymouth not passed the Cape yet (Elizabeth Allbon 2 May 1879)

Again there are very few active constructions, and out of three, two involve the agency of a crew member ('[the first mate] gave all the women handfull each'; 'he generally carries some with him'), while the third represents a collective action ('we left Plymouth'). There is no instance here of the first-person pronoun, and even though this is not a normalising entry, the emigrants are more acted upon than actors in their own drama.

Janice Gothard has pointed out that the verb 'to emigrate' was used transitively in the context of late nineteenth-century female emigration; officials 'emigrated' the women. Yet Gothard's conclusion would have applied to many of the men as well: 'The term "emigrate" used in this way denotes the taking away of agency from the people who were "emigrated"; they became the objects of the action rather than its subjects' (Gothard 98). The regulation of emigrants at sea left them as agents of only a limited number of significant actions, that is, as agents of actions considered significant enough to be recorded in a diary.

Two of the most important actions which permitted a sense of individual agency were the creation of accommodation space as home and the contesting of social space, both of which I have discussed in some detail in earlier chapters (Chapters 2 and 4). Through such actions emigrants managed to articulate a sense of themselves as agents, managed to employ the first person 'I' as the subject of an action sentence: 'After breakfast I cleared out our cabin and Martha well cleaned it, which occupied her till lunch time' (John Joseland 23 Mar. 1853); 'the Mate . . . swore he would give it me the next time he caught me there [on the poop deck]. I dared him & went again in the evening, but he took no notice' (John Fenwick 17 June 1854). In limited cases like these, the emigrants succeeded in countering the loss of agency imposed on them by the conditions of emigration and successfully portrayed themselves as initiators of significant actions in their own right.

But there is a paradox in this. I argued above that the obsession with detail is part of the grand scheme of the diary to arrest transgression and reduce the voyage to a normality that can be narrated. It would be logical, therefore, for diarists to achieve a sense of individual agency at the expense of the normal, the typical; transgressive moments would enable the diarists to articulate a sense of personal identity. Yet as I have pointed out before, emigrant diarists were not wholehearted voyagers and the kind of diary they wrote tended towards the domestic in order to contain the transgression implicit in journeying. It is not surprising, therefore, that the diaries show the emigrants achieving agency in the defence of domesticity. The articulation of a home and the contestation of social space, two actions taken by the emigrants of their own volition, both attempt to establish an idealised version of the old country and hence, for their imagined home audience, reinforce a sense of

[144]

normality. When emigrant diarists decided to take unilateral action, it usually had the paradoxical effect of eventually reinforcing their lack of mastery over both their situation and their environment.

*

The most common and certainly for me the most interesting significant act emigrants performed was writing a diary. Like the other significant acts, writing a diary allowed emigrant diarists to articulate themselves as the 'I' of an active construction: 'I am sitting at the scritoire writing this with my clothes off down to my waist and the 3 cabin windows open' (Jessie Campbell 8 Sept. 1840). To us such an entry may appear transgressive, so undermining my argument that diaries on the whole attempted to normalise the voyage, but it is the heat rather than the removal of her clothes that makes this entry appear transgressive. In fact, Jessie Campbell is within the codes that allow women to remove their clothes in their own domestic space and her presumption of normality reinforces the site that enables writing to take place, the private, feminine domain of home. This entry domesticates the voyage.

Writing a diary, then, is not inherently transgressive and indeed the most common stance taken by the narrator of the diary is one of self-effacement. In conjunction with an active avoidance of the first-person pronoun, the diary attempts to normalise the experience of the voyage by appeals to typicality, and to be effective such appeals involve a claim that anyone in the same circumstances could produce the same report. The diary was therefore assumed to be an unmediated transcription of a prior and natural reality. The types of informational discourses adopted by the diaries for this purpose, the discourses of navigation or natural history, for example, depend upon the establishment of a would-be objective viewpoint: '28th going 9 miles an hour. Cape hens, cape pigeons, Albatross black & white & Petterils flying about. A whale in sight on the 30th but did not see it' (Grace Tindall November 1856). A whale has been in sight but it does not need to be validated by the diarist having seen it; it is not the active, 'I have seen a whale,' but the passive, 'A whale in sight.' The informational discourses are essentially non-authored kinds of writing.

When it moves into the experiential mode, however, the diary becomes a first-person autobiographical genre, and this has fundamental implications for the notions of agency, personas, and self-effacement. Following Emile Benveniste, we can say that use of the first-person pronoun relates to two selves, the present subject that narrates (the subject of the *énonciation*) and the subject that is narrated (the subject of the *énoncé*) (Benveniste 218). In auto-biographical writing this division is commonly represented as the present self writing about the past self, and in the example I gave a moment ago Jessie Campbell is both the actor and the narrator. The same split is behind the two sorts of beginnings emigrant diaries have, one the beginning of the voyage and the other the beginning of the writing.

In an article written some years ago, Louis A. Renza looked specifically at the strategies used by autobiographers to deal with this split between the self as actor and narrator. Renza's interest was in literary autobiography, a topic different in some important respects from emigrant diaries, but some of his comments are worth considering in the present context. In terms of literary autobiography, Renza asks the following question: 'How can he [the autobiographer] keep using the first-person pronoun, his sense of self-reference, without its becoming in the course of writing something other than strictly his own self-referential sign – a de facto third-person pronoun?' (278–9). The autobiographer's 'I' gradually becomes a 'he' (or 'she'), a past self different from the narrating self. According to Renza there are three strategies the autobiographer can adopt to mitigate the unsettling division inherent in the self-referential pronoun 'I': 'One can try to suppress the consciousness of pastness; or one can "confess" it openly to oneself; or one can even extol it and emphasise the narcissism proposed by the autobiographical act' (279). Renza then goes on to suggest a typology of three modes of writing which correspond to these autobiographical strategies: the memoir, the confessional, and the narcissistic mode. In the memoir mode the autobiographer presents her or himself in public, intersubjective terms; in the confessional mode the autobiographer confesses that the self presented is different from the 'real' self; and in the narcissistic mode the autobiographer extols the split and emphasises the autonomy of the present, writing self.

Renza's premise is that the writer is already conscious of her or himself as the narrator, the problem for the autobiographer being that the past self written about is no longer congruent with the present self. In the case of the emigrant diary, the reverse is true. These diaries are neither introspective nor retrospective, they deal with the events of the day, and because the diarist is recording events close to their occurrence, the incongruity between the writing self and the self being written about is less obvious. In the majority of emigrant diaries, therefore, the memoir mode of writing is the dominant strategy because it relies less than the confessional or narcissistic modes on the foregrounding of a narrating self: the narrator is effaced by the presentation of a public self.

This intersubjective or public dimension can be gauged from the following extract from Annie Gratton's diary: 'There is an awning put over the Poop and I think I may picture us sitting in a large Gipsey's tent in all directions, it is very hot & we think we are not far from the line. We enjoyed our Tea on deck this afternoon & afterwards had a Dance' (28 June 1858). The diarist is using language here, as Renza puts it, 'to declassify information about his [*sic*] life' (280), to mitigate the division between herself as a private (classified) writing subject and herself as a public figure; in the above case, there is a mismatch between Annie Gratton as the 'I' who paints the 'picture' and the Annie Gratton who appears in the picture, but the first Annie Gratton becomes aligned with the second, the figure of the narrator being effaced by the more public persona. To construct that persona, Annie Gratton uses the collective pronoun 'we', and a public referent, the group 'picture' of the single women in a large gypsy's tent. Throughout the diaries events are legitimated by the social co-ordinates shared by the audience for whom the diarist imagines she or he is writing.

Here we might recall Mary Louise Pratt's 'effaced narrator' upon which the typical day recounted in Dr Livingstone's narrative depended. To the degree that such a voice 'bleaches out' transgression (in Livingstone's case the accompanying Africans), such a narrator is a spokesperson for the aspirations of not only Livingstone but his British audience. It is an imperialistic, mastering viewpoint. It seems to me that emigrant diaries are similarly imperialistic, though it is less obtrusive since most emigrants to Australia were British and most travelled on British ships; the mastery was less obviously a mastery of another culture, though when English emigrants were writing of Irish emigrants or cabin passengers of steerage passengers, it is easier to spot: 'it is a most ludicrous sight to stand on the poop and watch the emigrants trying to pace the deck, rolling from side to side and then making a sudden dash to the side of the vessel holding their head in their hands' (Margaret Walpole 16 June 1883). Margaret Walpole here presents the 'sight' as naturally available to anyone, though the ludicrousness of the steerage passengers being seasick depends on the reader accepting and adopting the privileged perspective of a cabin passenger viewing steerage 'emigrants' from the poop deck. It is a mastering viewpoint.

An acceptance of such norms as religious observance, appropriate ways of spending the day, and a stratified relationship between the social groups on board ship also made the self being written about 'transparently accessible to others', as Renza puts it, though the self became transparently accessible once again chiefly in terms of the imagined home audience. Acceptance of the norm not only made the voyage narratable, it offered an effaced position of mastery from which the voyage might be narrated. The identity diarists assumed through constructing a home and contesting space with other social groups was pre-eminently a public rather than a private identity. Emigrant diarists may have been reluctant autobiographers, but they had a keen sense of a public self in the way they presented events on board ship to an implied audience that shared their social references. Emigrants did not see travel as a way of altering their personality, and continuity of identity was largely unquestioned.

*

Emigrants are on the whole suspicious of their narrating voice, it makes them too self-conscious. In addressing their diaries either explicitly or implicitly to 'those at home', emigrants had somehow to find the right mode of address to a very diverse group of family, friends, and acquaintances. It was a collection of individuals that they would not normally be addressing as a group, and the tone of self-conscious humility adopted along with the claim that the diary was being written merely for self-amusement was a way of coping with the problem. This self-consciousness is most often found in this form either at the beginning or ending of the diary. Henry Widdowson makes the claim at the beginning: 'I cannot but again help expressing my fears that the perusal of this journal . . . will afford but little instruction or gratification' (18 Nov. 1825); Edward Towle makes the claim at the end of the diary: 'I am ashamed to send such a specimen to my friends to read, but I have written this journal more for the sake of occupying my mind than with the anticipation that it will afford any gratification or amusement to my friends' (Edward Towle 3 Sept. 1852). These moments demonstrate the diarist's unease ('my fears'; 'ashamed') when the act of writing is brought into consciousness at such crucial moments as the beginning and ending of a diary.

There is also a self-consciousness inherent in the very act of writing a diary for those unaccustomed to keeping one. As Trevor Field has put it, 'the personal diary itself is a type of writing which tends to make people self-conscious' (129). As a way of overcoming such self-consciousness, Field argues, diarists look for a figure to address as in the formula 'Dear Diary': ' "Dear Diary" is a form of mock address by means of which embarrassment is recognised and overcome' (129). Here is another reason why emigrant diarists might formally address their diaries to 'Dear Mother' or some such figure without sending the diary once it was written; providing the diarist could contain the proliferation of addressees, imagining an addressee overcame a self-consciousness at writing.

Diarists were therefore most at ease in writing their diaries when they were able to adopt and maintain a persona they assumed their imagined addressee would recognise:

> I hope when the day comes that I see you all again I shall
> remember some of the comical things I see and hear. One young
> man must needs take his sheet to sling up to the ceiling for a
> hammock and only being made of loose unbleached calico it gave
> way in the night and let him down unhurt. This is a curious life,
> totally different to what I have been used to. (Sophia Taylor 22
> Aug. 1851)

In this entry Sophia Taylor is saying one thing and meaning another; she is saying that she is living a different life at sea, yet she retains the outlook of the old life in order to describe it. The young man in the anecdote is being derided because he is trying to behave (albeit ineptly) in an appropriate nautical manner, but Sophia Taylor remains at home in a dialogue with her familiar audience, the one she hopes to see again. Most diarists adopted this strategy in order to guard against a discomfiting self-consciousness, they projected themselves as the same person who had left home, yet in the unsettling conditions of migration and despite the fact that many emigrants travelled out in the company of friends and family, such a strategy would not always have been easy. The new physical environment and the enforced company of passengers and crew from diverse social groups would have made the maintenance of any consistent, let alone familiar, public persona quite a task.

As British emigrants on British ships, the emigrants faced a challenge to their identities not so much from any breakdown of national identity but from a breakdown of gender roles. The ship as home, as I have already suggested, provided a space in which both men and women could adopt particular gender roles; while women were able to take nominal charge of domestic arrangements, the men could adopt the necessary distance from domestic tasks entailed in the role of head of the household. With many men travelling alone or in all male groups, this model of different gender roles necessarily failed in some cases: 'I have made a Pudding for the first time in my Life this morning for our Sunday Dinner' (William Thompson 26 July 1857). I have already quoted John Fenwick's remark ridiculing some of the men in steerage who had to make their own puddings: 'if there is no female in it [the mess], then some of the men tuck up their sleeves and set to work – some of them do well, but it is laughable to see some of the compounds of suet, potatoes, flour & raisins, thick & thin, sent to the Galley to be baked' (31 May 1854). Another who ridiculed male attempts to cook was William Shennan who wrote as he spoke in a pronounced Scots accent:

the School Master made something for tea yesterday what he called his mothers kake but no one could look at it   first he put a peice of past[e?] in the bottom of the baking tin then covered it with treeckle then another past untill he had five lares   five bounds of flower and four bounds of treeckle   he took it to the Bake house but they Laughed at him   well they put it in but when it began to heat it began not to like its hot ro[o]m so then it ran and spitted then the kook had to put it out   what a farce I cant explane what it was like it was more like taffy [toffee] than a kak (24 Mar. 1870)

Yet, while John Fenwick was a merchant travelling in cabin class, William Shennan was a blacksmith travelling steerage and the ironic tone of both their observations about men doing their own cooking stems not from a common class viewpoint but from the viewpoint of men who think of cooking as women's work. Indeed, William is quite able to laugh at his own attempts at cooking, as in this passage where he tries to retrieve something from the schoolmaster's 'mothers cake':

I am trying what I can make of it   I cut it up as small as I could then I put some water then squeesed it with my hands ind doe again what a lark then I put it into a bag and boiled it   iff that wont do I dont know what I will do with it make a Pratta loaf of it nex or give it to the Porposes   Dinner time all is anxious to see the the duff well I have done it at last but still it was very sickly   so endeth the Mothers Duff

In entries like this, the diarist's self-consciousness stems, if only in part, from a defensiveness about what kind of role the diarist's persona ought to adopt; any breakdown in gender roles threatened the diarist's public persona. As Thomas Severn put it with a similar self-consciousness: 'It would amuse many to see me making puddings – bread etc. for our mess' (11 Oct. 1852). This is hardly the persona of a seafaring adventurer, should any of the male emigrants have seen themselves as such. However, not only were the public identities of the men threatened, also threatened was the assumed dialogue with the imagined audience. The public persona of the diarist relied on maintaining the values of home; any questioning of those values not only threatened the identity of the diarist, it forced on her or him a self-consciousness which in its turn threatened the imagined dialogue. No longer could diarists imagine themselves as part of the community left behind. Hence the protective irony in descriptions of men performing domestic tasks:

> Arose with one of my mess mates at 4 o'clock this morning to wash out our dirty linen &c   laughable to see so many men in the washing Buckets up to their elbows lots of fun more fun than dirty clothes   I find I can do it smartish   think something about taking a Laundry Maids place upon arriving in Australia (Francis Taylor 22 Mar. 1850)

The tone of voice in this entry distances Francis Taylor as narrator from himself as a character on board ship. Men performing domestic tasks is seen as laughable and amusing in order to assert a community of interest with the diary's imagined audience, and in the same way as diarists might claim to be writing their diaries purely for self-amusement because they were unsure of themselves as narrators, so through the use of irony they distanced themselves as narrators from themselves as actors when they lost confidence in their public persona. It was a way of playing down transgression by playing up the division inherent in the use of the first-person 'I', a risky strategy given the diarists' general desire to avoid self-consciousness.

But not all diarists accepted all or even part of the dominant middle-class gender model, and neither did all react in the same way to transgressions of it. Some working men were able to cook and sew, and they wrote about such things unencumbered by middle-class pre-

[151]

judices. For example, even though William Shennan could be self-conscious about his cooking, he made no bones about patching his trousers: 'I got my hare cut by the cumertrees man and I put a peice in the knee of my trousers   I hope it will be the last patch I will have to put on them' (29 Apr. 1870). There is not the same use of irony here since the public persona is not threatened by the adoption of different gender roles. The same is true of the unnamed male diarist and his companion Tom on the *Scottish Admiral*: 'Tom hemmed up my bedsheets and we maded two nice cakes for tea and a fig pudding for tomorrow. Tom and me have started to cut hair has they keep on asking us to do it, we are going to share the money we take' (25 May 1883). There is no sense that these men are doing anything strange; if men could sew and cook before they left home, there was no need to make fun of sewing and cooking on board ship.

Similarly it was possible for some women to enter the male domain without feeling culturally threatened by the experience:

> A continuance of gales and squalls so much of it is quite fatiguing getting so little sleep for fear of being rolled out of bed. They persuaded me to go to the point of the ship to see the grand sight of the waves mountain high   the Ladys could not stand without two to support Gents to hold them themselves holding by something . . . It was a sight I think I never shall see such another, I expected a splash, but was determined to brave it come as it would, presently I caught it but never flinched, so bravo was sung out, the wind was fearful. (27 June 1863)

By going to the forward part of the ship to watch the waves, this unnamed woman sailing on the *Orient* was moving beyond the domestic sphere alloted her by middle-class culture, but her transgression was for her an act of self-assertion. When she wrote, 'I caught it but never flinched,' she was not writing ironically.

A second example is worth quoting, this time from the diary of Susan Meade:

> the companion being open I ventured to pop my head out to see the aspect of things – nobody on deck but the Captn – the sun shone brightly – the breeze pure mild & refreshing; this after the gloom & closeness of the cabin was too great a temptation to resist – I returned to my berth for my bonnet & cloak & was on the

deck in a trice, in spite of the huge waves which continually broke over the deck – the Captn assisted me to a seat under the round-house: when I was just beginning to enjoy myself a monstrous wave broke over & completely drenched me – the Captn heartily laughed & so did I – the purchase far outweighed the price & I returned to my berth refreshed in mind & body by the change. (27 June 1842)

The laughter here is not ironical, and the outcome of Susan Meade succumbing to 'temptation' and climbing on deck alone for a breath of fresh air does not threaten her self-image as a woman.

On the whole, it was the women rather than the men who were less likely to have to adapt to or resist new roles, and hence we are less likely to find the defensive use of irony in diaries by women. Because the emigrant ship was largely a domestic space, the only 'home' the emigrants had, women who had accepted the domestic roles ascribed to them by the culture in which they lived would have found their gender roles suited them to life at sea. From this point of view, the strict incarceration of single women would have provided little challenge to the identities of such women; they would not have found themselves taken to watch the waves at the stem of the ship like the unnamed woman on the *Orient*, and for much of the time they would have been involved in needlework donated by various charitable bodies, the finished products being either for the personal use of the women later or to be sold on arrival:

> the matron has given out knitting and sewing to the girls   thay
> are to make stockings & shumeses [chemises]   after thay are
> made thay are to wash them and [put] thair name on them and
> return them to the matron   after we have arrived thay are to be
> given to girls who have behaved themselves to the matrons
> satisfaction   I hope to merit some small token of good conduct.
> (Mary Maclean 21 Dec. 1864)

Threats to the gender roles of the emigrants should not be over-stated, and even where the domestic space of the ship posed a threat to the identity of men who were not accompanied by women who could prepare their food, they still had opportunities for climbing the rigging, catching fish, and other kinds of physical games through which they could assert their masculinity. Moreover, single working-men

[153]

especially do show themselves used to at least some of the kinds of domestic tasks shunned by middle-class men; and even among the domestic tasks in the married quarters there was a gender division which allowed the men to maintain their difference from women. The men maintained the gender difference by taking to themselves tasks which involved dealing with other men or physical strength: it was the men who collected the rations, who carried the prepared food to the cook, and who brushed and scrubbed out their quarters. Single women, however, were expected to scrub out their own quarters, and given that this was considered a masculine task in one part of the ship and a feminine task in another, this is clear evidence, if evidence were needed, that domesticity on board ship was largely a matter of culture rather than nature.

*

Paul Carter's discussion of self-reference in shipboard diaries traverses and I hope will illuminate my own discussion in this chapter of what I call self-consciousness, those occasions when a diarist becomes aware of her or himself as narrator. In *The Road to Botany Bay*, Carter identifies two types of self-referential diary entry: that which refers to the lack of events to record, and that which refers to the material conditions in which the diary is written (140–43). The way I see self-reference of the first type is perhaps different from how Carter sees it, and for him it represents 'a spatial occasion, a moment on the journey when the journey became an object of consciousness' (143). But for me references to the lack of events to record come into being when the diary is faced by repetition, a crisis of both time and space which threatens to disrupt the narrative progression of the voyage; one day is much like the previous and the diary is brought to a halt because there is nothing to differentiate the days: '*Wednesday, Thursday & Friday, 4th, 5th, 6th*: Fine weather, but nothing has occurred for me to note' (John Joseland 6 May 1853). This loss of differentiation is the result of the diary reducing the contingency of the voyage experience to the formulaic, a strategy similar to the one I looked at earlier where the diarist's experience is reduced to the typical or regulation daily routine; the reduction of the voyage to a series of normalising descriptions, be they descriptions of birds, cabins, or a typical day, leads towards the same silence that lies just beyond the 'nothing has occurred for me to note'. The self-consciousness that this produces is in turn related to the diarist's fear that dialogue between her or himself and the imagined audience at home is on the point of collapsing. The diarists are placed in a situation similar to when they find themselves adopting alien gender roles: a gap opens between the diarist as narrator and the diarist's public persona. The diarist is unable to keep the persona running, and when diarists are unable to write about themselves as actors, they are left with the residue, themselves as narrators, and a self-consciousness of the relative independence of their two narrative functions.

The second type of self-referential passage identified by Paul Carter is that which refers to the physical or material conditions in which the diary is being written. Unlike the other acts recorded in the diary, the act of writing a diary has the capacity to bring to the attention not merely the recorded action but the action of its own recording. Carter quotes the following example from the diary of the overland traveller Thomas Walker:

> I could write a great deal more to you than I do, but I have little convenience or time for the purpose. I can only do so at night when the others are asleep. I shall just describe to you my present situation; I am sitting on my mattrass in our tent . . . my paper is on my knees, the candle on my hat, in my left hand I hold my ink-stand. (141)

For Carter, this is a good example of what he calls 'a subject-and-predicate description'; for the diarist, 'the predicate of spatial details is, in fact, what brings his present situation fully into being.' Descriptions of cabins and steerage accommodation by emigrants could arguably have the same effect of bringing the diarist's situation fully into being, though I myself have also stressed that there are other ways of bringing a situation into consciousness without necessarily writing about it, for example, by the adoption of gender roles in the creation of the domestic domain on board ship. Nonetheless, the relationship between this kind of entry and a perception of shipboard space is important, not least because it involves a materiality which may distinguish this form of self-reference from the previous type in which there was nothing to record. As Carter himself puts it, 'This entry describes the material conditions of its own production. It reminds us that even the journal of travelling depends on moments of stasis: successive entries may symbolize the progress of the road, but they do not imitate the horse's motion' (141).

Moments of self-reference when shipboard diaries record the

material conditions in which they are kept fall into three broad categories: moments when the diary is reporting concurrent events, moments when the place or time of diary writing is remarkable, and those moments when diary writing is physically difficult. To take, first, those moments when the diary is reporting action occurring at the moment of composition, the writing self is brought into consciousness because it exists simultaneously with the events recorded (the emphases here are mine):

> Rachel & Mr Hunt are playing chess *while I write* now & Tregenna is looking on at another game between Captain Ward & Mr Tench. (Amy Henning 18 Sept. 1854)

> My dear old George . . . is just as silly as ever, even worse, I believe. *Whilst I write* he is busy reading 'Song & Seal,' it seems to interest him very much. (Isabella Turner 28 Mar. 1868)

> Fine fresh breeze with the sun shining, ship going along under the royals. To add to the effect, *while I am writing* this my fellow passengers are groaning at snails pace through some horribly low church hymns. (Thomas Miller 1 May 1870)

> This morning *while I am writing* they are burying an emigrant. (Thomas Coy 14 Feb. 1885)

The act of writing slides into consciousness because the diary has moved from retrospective narration to simultaneous narration. Transgression of the writing environment and a forced awareness of the present action of others has made the narrator self-conscious of her or his own present action. Domestic space as a site for writing is no longer neutral but worthy of comment.

In the second category are those moments when the time or place of narration is itself significant (my emphases):

> You can realise there is something remarkable happening since I am up at this hour *writing in my diary*. (Moses Melchior 3 Dec. 1853)

> I *write this* during my night's watch at 2 a.m. 29 July. In England it is only 4 p.m. 28 July. (John Fenwick 28 July 1854)

In these cases, focus has shifted completely from the events of the voyage to the writing of the diary. The cause is a mismatch between the circumstances in which the diary is being written and those the diarist assumes the imagined audience at home would consider normal or expect. In other words, the diarist's previous public persona has once again become unstable for the audiences as a point of reference and the diarist has been forced into a self-consciousness to explain the gap: 'It is difficult to realise at this moment that *as I write* with the wild elements raging and holding a grand carnival with lightning flashing and adding grandeur to the scene that it is midday at home in the beautiful English August' (Richard Watt 4 Aug. 1864). At moments like this, there is again a loss of shared, public co-ordinates and the diarist is forced to confront a shift of identity, is forced to admit that she or he is no longer one of the social group being addressed. The typical has been displaced and the normalising discourse fails.

However, the most frequent type of self-referential entry is my third category, that entry written when conditions make writing difficult or in some cases near impossible (my emphases once more):

> this night was very hot, *having hard work to write* this journal, on account of the perspiration running off my face in all directions. (Samuel Rawson 7 May 1838)

> It is so cold today that *I can hardly write*, however, I will do my best. (Moses Melchior 4 Nov. 1853)

> The vessel is pitching to such an extent *I cannot write any more* tonight. (Anna Fowler 16 July 1866)

> Ship pitching awfully, as it is now so *can't write very well*. A lot of the people queer. (Joseph Sams 11 Oct. 1874)

This type of self-referential entry is similar to the previous type where the diary recorded extraordinary times and places of narration, except that in this case the material conditions in which the diary is being written threaten the very writing of the diary. The self-referential 'as I write' of the earlier examples slides dangerously towards an 'I cannot write'. This in turn threatens the diarist not simply as the protagonist of the voyage but the diarist as the narrator of the voyage. The narrator is brought into focus because of the threat to the self as narrator, and it is not that there is nothing to write about, it is rather that the narrators are struggling to write and consequently to exist as narrators. Indeed, in cases where the diarist is trying to write during a gale, not only is

[157]

diary writing threatened but so too is the organised, narratable social space upon which the diary depends:

> Now *as I write* the ship rolls frightfully, upsetting everything movable and creating destructive havoc all about. Twice has my lamp been pitched off the table and Mr Smith has just informed me that our berth is in the greatest disorder from the fact of my box having changed its position so that it now rests in the middle of the floor on the deck. (Richard Watt 27 June 1864)
>
> 11 p.m.: Ship labouring heavily. She keeps breaking off every now and then. Every time she does so, of course, her way through the water is almost stopped and she gets the seas broadside on. Oh, Moses, she does kick up old Dido at these times! *It is very hard to write* under these circumstances, I can tell you. (Henry Lightoller 8 Oct. 1878) (my emphases)

It is precisely at these moments when the journey threatens to engulf the 'floating home' from which the diary is written that the diary entry becomes a self-referential narrative occasion, with the first-person pronoun referring to the narrator rather than to the protagonist. During moments of self-reference when the predominant memoir mode is suspended, when the diary, that is, refers primarily to the material conditions of its production rather than to any public, social event, the otherwise effaced narrator is brought sharply into focus.

The words 'as I write' suggest a simultaneity of existence between the narrator figure and the diarist as protagonist or actor of the drama. The two reference points for the use of the first person 'I' seem to coincide: the one who is writing is also the one being tossed about in the ship. At moments of spatial crisis on board ship when the diarist is struggling to write, the split caused by the use of the first person may be somehow resolved. It could be said that the telescoping of the autobiographical past and the writing present has the effect of similarly telescoping the two selves into one subject position. This is the same point raised by Jonathan Rée in his discussion of the eighteenth-century philosopher Descartes: 'In a pure diary like the *Meditations* there is no scope for the autobiographer's wisdom-after-the-event: there is no distinction between the present "I" and the past "I", for the dominant time of a diarist's thoughts is discursive, not historic: it is the fugitive present of their own inscription' (19). I am unsure how far Rée himself accepts this, but it has clear implications for Descartes's *cogito ergo sum*, 'I think, therefore I am.' The 'pure diary' here is a commentary on thoughts and events as they occur, and the writing self is held to be present unto its thinking self.

However, it is a mistake to assume that the diary is a mode of narration that can somehow make whole that split between narrator and protagonist to be found in the first-person autobiography, can somehow make the diarist more self-present than the autobiographer. It is possible to efface the narrator, as is the overwhelming case in emigrant diaries: diarists become defensive when forced to consider the act of narration. It is also possible to foreground the narrator, as happens when the diarist's public persona comes under threat. But the diarist's role as narrator and her or his role as a protagonist remain linguistically separate, and as in the classical autobiography that was the subject of Renza's enquiry, the use of 'I' in the diary will always create a speaking persona that is an effect of the text rather than a guarantee of Descartes's *cogito ergo sum*. The diarist comes into being through writing a diary, and is dependent on language; the 'I' of Descartes's 'I am' exists only at the moment of narration.

The irony in all this is that the division inherent in the self-referential pronoun 'I', the division between the 'I' of the narrator and the 'I' of the protagonist, becomes most apparent in those entries which seem to collapse the time lapse between the writing and what is written about, when the diarist is attempting to write in the present time to attest to the authenticity of the present and her or his own sense of personal agency. The previously effaced narrator is brought into focus at moments of spatial crisis, when the normal regulated spaces of the ship are thrown into a 'confusion' comparable to that of embarkation, and this suggests not only that diarists avoided using a dramatised narrator because it made them self-conscious, but that the memoir mode of narration, which is aligned very strongly with Pratt's normalising discourse, was a way of managing shipboard life and controlling the transgressive potential of the journey. At moments of spatial crisis, this mode fails, and a gap opens between narrator and audience, between the narrator and the public persona: 'tonight *as I write* the elements are raging outside I fear we are going to have another terrible night – what between sickness, pain & want of sleep, I fear I shall arrive a poor sight in Melbourne – if Providence allows us to get there' (Elizabeth Ankatell 10 Mar. 1865). At moments like this, diarists attempt to write themselves back into the diary not as agents in control of their environment but as narrators in control of a diary. Yet the self-reference which follows produces in turn a self-consciousness which leaves the diarist spatially embarrassed and lacking the controlled, imperial viewpoint of the effaced narrator: 'I write under the greatest difficulty on account of the Ro-o-lling' (Richard Watt 29 June 1864). Here the representation of the present motion of the ship ('Ro-o-lling') attests to the self-conscious embarrassment of the diarist, an embarrassment caused precisely by the split between his sensory experience and its recording; the self represented is at once both the subject tossed around by the sea and the narrating subject aware of himself as reporter. Ironically, writing the words 'as I write' does not so much unite the divided self as reduce self to a repeatable mark on the page, the first-person pronoun 'I'; and any sense of agency that the diarist might grasp at moments of crisis by writing a diary evaporate as the narrator becomes purely specular, a ghostly figure not of the ship but of the diary.

Chapter 6

Writing the coastline

'At 6 o'clock the land of promise came into view'

This afternoon about 4 O. C. we heard that land could be seen – I went up and looking could see in the distance what looked like a long dark cloud on the horizon – it was the land! I called Naomi up and in half an hour we could see it quite distinctly. And still more plainly in the course of the Evening, as we continued to bear towards it. It was a pleasant sight indeed, after looking at nothing but sky and sea for so long, to see something different. Every one crowded to the ships side, and looked, and looked as tho' they would never be tired. (George Randall 3 Oct. 1868)

Emigrants did of course grow tired of the looking, particularly if they had three or four days of coastline to pass before they reached their destination, but 'after looking at sea and sky for so long' that first sight of land was a moment to be cherished. It would be hard to under-estimate the effect of being out of sight of land for three or four months, and it is clear from the accounts that the 'looking' was intensified by the prolonged absence of distant objects. On the steamer up to Brisbane, Joshua Hughes noted: 'Great excitement was produced at the sight of the first cow, one calling to another "There's a cow, look at it" ' (23 July 1863). Alfred Joyce recalls the approach to Port Phillip in 1843: 'After four months on the continuous expanse of the ocean, the entrance through the heads at Queenscliff seemed almost like running ashore, everything was so near and contracted. A babel of exclamations was kept up as every new object came into view' (29). The visual deprivation intensified the looking, distant objects appeared nearer than normal, the effect conspiring with the heart's desire to reach out for the land.

Differentiation was equally important. The failure of 'blue scenery' lay in its lack of differentiation, there were no fixed objects and no ways of constructing a sense of place. The land provided the emigrants with stimuli which suited their ways of seeing and allowed objects to be identified and placed in relation to others: 'As we continued to steer toward the land we could see it plainer every moment. We could see the lighthouse on the point, and the keepers house; soon after we could see the color of the rock and the grass and trees. It looked a very pretty, tho' solitary spot' (George Randall 4 Oct. 1868). George Randall here is organising his world and constructing a place, 'a very pretty spot', something he has not been able to do beyond the space of the ship since his last sighting of the English coastline four months earlier. When the landscape failed to allow differentiation, when no objects could be identified, the landscape shared the monotony previously ascribed to the seascape: 'On getting nearer land, I must confess that I was more disappointed by its monotonous outline, regularity of shape in the hills, and especially the unvarying colour of the vegetation, than I could well have expected to be' (Richard Watt 9 Aug. 1864). This description is more like a description of the sea than the land.

There was nothing particular about the Australian coastline that gave rise to the emotive response of seeing land; the heightened 'looking' was purely a response to visual deprivation. It operated, for example, in the reverse direction, as in Louise Buchan's description of the coast of Ireland after a two month voyage on the SS *Great Britain* from Melbourne to Liverpool: 'The green fields looked so fresh to our unaccustomed eyes, and altogether everything looked deliciously fresh' (27 May 1872). Henry Curr, a Roman Catholic priest, noted the same effect when sailing in sight of an island in the South Atlantic: 'You cannot imagine what an object of interest this barren island became to all of us, and presume only those whose eyes have rested on nothing else but sky and water for a whole month can fully appreciate the sight' (8 Aug. 1856). In this respect it mattered little what the coastline of Australia looked like; emigrants were happy merely to have sight of land:

at 4 Oclock Wilson's Promontory was visible to all   I got up earlier than usual to see the long wished for sight & was much gratified for although this part of the coast of New Holland is extremely bleak & barren it was delightful to see land of any kind after 3 months with nothing but the deep blue sea to feast our eyes on. (Margaret Menzies 29 Dec. 1838).

Or as 'N. C.' put it: 'As for Kangaroo Island, it seems a very uninviting place; nothing but cliffs, sand, and scrub; still, it is land, and our land of promise too' (21 Jan. 1849).

But if emigrants were pleased merely to have a sight of land after the long voyage out, they were nonetheless quick to make aesthetic judgements about the beauty of the land. Some writers, especially some of the men in the earlier years of the nineteenth century, looked on the coastline from the perspective of a surveyor or amateur geologist; they attempted to formulate what they saw in terms of an objective scientific discourse. It was in geological terms that J. Kidd Walpole described the islands and rocks of Bass Strait, through which most ships heading for Sydney and the east coast had to sail: 'Rodondo (round?) is granite, & *so steep that the deer cannot lodge on its sides* – it is 17 miles from Curtis – The Kents are granite – the Judgment has a reddish tint – & Curtis looks white like a big pumice stone. Thro the glass – the face & corners, edges, & angles of the rock looks every where rounded, as if soft – but I may not be right as to its formation' (25 Oct. 1837). But even where geology is being called upon to validate the description, the diarist would slip into an alternative aesthetic discourse:

Jervis Bay – *picturesque* – Bowen I[slan]^d – p[oin]^t Perpendicular 650 feet high. Stratum like coal in the face of the cliff – *fire* & smoke at the head of the Bay – Setting sun on Cape S. George – cliffs – ravines – heather – forests – lovely – the line of coast in sight at the time presented all tints, from the *faintest* hue to the richest purple – in short all imaginable, or possible varieties, of the spectral tint. (J. Kidd Walpole 29 Oct. 1837)

Here the coastline is doubly inscribed, in terms both of geology ('Stratum like coal') and aesthetics ('picturesque'), but it is the aesthetic which prevails as in almost all of the descriptions of the coastline contained in the diaries.

The aesthetics of the early diaries are fairly easy to specify because the diarists, as members of a cultural élite, were well-schooled in contemporary debates concerning landscape representation. Felton Mathew, later to become Surveyor-General of New Zealand, described Madeira on his voyage out, and his description demonstrates what many early settlers were looking for in a coastline:

The view of Madeira is exceedingly fine & romantic – the bold &

[163]

rugged outline of it's lofty 'cloud capp'd' peaks – some of them apparently clothed with wood – it's deep ravines and broken cliffs – it's precipitation & richly varied sides studded with here and there a neat little white cottage – the whole, of that rich azure or almost purple hue, which we see in some of Claud's pictures, but to which English scenery is a stranger – this combined with the brilliant & varied colours of the sea, every wave crowned with foam, forms certainly the most beautiful scene I ever beheld. (24 Aug. 1829)

What makes this landscape 'romantic' in the terminology of the time is the contrast between its 'lofty "cloud-capp'd" peaks' and its 'deep ravines', a contrast expected to evoke in the viewer a feeling not so much of beauty as of awe. The 'little' white cottages studding the sides of the mountains have to be 'little' to emphasise the insignificance of human habitations when compared with the scale of the natural land-scape. Overlaid on this, however, is the less awesome influence of the seventeenth-century Neapolitan painter Claude Lorrain whose works depicted a much more cultivated and less threatening landscape than that implied by the term Romantic; 'that rich azure or almost purple hue' ascribed by Felton Mathew to Claude is echoed in J. Kidd Walpole's observation above that 'the line of coast in sight at the time presented all tints, from the faintest hue to the richest purple' and evokes an idealised beauty appropriate to a land the emigrant had travelled halfway round the world to see. The emigrant with knowledge of early nineteenth-century aesthetics might hope to be overawed by the land-scape in the Romantic tradition, but that awe would need to be tem-pered by the idealised pastoral of a Claude composition if the land were to invite settlement. The best landscape would be, to use the terms as they were adopted from Edmund Burke in the eighteenth century, both sublime and beautiful.

Most of the free emigration to Australia up to about 1840 was centred on Hobart and Sydney; South Australia was founded in 1836 and Port Phillip (Melbourne) began to attract emigrants in number only in the 1840s. The coastline around Hobart in particular was highly accommo-dating in terms of landscape aesthetics, as in the diary of William Hamilton, one of a group of Scottish Presbyterian ministers, sailing up the River Derwent towards Hobart in the aptly named *North Briton*:

About two o'clock this morning land was descried several hours

earlier than was expected. Now we pass along the shores of Van
Diemen's land. We see several thick forests rising from the shore
to the summit of pretty lofty hills. The outline is very like that of
Argyleshire in Scotland i.e. nearly mountainous . . . the shores of
the firth were distinctly visible. They were interesting & highly
beautiful beyond any thing I could have anticipated. The hills
were much like those which environ the Gare loch & clothed with
wood from the water's edge to the summit unless where a
precipitous rock presented its naked face or a cottage had been set
down & some fields reclaimed & laid under crop. As we advanced
cottages and cultivated spots became more numerous & in fact
almost continuous along the western shore. . . . On the whole it
was the impression of every one that the land was exceedingly
beautiful and decidedly surpassed the most admired parts of
Scotland in point of scenery. (4 Sept. 1837)

This is a very positive assessment of the landscape, not least because the
features remind William of his native Scotland, a point also made by
another Scottish Presbyterian minister on the same vessel: 'The
scenery of the Derwent and indeed of the whole island is very Scottish in
its aspects, a circumstance that has attracted many Scotch men to it in
preference to New South Wales' (Mr Tait 4 Sept. 1837). Of course,
Scotland is no more naturally Romantic than Van Diemen's Land, and
Scottish landscape itself could be read in terms of a Romantic aesthetic
because of its perceived similarity to the primary site of Romantic
landscape, the Alps. The Romantic was largely a way of seeing, and if we
compare William Hamilton's description of Van Diemen's Land as
Caledonia with Felton Mathew's Madeira, both praise the 'outline' of the
coast, its 'lofty' peaks and the woods that 'clothe' the hillsides, and both
contrast the 'precipitous' rocks with the 'cottages' of the inhabitants.
In all these aspects the vocabulary is identical and points to a highly
conventionalised way of seeing the land. Moreover, the Romantic aesthetic in William Hamilton's description is again tempered by an earlier
pastoral, and the rugged mountain scenery is tamed by settlement:
'some fields reclaimed & laid under crop'. As Thomas Mort said of the
Derwent earlier in the same year as William Hamilton: 'it had all the
beauty of the Clyde scenery with the grandeur of the Alpine inter-
mingled' (13 Jan. 1837). It was a country to be both desired and feared at
the same time.

Because of its readiness to be accommodated within the aesthetics of landscape, there are rarely any negative assessments of the coastline on the voyage up the Derwent to Hobart. South Australia, however, fares less well primarily because of the failure of Kangaroo Island, an island roughly one hundred miles long which ships had to coast along in order to reach Adelaide: 'It is very barren & rocky in some places, and in others fertile, but for the most part it seemed scrubby: we could not see any thing like a large tree upon it. I believe there are a few *squatters* on it' (S. E. Roberts 9 Nov. 1848). Kangaroo Island could provide a moment of jubilation: 'At daylight this morning we were still beating to windward, but, oh welcome sight! Kangaroo Island only a few miles ahead' (N. C. 21 Jan. 1849). But as Kangaroo Island became more distinct, the jubilation subsided: 'As for Kangaroo Island, it seems a very uninviting place; nothing but cliffs, sand, and scrub' (N. C. 21 Jan. 1849).

The problem with Kangaroo Island was that it was neither the Alps nor a Claudean pastoral. Or more exactly, Kangaroo Island could not be read in terms of a landscape aesthetics based on regions of Europe like the Alps, and it failed on all the points of concurrence between William Hamilton's Derwent and Felton Mathew's Madeira. Its outline was unvarying, being mainly low cliffs, it had no 'lofty' peaks which might stand up above the cliffs, and it had no woods, only what was almost universally described as 'scrub'. It had no towering and awe-inspiring rock faces, and it had no signs of habitation, none of those little cottages nestling against a mountainous backdrop. In short it was, as 'N.C.' put it above, 'uninviting'. Or as Stephen Brennand noted: 'one young fellow wished he had gone to the bottom instead of coming to such a dreary looking shop' (12 Nov. 1883).

*

Such assessments of the coastline, whether negative or positive, demonstrate that the European cultural background of the emigrants gave them an identifiable set of categories by which to evaluate the landscape. Emigrants were looking for a coastline with a clear outline, a line of high hills or mountains, thick woods or forests, evidence of cultivation, and evidence of habitation. Such categories may be found embedded in the competing landscape aesthetics of the early-nineteenth century, yet it is clear that they persist even when the terminology of the Romantic, the picturesque, and the sublime fall from use as the century progresses. The generations which make up the mass migration to Australia from the late 1840s on were less schooled in the aesthetics of landscape than the more formally educated early free-emigrants, though a number of later emigrants from the middle classes were amateur artists and continued the practice of illustrating their diaries. The ability to make a passable sketch still counted as a necessary accomplishment attendant on membership of a cultural élite, and one of the pleasures of looking through emigrants' diaries is finding some of them illustrated; since there was no snapshot photography at this time, these sketches provide a rarely published pictorial account of the voyage out.

More striking, though, is the persistence of the categories by which the coastline is evaluated in the diaries of those who probably had no upbringing in landscape appreciation. William Reay, a butcher and a man who had certainly never travelled to the Alps, used the Alpine landscape like the well-educated Thomas Mort forty years earlier as a point of reference when addressing those left at home: 'we expect to sight Cape Howe to night late on   Sydney is 240 miles from this cape   the coast that we saw yesterday is the roughest ever I saw   if the Alps is any rougher than them they over rough for anything' (3 Dec. 1877). What is missing from working-class accounts is the literary rhetoric, compare William Reay with Louisa Clifton:

> The moment any eyes first rested on that 'dim discovered scene' was one the remembrance of which the longest life can never obliterate; none who have not known what it is to sigh, to long with sickening longing for land after a voyage of more than 3 months can fully understand with what ecstacy of feeling the first view and scent of land greets the weary senses. (17 Mar. 1841)

Working-class emigrants, though they continued to evaluate the landscape using the same categories as middle-class emigrants, had probably learned their aesthetics more from visual than literary sources: 'this morning when looking at the land I thought of a picture I saw   it represented a man and his wife looking wistfully over the sea' (Mary Maclean 15 Mar. 1865). The adoption by the working classes of an aesthetics which had already been passed down from the landed classes to the middle classes was probably largely due to those aesthetics permeating popular art forms. Inexpensive engravings like those which popularised the Scotland of Sir Edwin Landseer could now be produced, and with the development of illustrated newspapers from the 1840s forward, working-class households had access to landscape scenes which could be cut out and pinned on a wall. Such scenes may then have been reinforced by those buildings and landscape gardens which emigrants knew from personal experience: 'in many prospects it resembles the Woburn Abbey estate though superior in grandiour' (William Nichols 9 June 1849).

Yet I also want to suggest that the persistence of the aesthetic conventions of landscape evaluation was supported by the specific historical circumstances of nineteenth-century Australian migration, both physically and ideologically. Emigrants used aesthetic conventions flexibly and in a way which suited their needs at a particular moment in time. Landscape descriptions were not dictated solely by the educational background of the emigrants or by the form through which landscape conventions were mediated. The emigrant way of looking at the coastline was functional, and it sprang from being an emigrant.

The demand that the outline of the coast should be 'bold' echoes through the diaries. It occurs, of course, in Felton Mathew's description of Madeira – 'the bold & rugged outline of it's lofty "cloud capp'd" peaks' – and is part of the aesthetics of the picturesque which demanded variety of outline if the scene were to evoke pleasure in the viewer. This is clear from Anna Fowler's description of Cape Howe, a point of land important for navigation and often an emigrant's first sight of Australia:

I am delighted with the first distinct view of my new adopted country. The 20 or 30 miles of coast spread out before us forms a really beautiful panoramic view. In the foreground is the rather low and sandy projection of C. Howe which shines like gold in the sun. From the verge of the water rises the lofty and elegant lighthouse. Immediately behind the sand hills rise steep rugged hills, almost mountains, clothed with dark verdure, probably forests of gum trees to the very summits. Behind these again and stretching away far on either hand I can count five or six ranges of hills, some covered with trees, some conical, some dome shaped. The most distant are quite blue and evidently lofty mountains, 20 or 30 miles in the interior. The undulations of these hills form a most beautiful outline. There is every variety of shape, some of them remind me of the hills seen from Hatton House. (17 Sept. 1866)

This is a highly-organised description and made by someone clearly competent in landscape conventions; its painterly aspirations make it easy to visualise. The 'panoramic view' begins with the foreground, 'the low sandy projection' of Cape Howe shining 'like gold', in order to draw the eye to focus on 'the lofty and elegant lighthouse' before allowing the eye to move back to the 'rugged hills' immediately behind the Cape and then further away across the 'five or six ranges of hills' until it makes out the far distant 'lofty mountains'. There is nothing random in the organisation of this description.

Yet any specific description of the coastline is only partly explained by considering the dominant landscape conventions, and Paul Carter makes the point that mountains may be read in different ways depending on the specific circumstances of the observer, on whether the viewer is a traveller or a settler: 'It is only the settler, looking reflectively back towards his cottage, and beyond it to the nestling horizon, who finds the backdrop of hills attractive: to the traveller they are merely an obstacle' (*Botany Bay* 246). In the case of the emigrant at sea, the hills do provide a protective backdrop to the picturesque 'cottage':

> As we came further into the bay the country improved very much
> in appearance on both sides and near the Heads it was really
> beautiful. High hills covered with woods and houses scattered
> about. We saw one very pretty English looking house near the
> shore, in amongst the trees, with a nice garden looking quite like
> a home. (Annie Henning 16 Oct. 1853)

This is the image of the 'home' on land that the migrant is seeking, a home substituted in Anna Fowler's description above by the 'lofty and elegant' lighthouse standing on the golden projection. No protective image of home is possible on 'low' country, and because it offers no image of settlement, a flat coastline seems 'uninviting': 'The land sighted proved to be a part of the mainland of Australia; its appearance was not very inviting, as with the exception of two or three detached hills it was very low' (Samuel Pillow 24 Apr. 1853). But hills and mountains are less of an obstacle for the voyager than for the land traveller, and in the same way as the eyes are led further away from the coast, from one range to another as in Anna Fowler's description, so they dramatise the movement towards a destination, the migrant's goal. The contrast between the mountains and the cottage in the ideal coastal landscape offer comforting, if conflicting, images of both movement and settlement to an emigrant viewing the coastline from on

[169]

board her or his 'floating home'. How the landscape is seen depends on the specific position of the observer.

Signs of habitation are particularly important in offsetting the potentially awesome effect of a bold and rugged outline. Too much in the way of ravines and precipices, while they may appear sublime, produces a landscape onto which it is difficult to project a home:

> The scenery all along the coast from Melbourne to Sydney is very fine, but much more melancholy than English scenery in spite of the cleaner atmosphere & more brilliant sun. All the foliage is of the same grey green, peculiarly monotonous when spread over such immense tracts of land. Sometimes we found ourselves sailing under richly wooded capes while the land behind seemed to pile itself up into awful tiers of dark green forest. – Then some solitary rocks broke the dark monotony & rose precipitously from the sea, sometimes crowned with a small lighthouse and always covered with sea birds & white with flying foam. (Margaret Walpole 8 Aug. 1883)

Many of the elements in Anna Fowler's positive description of the land I quoted earlier are present here in Margaret Walpole's negative assessment: sunshine, the cape, the lighthouse, and the tiers of tree-covered hills are present in both, but while Anna Fowler praises the 'rugged hills, almost mountains, clothed with dark verdure, probably forests of gum trees to the very summits,' Margaret Walpole's image of the land piling 'itself up into awful tiers of dark green forest' causes a shudder.

What is especially odd is that, in general, the sight of forestry usually produced admiration in the viewer. Forestry was, of course, the raw material of settlement, with wood being needed for housing, for heating, for fencing, and for waggons; wood could be and was exported from the earliest days of settlement, and to this day what is left of the rainforests bear the scars of the destruction of the red cedar. Coal it is true was vital if any steam dependent industry was to be established, and that may unconsciously have been behind J. Kidd Walpole's observation of 'Stratum like coal in the face of the cliff' which I quoted earlier. But coal would be hidden, certainly unobservable from the sea, and this left timber as the index of Australia's natural resources. No matter that most of this wood itself turned out to behave differently from deciduous British trees, sometimes proving almost impossible to cut with an axe, emigrants were quick to praise what seemed like an over-abundance:

My anticipation of the Coast Scenery I find exactly reversed – I had
pictured to myself a low sandy beach, almost a flat for as far as the
eye could reach & devoid of Timber – On the contrary it is a fine
bold coast with a succession of hill & dale & covered (as far as we
could see by means of the Telescope) with timber. (Oswald
Bloxsome 1 Aug. 1838)

This is the squatter's landscape and behind all the eulogies to the woods
and the forests, behind all the claims for sublimity and beauty, lies that
word 'timber'.

So it was not the timber of her 'richly wooded capes' that produced
Margaret Walpole's antipathy to the coastline; the difference between
Margaret Walpole's description and that of Anna Fowler is that where
Anna Fowler was able to transform the lighthouse into an icon of home,
Margaret Walpole could do no more than see the rocks with the
occasional lighthouse perched on top as an image of her isolation at sea;
Anna Fowler's 'lofty and elegant lighthouse' stands on a 'low and sandy
projection' while Margaret Walpole's 'small' lighthouse perches on a
precipitous 'solitary' rock. If the 'monotonous' grey green of the
eucalypts in Margaret's description mimicked the sea, the size and scale
of the lighthouse mimicked the isolated ship. It was a way of looking
that was expressed in almost exactly the same terms by Rosamond
D'Ouseley:

At 10 to 7 o'clock a sailor of the top gallant mast sung out 'Land on
the port bow' but we could not see more than a faint streak on the
horizon for a long time. Then as we came nearer we saw a wild
hilly country covered with trees & scrub, no human habitation
near except at the extreme point a solitary light-house; so our first
view of land was not at all exhilarating. (13 Oct. 1869)

It was all too much like the undifferentiated experience of being at sea,
and if emigrants could praise a Romantic scene, they had little desire to
be cast away on an isolated outcrop. They expected much more of
Australia than that.

If human habitation could mitigate a potential antipathy towards a
monotonous landscape, so too could its associated feature, cultivation.
The sight of timber might promise settlement, but there was nothing
quite like a cleared area of the coast to arouse enthusiasm: 'The country
on either side is but partially cleared, a large portion of it being thickly

wooded to the water's edge. The farm and cultivated land in some parts you may imagine was not slight refreshment to us' (William Johnstone 30 Mar. 1842). Cultivation seemed to show the land was fertile, and if the problem with Kangaroo Island was that it was too flat, it was also, fatally, considered infertile: 'We had a glimpse of the Island last night but this morning we have been very near; it looks a large, rocky, barren place 100 miles in length, with good harbour, and as it stands very high it would be a healthy place to live if the land were fertile. There are here and there spots of fertile ground, but the most part is barren' (Sophia Taylor 29 Nov. 1851). Emigrants did not like 'barren' landscapes, and one of the ambiguities of the image of the rock (and there were many rocks along the coast) was that it could be the noble Romantic precipice, but it could also be an index of infertility: 'it looks a large, rocky, barren place.' Even Sydney Harbour, though nearly always praised for its great natural beauty, could fall foul of this double reading. In one way of looking, the rocks were clearly what gave the harbour its beauty:

> as we entered the Bay it was a beautiful prospect to view the lofty rocks that surrounded us many of them being quite perpendicular and of an emmence hight in many places   they appear as though they were built by human hands   many of the rocks are falling down and large stones are laying on the beach the size of a Waggon   it causes a noble appearance something similar to the ruins of an ancient Castle   the tops of the rocks are coverd with evergreens and in many places we observe a beautiful Cottage built of white stone   in many prospects it resembles the Woburn Abbey estate though superior in grandiour. (William Nichols 9 June 1849)

William Nichols, recorded in the passenger lists as a labourer, was almost as fond of the word 'lofty' as he evidently was of Gothicism, and some of the 'loftiness' of the mountains he had observed earlier on the voyage along the coast has found its way to the rocks of Sydney Harbour: 'on A lofty rock stands Govement house with the Union Jack flying on top of it' (10 June 1849). On the other hand, because of an ambivalence in what rocks represented, the rocks in the harbour could also indicate barrenness and result in a highly disparaging description: 'Now for a small account of Sidney whose first appearance is neither tempting nor inviting   the Government domain looks very well but when you look a little to the right at the town it is like a lump of house

[172]

built upon and among barren rocks and all around us appears to be nothing but rocks and stunted trees' (Thomas Mitchell 16 Mar. 1834). Stunted trees are not what are needed. Some of this negative assessment may be due to the diarist being a surgeon who was intending to return to Britain, something may also be due to the time gap between the two accounts and developments around the harbour. But the association of rocks and barrenness was made by many others and it remained a potential throughout the period in which such diaries were kept.

George Seddon has tried to account for differences in the way the landscape of Australia was assessed by making a division between picturesque and utilitarian ways of looking; positive assessments belonged to the picturesque, negative ones to the utilitarian (10–11). This is useful in terms of the language of the early-nineteenth century, but the picturesque way of looking is nonetheless still linked, if in a slightly different sense, to questions of land use. There may be some sense in talking about the difference between a surveyor's discourse and that of the landscape painter, but that is not the same as arguing that how we construct our landscapes in any cultural form can be divorced from material considerations. It would be the same as arguing, as it is tempting to do, that the evaluations of the land in terms of its beauty are most likely to be made by women, and evaluations in terms of productive capabilities are most likely to be made by men. Such a division not only ignores the evidence, it disregards the factors leading to the creation of aesthetic conventions.

Denis Cosgrove has argued that the European ability to praise land that did not sustain a settled community was linked to the commodification of the land; with the development of industrial capitalism in Britain, land became capital and its value became divorced from its use-value (*Social Formation* 231). Cosgrove gives as example the Scottish Highlands where land clearance increased the exchange value (rather than the productive potential) of the moors and glens for the large landowners (232). Another obvious example would be the high exchange value of unproductive English parkland, and many of the emigrants read the coastal scenery in terms of parks surrounding large country houses: 'At 4 a.m. I and most of the passengers got up to watch our progress in proximity to several uninhabited rocky islands; on one island we passed is a light house the top of which is elevated on a rock a thousand feet above the level of the sea; and amongst some wild and park-like scenery are two or three dwelling houses' (unnamed passenger on board the *Kate* 23 Oct. 1853). These islands of Bass Strait can be praised in aesthetic terms not because they are worthless but because such land has been invested with a cultural, aesthetic value linked to the exchange value of analogous land in Britain.

Similarly, land under cultivation also had an aesthetics of its own. Parkland, of course, could be used for grazing, but an aesthetics of farmland corresponded with the development of intensive agricultural production, the enclosure of commonland and open field arable land (Barrell 61). In the later eighteenth century this was largely supplanted by the picturesque vogue and its preference for uncultivated land, but during the Napoleonic Wars in the early nineteeth century, in response to the need for a sense of national unity, there was a revival of landscape painting depicting a harmonious and productive English countryside populated by landowners and their well-fed labourers (Cosgrove 66). This did not guarantee, of course, that land in Australia that looked like English grazing or arable land would be productive; the aesthetics might be transportable but not the material conditions to which it was linked. Yet this did not prevent a link being assumed between aesthetic beauty and productive potential. Simon Ryan has noted this link in explorers' journals: 'In the explorers' journals there is a strong association of the picturesque and the beautiful with the land's "richness" or use-value' (287). And Brian Birch has pointed out something similar with regard to nineteenth-century British settlement in middle western America:

> What is interesting is that these evaluations [of the prairie edges] were sometimes based less on the character of the vegetation and soil cover and more on the visual beauty of the landscape, perhaps because to English eyes a landscape of aesthetic quality would obviously be free of swamps, infertility, and other drawbacks to prosperous settlement. (177)

The aesthetic, then, is not a way of looking divorced from material considerations, and as may be remembered, the aesthetic was one among many of Mary Louise Pratt's 'interlocking informational orders' through which white explorers exerted mastery over the lands of Africa. When emigrants described the coastline, be they male or female, be they talking in terms of wild Romantic scenery or the beauty of cultivated land, they were also taking possession. Nineteenth-century British emigrants to Australia were in search of a landscape that was aesthetically pleasing, a landscape that would offer a contrast to the monotonous seascapes of the previous months; this was a landscape that would be bold, varied, and Romantic. But they were also looking for a land that would offer them a home, a land to settle, a land not so much sublime as beautiful. Forestry offered both the raw material of settlement and an apparent confirmation that the land would be fertile, while fields and, above all, evidence of European habitation could be read as a welcoming feature of the landscape itself. Ultimately, emigrants were looking for a landscape that would offer them what they desired.

*

The descriptions of the coastline found in emigrants' diaries clearly need to be read in terms of both contemporary landscape aesthetics and the nuances which result from the coastline being the diarist's first sight of land for three or more months. But an additional factor in danger of being forgotten here is the physical relationship between the observer and the observed. If land was seen in a particular way because of the long period emigrants had spent out of sight of land, how the land was assessed also owed much to the physical viewpoint of the emigrant. To view a coastline from on board a ship is radically different from viewing it from on land, and the stretch of water dividing the observer from the observed allowed emigrants to view the land pictorially as an aesthetic object. On land we need to climb a hill or similar vantage point if we are to see a landscape, but at sea the physical and aesthetic distancing needs no contriving; it is there in the distance from the ship to the shore. The sea offers no features in the immediate foreground of vision to distract the eye from the land, and it is this detachment from the land which enables the emigrant to view the coast as a picture. As Abijou Good noted of Queenstown (Cobh) in Ireland which he visited en route from London to Rockhampton: 'alltho the town looked beautifull from the vessells deck, when i was on shore & could take a nearer veiw they appeared wretched dwellings but they were all whitewashed or painted & this was the cause of the fine effect from a distance' (20 Mar. 1863). This effect of distance is the same as that noted by John Barrell with regard to the elevated viewpoint in classical landscape painting: 'it creates a space between the landscape and the observer, similar in effect to the space between a picture and whoever is looking at it' (Barrell 21). Descriptions of the land are dependent on the emigrant viewing the coast from the water.

[175]

Emigrants quite often use the term 'panorama' to express the effect of seeing the coast from on board ship: 'we again rounded Cape F. Henry and anchor'd in the interior of Adventure Bay near and in a straight line to the North of Penguin island   we have here a most beautiful Panoramic view' (Henry Widdowson 3 May 1826). The word 'panorama' was coined in the late eighteenth century by an unnamed friend of Robert Barker for Barker's specially designed and patented circular exhibition room in London (Altick 132). This exhibition room housed a 360° painting which the observer viewed from a platform in the centre. The scene, usually topical or topographical (i.e. a battle or a city), completely encircled the observer and gained its effect by a kind of *trompel'oeil*; by masking the top and the bottom of the painting, the exhibition space tried to create the illusion of actuality (Altick 188). Unfortunately, judging from the comments of a New Zealand settler who viewed S. C. Brees's 'Panorama of New Zealand' in London in 1849, the illusion of reality was not always achieved:

> All inanimate objects are admirably handled; but almost every living creature appears as magnified to nearly twice its natural proportions . . . Horses stand near stables into which they could never get; and a short milkmaid would almost need steps to reach the cows . . . One scene exhibits the arrival of Governor Grey: here is seen a gigantic sailor who would sink any small craft . . . I took some ladies of a family who were hesitating between New Zealand and the United States. They were naturally alarmed at the ferocity of aspect and Brobdignagian proportions of the natives – so different to reality: they say it is a sweet country; but certainly not a *safe* one – at least for the 'Unprotected Female'. (*Canterbury Papers* 83–4)

Robert Barker's main panorama building was opened in Leicester Square in 1794, and though other panorama buildings followed, most notably the ill-fated Colosseum in the late 1820s, it was one of the longest survivors and it continued to show its canvases until 1863 (Altick 140ff).

It is in this precise sense that the term 'panorama' is employed by Edward Snell of eight sketches he made in his diary of Plymouth Sound at the beginning of his voyage to Adelaide: 'The foregoing sketches are a complete panorama of the Sound' (15 Aug. 1849). The sketches if joined together would form a 360° panorama. Given that such pictures situate both the painter and observer at a very precise and unobstructed viewpoint (in Edward Snell's case, the position was the ship's anchorage in Plymouth Harbour), this is a good example of the subjection of the land to the all-seeing gaze of the post-Enlightenment subject to which Mary Louise Pratt alludes in her work on explorers. Jeremy Bentham's Panopticon, a circular prison in which prisoners were kept under constant surveillance by the warders in the centre, dates from the same period as Robert Barker's device, though with the more overt subjugating intentions analysed by Michel Foucault in *Discipline and Punish* (1975).

In its most common form in the diaries, the term 'panorama' merely indicates that the diarist enjoyed a wide view of the coastline: 'The 20 or 30 miles of coast spread out before us forms a really beautiful panoramic view' (Anna Fowler 17 Sept. 1866). Wide views like these were popularised from the 1840s to the end of the century by the illustrated newspapers, most notably by the *Illustrated London News* and the *Graphic* which both issued panorama giveaways (Hyde *Gilded Scenes* 33–5), and as well as showing a debt to 360° panoramas, wide views also called on a long tradition of engraved 'long views' or 'prospects' dating back to the Renaissance (Hyde *Gilded Scenes* 11); interestingly, Richard Altick argues that 'the topographical panoramas as a group were a bourgeois public's substitute for the Grand Tour, that seventeenth- and eighteenth-century *rite de passage* of upper-class society' (180).

In their descriptions of the coastline, many diarists were working within very precise if not altogether consistent pictorial conventions, but in most cases the specific source of the conventions is impossible to pinpoint. Occasionally, however, the diarist uses a particular reference point. Felton Matthew's allusion to the paintings of Claude Lorrain is a case in point, as is William Nichols's reference to Woburn Abbey in his evocation of a naturally Gothicised Sydney Harbour. One of the most specific admissions of this sort comes from the diary of Henry Whittingham, and it is a useful reminder that it may not be high art forms that are the most direct influence on how the coastline is seen. Two weeks out of London, Henry Whittingham's ship passes Palma in the Canary Isles:

Now abreast of Palma (lying S.E.): we still sailing S.W., at a distance of, perhaps, 8 or 10 miles. Splendid view. Hitherto, my ideas of such views have been formed, principally, by reading;

[177]

seeing panoramas: ect[a]. I was, therefore, surprized and pleased to find that they had been formed with much accuracy. I wanted only the actual observation to complete them. Here is full material. Witnessing the Panorama of the Nile: the effective painting in the Surrey Gardens: reading the shortlived 'Literary Herald': & a few other similar stimulants first inspired within me a strong love for oriental Scenes. Looking through a small Telescope, I am able to see several dwellings – dots of white – and also to learn that scenery of the Country is wild & romantic. Towards evening it plays the dissolving view to perfection, & leaves me pondering upon the wonderful effect that light, shade, color, & all that makes a fine view, has upon the mind. (10 Feb. 1853)

There is a self-conscious tone in this passage, indeed, in Henry Whittingham's whole diary, that makes me wary of taking it at face value, but I quote it to show the more popular kinds of pictorial material that might have influenced a large number of emigrants. Reading, of course, played its part, and Henry Whittingham specifically mentions the *Literary Herald*, an illustrated journal which ran for only eight issues in 1846. In the absence of photography, illustrated newpapers like the *Illustrated London News* carried engravings not just of contemporary events but of sentimental or picturesque scenes that could be cut out and either framed or pasted up. These could inform the taste of those who were less inclined or less able to read. Henry Whittingham also mentions the Surrey Gardens, opened in London in 1831, which were pleasure gardens frequented by the suburban middle classes in the summer; here, giant three-dimensional panoramas made out of canvas and wood, like the 'Panorama of the Nile' seen by Henry Whittingham, provided a backdrop to spectacular nightly firework displays in front of a three-acre lake (Altick 322–31). Judging from the diary of Daniel Higson, other pleasure gardens such as the Belle Vue Zoological Gardens in Manchester had a similar effect on the way in which emigrants saw the coastline of Australia: 'Land on the port-bow at 6.30 but we could not see it from our window till 8 oclock. Now we are close to it, it seems to rise from the sea like one of the scenes at Belle Vue, we can see the lighthouse on Cape Otway. It is a wild looking coast with breakers all along the shore' (Daniel Higson 13 Oct. 1869); the reference here is again to a giant three-dimensional open-air panorama situated behind a lake. Dissolving views, a third source mentioned by

Henry Whittingham, provided a different form of popular pictorial display; they were developed during the 1830s out of the older magic lantern displays, the invention of the limelight allowing one projected image to be 'dissolved' into another (Altick 219–20). Such images were often used to illustrate an educational lecture given, for example, at a Mechanics Institute or by a temperance lecturer, though they were also employed as entertainments in their own right, and unlike the Leicester Square Panorama or the Surrey Gardens, they could be enjoyed by a popular non-metropolitan audience. In such ways, or so he says, Henry Whittingham developed his 'strong love for oriental scenes'.

But in all the forms so far discussed, the relationship between the viewer and the view was relatively fixed. It is true that in Robert Barker's 360° panoramas the spectator might turn round in the centre to see different aspects of the scene, and even in the wide-angle panoramas of the pleasure gardens the spectator could look from one part of the scene to another, as in a modern widescreen cinema. But unlike, say, a cinematic tracking shot in which the camera follows, say, an actor or a car, in these panoramas there was no sense of the observer being on the move. Yet if one implication of the emigrant arriving by ship is that the coastline was viewed as a pictorial scene, a second is that some descriptions are dynamic rather than static, with various features of the shoreline being described sequentially. Here there is again the distancing necessary for the pictorial effect, but there is also an additional narrative effect as the ship tacks parallel to the shore.

Edward Snell's sketch of Plymouth Harbour, while it draws on Robert Barker's circular panorama, had another forbear and it is also indebted to the sketches made by navigators and surveyors as they sailed along unfamiliar coastlines. Once joined together, such sketches provided a continuous outline of the coast stretching for a number of metres, and even if those found in the diaries are not so ambitious, this type of sketch nonetheless remained a convention for representing the coastline, as in the diaries of J. Kidd Walpole (1837) or Anna Fowler (1866). In this sense they are more akin to the *moving* panorama, a device dating from the early nineteenth century which reached the high point of its popularity in the late 1840s and early 1850s (Altick 198ff). The moving panorama had a portable version which wound in and out of a wooden drum (Hyde *Gilded Scenes* 33), but in its theatrical form it consisted of a painted canvas sometimes several hundred metres long and perhaps three or four metres high which passed across a stage from one roller to another for the gratification of a paying audience. In some cases, the moving panorama might depict several different scenes one after the other, as in John Skinner Prout's illustration of 'the Voyage to Australia and a Visit to the Gold Fields' in 1852 ('exhibited daily at 309 Regent Street') which contained a dozen or so illustrations of the voyage out. In other cases, one continuous scene was painted onto the canvas to give an impression, as in the cinematic tracking shot, that the audience was on a journey, waterfronts and river views being particularly popular subjects; indeed, as well as the panorama of the Nile in the Surrey Gardens, Henry Whittingham could also have enjoyed a moving panorama of the Nile which opened in the Egyptian Hall in London in July 1849 (Altick 206). Some such panorama appears to have been in the mind of Abijou Good, whom I mentioned earlier, when his ship put into Queenstown (Cobh) in Ireland en route from London to Rockhampton: 'a more beautifull sight i do not recollect to have seen, the white houses were scattered on the green hills & as they passed before us like a panorama it was a splendid scene' (10 Mar. 1863). The reference here seems to be to a moving panorama of a waterfront painted in the picturesque mode.

Moving panoramas tried to recreate the sense of narrative direction which could be given to a coastline or river bank by the physical movement of the observer along it. In the case of cities like Brisbane or Melbourne, the emigrant was usually transferred to a river steamer for the final part of the voyage and this resulted in a narrative with a strong sense of progression, as here in Susan Meade's description of her voyage up the river Yarra Yarra in 1842:

> About 10 o'clock got on board the Governor Arthur steamer to proceed on our way to Melbourne 9 miles up the Yarra Yarra. – This is the most beautiful river I have ever seen, even the ever-winding graceful Wye with all its natural attractions sinks into insignificance compared with it. – As the bay disappeared I became transfixed with admiration at the transcendent beauty of this highly favored land. – No language can convey a correct idea of its loveliness. – The untrimmed trees present to the eye three distinct generations. – The tender plant just springing from the ground – The full grown budding and blossoming, and the forest tree of years almost branchless & leafless bearing its whitened head far above the whole. (Susan Meade 9 Aug. 1842)

The observer moves from the bay to an 'ever-winding' river like the Wye which, presumably, will reveal new sights, its 'natural attractions', at every turn; indeed, it was the progressive views provided by river trips which, by the end of the eighteenth century, had made a trip down the Wye a popular attraction for tourists in search of the picturesque: 'Unlike travel in a jolting carriage, the smooth passage of the boat relaxed the tourist and encouraged concentration on the very steady unfolding of the views' (Andrews 89). Yet what gives this description its narrative direction are 'the untrimmed trees', and though they 'present to the eye' three generations at once, it is difficult to avoid seeing these generations as coming progressively into sight. By combining the linearity of language and the movement of the observer, the description of the trees is itself directional and the movement of the steamer towards Melbourne is aligned with a 'natural' progression. This is an evolutionary narrative, and one which gives the voyage out as a whole a natural direction and a sense of destiny being fulfilled.

With the coming of the gold rush in the early 1850s, it was not long before Susan Meade's Yarra became less able to participate in the emigrant's understandable desire to find an earthly paradise in Australia: 'at the expiration of nearly 4 hours we came to the end of our meanderings on that narrow shallow dirty meandering "Yarra" and with what bounds did I leap across the steamers then lying between us and the land' (Robert Saddington 16 Oct. 1853). This, however, did not prevent Annie Henning on the same voyage as Robert Saddington from finding a positive narrative earlier in the day: 'As we came further into the bay the country improved very much in appearance on both sides and near the Heads it was really beautiful' (16 Oct. 1853).

In deep-water ports like Hobart or Sydney, the emigrant ship could sail right up to the city, and one of the most instructive accounts of the way in which the coastline might participate in its own narrative reading is Elizabeth Fenton's on a voyage up the Derwent to Hobart:

> As we sail up this beautiful Derwent, every mile most distinctly marks the progress of civilisation. We *now* are in sight of Hobarton, a small and irregularly built town, viewing it at this distance, but with an indefinable 'English air'. Mount Wellington, yonder table mountain, rising abruptly over the town, is topped with snow . . .
>
> As we advance, pretty cottage residences are visible in what appeared impervious jungle. I wonder if these are 'farm houses'.

There are streaks of lovely yellow sand, fringing each diminutive
bay or inlet of the waters among the hills; there are wide fields
freshly ploughed, and ploughmen and sowers all busy at their
labour with English smock-frocks. (11 Aug. 1829)

The key term in this description is, for me, 'the progress of civilisation'.
In the first instance, 'civilisation' refers to the cultivation of the land by
the settlers and suggests that what was previously 'impervious jungle'
(Elizabeth Fenton has just arrived from India) is now being ploughed
and sown. As I argued above, emigrants looked for signs of successful
colonisation. Of course, there is also the hidden implication that
civilisation equates to a specifically English social order, the 'English
air', and the description might be less enthusiastic were the labourers
French settlers or African slaves. Needless to say, evidence of Aboriginal
settlement would not have been written in the same terms.

But there is a paradox in this description arising from a specific
ambiguity in the word 'progress'. Settlement is in one sense being seen
as a progression in three stages from jungle to farm to town, a temporal
progression. But the spatial progress of settlement at that time would
be occurring outwards from Hobart in precisely the opposite direction
to the progress of the ship upriver to the town; new settlers would reach
the town and then go beyond the current farms to cultivate new
farmland further away. Rather than describing the centrifugal 'progress
of civilisation' as it might be occurring from town to farm to jungle,
Fenton's progress upriver turns the landscape into something akin to a
moving panorama in which each scene depicts a stage in the temporal
'progress of civilisation' – forest to cottage to town. This narrative
sequence is particularly tenacious and versatile, emerging as late as
1904 as part of a nationalist mythology in Frederick McCubbins's
triptych *The Pioneer*. With the conflation of the temporal and the
spatial, the observer becomes static and the landscape the actor
naturally civilising itself.

When emigrants wrote the coastline as a narrative, they were looking
to write a narrative which mirrored their own desires. The first
narrative model they used was that of a progressively more beautiful
landscape: 'The coast improves as we run North. More signs of Wood,
and quality of Land' (Henry Whittingham 14 May 1853); 'At first there
was nothing interesting in the low swampy islands near the mouth, but
after winding some four or five miles, the scenery was truly beautiful'
(Richard Watt 15 Aug. 1864). As in Susan Meade's description of her

voyage up the Yarra, what I will call the 'nature' paradigm was founded on a kind of natural progression; the landscape naturally grew more superior towards the emigrant's destination until, as in this example, the diary reaches an aesthetic critical mass in danger of spontaneous fusion:

> This morning land became quite distinct like a lot of stone quarries   it looked bold, but toward 8 or 9 o'clock it was very pretty at half past 9 the Pilot came on board to take [us] into the bay and after that time it gradually grew more varried and interesting untill it quite surpassed every thing I ever saw or imagined of the picturesque and Romantic   it is utterly impossible to do justice to the view nothing but the skill of an artist could and then he must use some hundred yards of canvas to convey an idea of its beauty and sublimity . . . every body seems enchanted and well they may for it looks like fairey land.
> ('Jemima' 4 Oct. 1853)

'Fairey land' is an appropriate metaphor for this woman's panoramic view as it successfully displaces responsibility for seeing the landscape as both beautiful and sublime from culture to (super)nature – it is the work of the fairies. The agency of the 'looker' in constructing the scene is doubly effaced, first by the adoption of a conventional aesthetic response and second by the suggestion that its beauty is the result of enchantment. In this way of looking, Australia is a land without a history.

The other narrative paradigm is more overt in its acceptance of the role of culture in constructing the emigrants' destination, though it remains nonetheless another specific way of looking. We could call this paradigm the 'culture' paradigm as it presents the landscape as progressively more cultivated; in this model the sequence wilderness-hut-city is read into the coastline as the ship sails along: 'As we come nearer to Hobart we find the land is more cultivated. It is thickly dotted with houses and large gardens. Also some gentlemens houses which are very fine ones. Hobart is now in view' (Thomas Coy 17 Feb. 1885). Thomas Coy's description here is the same, though in a less developed form, as that adopted by Elizabeth Fenton almost sixty years earlier, and Hobart, probably because of its position on the Derwent, seems particularly susceptible to it. Arrival by ship re-enacts for the emigrant a cultural paradigm of civilisation and the features which parade past the ship are formed into a narrative of settlement, making the destination of the voyage precisely 'destined' or providential – the settlers' town appears as the endpoint both of the voyage and civilisation. Indeed, judging from the following account where the flag is substituted for the town, it is also a specifically British destiny:

> As we neared the land, many were the wonders each of us with our telescopes thought we discovered. At length, I espied a hut and then another and then again beheld the British ensign in token of recognition of welcome hoisted as our welcome. This was about 9 A.M. When we were not more than 2 miles distant from the shore we sounded, found 25 fathoms, hoisted our flag in return and hove the ship about, the wind being right ahead but the weather now delightfully fine. (Jonathan Binns Were 12 Nov. 1839)

The exchange of signals, the recognition of the flag, is essentially a misrecognition, a failure to read the land in a non-imperialist manner. The landscape appears to collude in a cultural paradigm of colonisation, validating emigration as a providential and inevitable phenomenon.

Narrative descriptions of the coastline from on board ship give direction to the ship, and to the extent that the landscape mirrors the desires of the emigrant, such narratives make the entire voyage out, not just the voyage up river, appear providential. Clearly what would suit most nineteenth-century British emigrants would be a coastline that could be read through a conflation of both narrative paradigms, with the endpoint a kind of British fairyland, a destination/destiny that is not only naturally beautiful but is providentially a British colony. Moreover, this was a narrative which, unlike previous narrative sequences begun on ship, could not peter out: 'it is not so weariesome now as we are in sight of land And I expect we will be in sight of it all the way now as we are still sailing along the coast' (Alexander Turner 14 Oct. 1883). Once the coastline of Australia had been sighted the journey would be 'not so weariesome' as there would be something to write about every day until the endpoint of the voyage was reached; a panorama could be drawn which would lead directly to the diarist's destination, the long wished-for promised land of the emigrant.

*

Emigrant diarists attempted to give voice to their desire for a providential destiny by calling Australia 'the land of promise'. The phrase is usually dismissed today not only as a cliché but as a cliché previously applied to America, earning a double condemnation from Australians keen to preserve a sense of Australia's difference from the United States. The phrase was certainly applied to America in the nineteenth century, and both Oliver MacDonagh and Terry Coleman quote a letter from Thomas Garry, an Irish immigrant to America, to his wife in Ireland hoping she would shortly be joining him; the letter was sent in March 1848 and ended: 'Keep your heart as god spareed you, you will shortly be in the lands of promise and live happy with me and our children' (MacDonagh 21; Coleman 27).

Ross Gibson in *The Diminishing Paradise* has looked in detail at the European dream of a southern paradise, noting how what in medieval times was a myth of an antipodean El Dorado was still strong enough in the nineteenth century to lure white explorers to the very centre of Australia. The earliest examples cited by Gibson of the phrase 'the land of promise' are by the New South Wales judge Barron Field and by the explorer Charles Sturt. Field used it to describe the land beyond the Blue Mountains in 1822, while Sturt applied it to the lower reaches of the Murray River in 1830:

> Whilst the expedition was toiling down the rivers, no rich country opened upon the view to reward or to cheer the perseverance of those who composed it, and when, at length, the land of promise lay smiling before them, their strength and their means were too much exhausted to allow of their commencing an examination, of the result of which there could be but little doubt. (Sturt 223)

The land of promise here, as in the Field passage, is a region whose occupation is forever deferred. Like the end of a rainbow, the land of promise may beckon but never be reached.

By the 1850s, the phrase 'the land of promise', like the literature on Australia, had proliferated and it was used predictably enough by such propagandists of emigration as Samuel Sidney in *The Three Colonies of Australia* (1852), and by W. H. G. Kingston in *How to Emigrate* (1855): 'Let some one in whom they [the British people] have confidence bring back the bunches of grapes from the land of promise, and they, like the Israelites of old, will only be too eager to reach it' (21). It was also used as the subtitle of William Stones's emigrant handbook, *New Zealand (The Land of Promise) and its Resources* (1859), and applied again to New Zealand in 1873 by the editor of the *Labourers' Union Chronicle* in a colourful editorial exhorting unemployed agricultural labourers to

[185]

emigrate to where the union thought they would be better treated: 'Not a farm labourer in England but should rush from the old doomed country to such a paradise as New Zealand ... Away, then, farm labourers, away! New Zealand is the promised land for you; and the Moses that will lead you is ready' (in Arnold 51). The Moses in this instance was Christopher Holloway, an official of the National Agricultural Labourers' Union.

Emigrants who called Australia 'the land of promise' in their diaries were therefore using a phrase that was already a cliché. That many of the emigrants were still prepared to use the phrase is evidence that avoiding clichés was not a matter to which emigrant diarists gave much thought. The remarkable similarity between diaries written at sea during the long voyage out suggests in fact that the use of clichés is an indicator of the successful diary rather than the reverse. The unsuccessful diarist was the one who was unable to turn the utterly alien experience of being at sea for three or more months into something familiar and knowable that could be narrated; to lack a suitable cliché was to lack a way of expressing what so comprehensively lay outside the diarist's previous experience. The successful diarist transformed the foreign into the stereotype; the more the diary was like any other diary of the voyage out, the more the voyage experience could be communicated to those left behind. Emigrants called Australia 'the land of promise' because in their particular circumstances it was useful for them to do so.

The phrase 'the land of promise', of course, refers to the Biblical epic of Moses leading the people of Israel out of Egypt towards the land of Canaan, and as such it provides a very useful analogy of the voyage out. As the Israelites battled against natural, human, and divine obstacles, so emigrants might pose their voyage as an epic narrative in which they have been led by the hand of providence to a pre-ordained destination. As the final sentence of Mr Barton's diary demonstrates, emigrants could allude to it as a way of ending a diary on a high note: 'We are now within a few miles of the light-ship, the twinkle of wh[ich] appears at intervals. Hurrah for the land of Canaan!' (5 Dec. 1853). There is, of course, a certain self-consciousness in Mr Barton's tone, partly I suspect because he has come as a gold-digger rather than as a religious refugee, and emigrants generally did not see emigration primarily in religious or spiritual terms, despite the work of certain propagandists like W. H. G. Kingston. For the returned colonist in Kingston's story *How to Emigrate*, emigration was more than a search for a better standard of living: 'We have a solemn duty before us – a noble destiny to work out' (44); emigrating in search of higher wages, he points out, is one thing, but 'to make money is not the sole object of emigrating, certainly not of colonizing' (43). Nonetheless, despite the fact that most British emigrants were in search of an improved standard of living, Christian journey-stories were useful in giving meaning to the voyage out because of their widespread currency.

Dependence on cliché does not mean that the language of the diary was unresponsive to the particular circumstances in which the emigrants found themselves, and although the cliché domesticates the alien, it remains a response to a specific situation. 'The land of promise' might be used by emigration propagandists trying to raise the rhetorical level of their arguments, but during the voyage out the phrase is connected exclusively to the nodal points of the voyage, departure and arrival.

Susan Meade, travelling out with her sister and her sister's husband, uses it early in the voyage:

> The white cliffs of my native isle have faded from my sight – where
> the happy years of childhood have glided swiftly away in the
> society of my affectionate parents, sisters & brothers of my
> happier hours – but for these dear ones I have left I do not regret
> leaving England – I am fond of travel, & hope seems to shed a halo
> round my pathway whispering scenes of happiness yet to come in
> the terrestial land of promise to which I am bound – God grant
> that these my pleasing day-dreams may be realized, yet not my
> will 'O! Lord but Thine be done.' (14 Apr. 1842)

Susan Meade is very careful to distinguish between her 'terrest[r]ial land of promise' and a presumably more heavenly promised land, something perhaps like Christian's Celestial City in another epic journey-story popular in the nineteenth century, *Pilgrim's Progress*. Yet even with her recognition of the terrestrial nature of her promised land, Susan Meade admits that as yet it is a promised land only in her imagination, a 'pleasing day-dream'. The land of promise is always dreamlike because it is always a projection of the mind elsewhere. At the beginning of his voyage in 1863, Joshua Hughes noted how looking forward to the land of promise took the mind off the past: 'Steam tug still has us in tow. Welch coast plainly visible. Did not see much evidence of grief anywhere visible, every one appeared to be in good

[187]

spirits & more inclined to look forward with hope to our future land of promise, than to look back with regret on the past' (Joshua Hughes 13 Apr. 1863). The land of promise is a way of mediating the present by an appeal to the future.

'The land of promise' is part of a vocabulary of transition rather than settlement, it functions only when there is a clear sense of time past and time future. During the long voyage out, this sense of transition is lost and as the days sink into monotony, so there is a sense of time standing still. This timelessness corresponds to a period of temporary settlement. Only when the ship draws towards its destination does the sense of transition return, and with it the conditions for using the phrase 'the land of promise'. As the ship catches the westerlies and passes south of the Cape of Good Hope, so emigrants like Thomas Davies began to think of arrival: 'the vessel was going about 12 knots an hour, which put all in good spirits as we all longed to see the shores of the land of Promise' (Thomas Davies 26 Sept. 1854). This longing was what made the metaphor valid: 'Wind still fair. Passed Cape Howe at the rate of 10 knots. Much talk about the Promised Land' (Henry Knight 21 Apr. 1852).

So it is that the promised land can never be reached; the promised land was a place to which one looked forward, it was not a place at which one arrived. Even in the Biblical story, the promised land was 'much talked about', to use Henry Knight's phrase above, but never reached by Moses and the others who left Egypt. Moses led his people across the Red Sea and out of Egypt, but because of a broken divine injunction, only the descendants of those who left Egypt were allowed to occupy the land of Canaan; Moses died and it was Joshua, not Moses, who led the Israelites across the Jordan. It was this that made the land of promise a useful metaphor because however close emigrants came to it, the promised land could never be entered. The promised land might be glimpsed: 'Rose this morning at ½ past four, and at 6 oclock the land of promise came into view   it appeared like a haze on the horizon and many could not see it for a few hours' (Andrew Hamilton 8 Oct. 1853). But however near it appeared to be, it remained like the end of the rainbow, just beyond their reach, as William Bray discovered when he and his fellow emigrants were put into quarantine in Port Phillip Bay: 'Countenances which two days ago were lit up with cheerfulness & joy at their safe arrival are now marked with sorrow & sadness at their very trying and unexpected imprisonment, looking over on the land of promise, in full sight of Melbourne, but not allowed to put foot thereon'

(19 Aug. 1854). Emigrants were kept out of the land of promise not because of any quarantine laws but because it is a dream which exists only for those in transition. The land of promise can never be inhabited, it exists only for those who are outsiders.

Denis Cosgrove, using the work of David Lowenthal and others, has helpfully discussed the difference between an external observer of landscape and its inhabitants, what are called the insider-participants (*Social Formation* 18–19). Whereas the external observer might walk away from the land, the insider-participant enjoys a social rather than an aesthetic response to a land which is part of her or his daily life. Cosgrove's argument, although based on the distinction between a feudal and a capitalist Britain, could correspond in an Australian context to the difference between the land as it might be lived by the indigenous peoples and a view of the coast as seen by an immigrant:

> In a natural economy the relationship between human beings and land is dominantly that of the insider, an unalienated relationship based on use values and interpreted analogically. In a capitalist economy it is a relationship between owner and commodity, an alienated relationship wherein man stands as outsider and interprets nature causally. (64)

While Aboriginal culture does not contain a notion of private ownership of the land, for the European settler Australia was a land ripe for private ownership: 'Here is a tract of Country of Hundreds of miles in extent that may belong to any one who chooses to set himself down & in all probability would never be turned off the land at least till he had made a fortune out of it' (Oswald Bloxsome 2 Aug. 1838). Here is a land fit for white squatters.

Ross Gibson in *South of the West* offers a similar indictment of European ways of seeing the Australian landscape: 'the white Australian attitude to the South Land is unequivocally derived from the Renaissance imperial ethic' (6). With the coming of printing, so Gibson argues, space seemed to offer itself as an object to be known, to be read, by those searching for new knowledge; land became an object or a commodity: 'white Australia is a product of the Renaissance mentality that is predicated on the notion of an environment *other than* and *external to* the individual ego' (8). This is precisely the view constructed of the coastline by the emigrants as they came in sight of Australia; the

[189]

promised land was always a prospect, a land to be viewed from the outside.

In this view from the outside, Aboriginal people were almost totally erased from the landscape, their presence being invoked only in a causal relationship to the fire and smoke sometimes seen inland: 'saw a single light on the Beach supposed to be the Natives cooking the Kangaroo' (Harriet Taylor 24 Jan. 1840). White Australians also ate kangaroo: 'Dined after church service yesterday on delicious kangaroo soup, a fine haunch of ditto, lamb, a pair of fowls, ham and sausages, turnips, lettuce, onions, fruit-pies, and plum and custard puddings' (George Fletcher Moore 22 Aug. 1831). The image of 'Natives cooking the Kangaroo', however, depends not on 'natives' occasionally eating kangaroo but on a relationship between the two whereby the image of one automatically conjures up an image of the other. In other words, this image of 'Natives cooking the Kangaroo' is an icon, a culturally constructed white image of Australia from the outside, though Harriet Taylor does have the honesty to admit that this was only a 'supposed' cause of the fire and smoke.

Yet even this 'supposed' is characteristic of the diaries; unless they happened to be working for white settlers, the Aboriginals noted in the diaries were more of the imagination than of the flesh, as in this passage concerning a party of emigrants who rowed to the shore from their becalmed ship: 'They saw the columns of smoke inland, & surmising it to be some native feast, or such like, determined if they went ashore (w^h. they did not) to keep altogether, for fear of treachery' (J. Kidd Walpole 27 Oct. 1837). Supposition and surmise. Such fantasies would be laughable had not genocide quickly made any return of the coloniser's gaze impossible. The people who lived the land were destroyed by those outsiders who looked at the land as a commodity to be bought and commercially exploited.

It was their distance from it that allowed the immigrants to project onto the land their fear of the Aboriginal people and their desire for the land of promise. The initial sight of land from the sea was often mistaken for a cloud: 'The promised land is but a cloud as yet – but in an hour it ought to be well up' (Marjory MacGillivray 24 Jan. 1894). The cloud-like appearance of the land increased the anticipation of the emigrants as they waited to see what the coast would look like. But, as in the case of the kangaroo-eating pantomime Aboriginals conjured up by the emigrants at sea, the coast was always cloud-like, was always specular; as we project shapes onto clouds, some looking like familiar faces, others looking like mythical beasts, so those on board ship projected a destination moulded by their desires:

> As we approached the cape of Maria Van Dieman, which is the
> extreme North Westerly point of the North Island – many were
> the speculations as to objects rendered visible. – One swore he
> could see by the aid of his glass a homestead & afterwards a couple
> of men on horseback galloping up the side of a hill – another
> fellow went as far as to state that he could see a couple of Maoris –
> one digging young potatoes & the other shelling green peas!
> another – thinking no doubt he had hit upon a capital joke –
> informed those situated near him that he could distinctly discern
> black men with white faces on the shore! (George Pearson 31 Dec.
> 1880)

This may be the coast of New Zealand rather than Australia but the projection of a destination operates the same. Icons of British settlement are invoked, the homestead and the men on horses, even Maoris are conjured up to look like Europeans. They may think they are joking, but George Pearson and his fellow emigrants are creating the kind of promised land a fanciful exhibitor of dissolving views might have shown in London. The promised land was a fairyland, a daydream, a bank of clouds, a site of supposition and surmise, a land for speculators indeed. Australia was objectified by emigrants in their diaries through a range of metaphors, but such metaphors worked only for the emigrant at sea. As verbal currency, they became worthless once the emigrant stepped on land.

Chapter 7

Making an end

'I was once more treading on terra firma'

A couple of years ago I spent an afternoon at the Merseyside Maritime Museum in Liverpool looking round a permanent exhibition illustrating nineteenth-century emigration to America and Australia. One of the exhibits which demanded my attention was a boardgame dating from the 1850s called 'Race to the Gold Diggings', and it comprised a book of rules, a teetotum, a board, and three miniature clipper ships. The object of the game was for each player to move her or his ship to the spin of the teetotum around an oval course which represented the sea route to Australia, the winner being the first to get to the goldfields. Apart from the fact that the Museum had missed what seemed to me an obvious opportunity for making money by selling reproductions of 'Race to the Gold Diggings' (at least, I desperately wanted one for myself), my other thought was of the link between boardgames and journey-stories that Jonathan Rée makes in his *Philosophical Tales*.

Rée discusses boardgames and journey-stories in the context of an essay on Hegel's *The Phenomenology of Spirit* (1807) and Hegel's vision of a consciousness called Spirit travelling on a journey towards enlightenment or 'absolute knowledge'. Rée first looks at the development of what he calls the Christian journey-of-enlightenment story, stories like the anonymous thirteenth-century *Quest of the Holy Grail* or, in the fourteenth century, Dante's *Divine Comedy*, in which a hero sets out to overcome a series of trials and achieve a spiritual enlightenment. If in classical epics like Homer's *Odyssey* or Virgil's *Aeneid* the hero remains essentially the same person who set out despite his experiences, in journey-of-enlightenment stories the hero reaches a vantage point from which he can reappraise the meaning of this journey: 'the travellers are gradually educated and transformed, so that they can conclude by looking back down the road they have taken, seeing it spread out beneath them with its obstacles reduced to their true proportions and its hazards and false-turnings obvious at last' (68). Rée points out how, for the reader, one of the fascinations of such journey-stories lies in their play of perspectives. The reader at one and the same time has to negotiate between the viewpoint of the traveller who is straining to see over the horizon and the viewpoint of the gods who have the journey mapped out below them: 'The art of the journey-story is inescapably visual and perspectival: it depends on getting the reader to see the journey both from the point of view of the traveller, and from the point of view of the gods or the birds, who can see the path beyond the traveller's horizon' (67). It is then a short step for Rée to point out how this interplay of perspectives is also to be found in board games which involve a journey, with the players having the route spread out before them but also having to adopt the perspective of their token as it travels the route. In playing 'Race to the Gold Diggings', therefore, players have continually to switch perspectives between an overview of the route and the point of view of their miniature clipper as it struggles past the obstacles on its voyage from Britain to Australia.

In Chapter 3 I looked at the way in which maps provided emigrants with a sense of space but no sense of place. It was possible to chart the progress of the voyage on the map, but there were no landmarks to correlate with the ship's position on the map; visually, the ship might be always in the same place. My argument there was, first, that contrary to what might be expected from a journey-story, the diaries concentrated not on any places passed through on the journey, but on the mode of transport; the place in which emigrants seemed to remain was the ship itself. Second, I argued that emigrants could gain a sense of physical progress by keeping a diary, but that transgressive incidents were needed if the diary was to avoid repetition and monotony. In this chapter, however, I want to look at these aspects of the journey in terms of arrival at the destination when we might expect many of the problems of being caught at sea between the old world and the new to be resolved. In short, I want to ask, what happens when the emigrant/board-player reaches the end of the voyage/game?

For Rée, as I pointed out above, arrival at the end of the Christian journey-story allowed the heroes to achieve something like the god's-eye view of their trials: 'they can conclude by looking back down the road they have taken, seeing it spread out beneath them with its obstacles reduced to their true proportions and its hazards and false-turnings obvious at last' (68). The journey-story is like a spiritual boardgame and the success of the traveller/player is gauged by her or his success in arriving at a vantage point where the two perspectives converge, the journey is halted, and the game won.

A similar kind of enlightenment is claimed by Louis O. Mink in his discussion of narrative as an explanatory mode of human understanding. Mink is interested in the role played in historiography by storytelling, and to make his case he draws a distinction between two types of narrative cognition: 'to know an event by retrospection is categorically, not incidentally, different from knowing it by prediction and anticipation' ('History and Fiction' 546). Of course, an emigrant at sea has a great deal of predicting and anticipating to do; what Mink's work suggests is that once the voyage is over, once it can be seen as a single narrative that has been followed, a different form of understanding the voyage comes into play, what Mink calls configurational comprehension:

> in the configurational comprehension of a story which one *has followed*, the end is connected with the promise of the beginning as well as the beginning with the promise of the end, and the necessity of the backward references cancels out, so to speak, the contingency of the forward references. To comprehend temporal succession means to think of it in both directions at once, and then time is no longer the river which bears us along but the river in aeriel view, upstream and downstream seen in a single survey. (554–5)

At the end of the story/voyage, Mink suggests, the reader/emigrant achieves that god's-eye aerial view which Rée holds to be characteristic of the journey-story. If the emigrant is writing a book of the voyage out because she or he shares the cultural belief that the voyage is already structured as a narrative, her or his particular voyage cannot be understood as a single story until the end of the voyage is reached. In this sense the emigrant diarist travels with, to use Peter Brooks's phrase, 'the anticipation of retrospection' (23); the voyage can only be comprehended in retrospect.

*

As the ship drew closer to its destination, it was not just the crew who were preparing for the ending of the voyage:

A bright clear day, with steady breeze blowing, and the ship going
about 8 knots. The sailors high[ly] busy washing paintwork
scraping, &c they use a preparation called scrugy mugy by them
consisting a good deal of potash. Crosby and I busy fitting lids to
the cases and making them look decent, in the evening the [we?]
packed one with dirty linen, putting the soda water machine in
the middle, for the time our cabin was like a carpenter's shop,
with hardly room to move. (Charles Bolton 21 May 1872)

Both passengers and crew commenced rituals which punctuated the
voyage, cleaning the ship and repacking belongings. But for many
passengers, there were also diaries and letters to be brought up to date:

The sailors are all busy cleaning down and making everything
bright – this morning the volunteers sanded and scrubbed the
poop until it was almost white.
    In other parts of the ship busy letter writers are squatted here
and there jotting down their yarns and adventures. (Richard Watt
6 Aug. 1864)

While the sailors had to prepare the ship for inspection by the
immigration officers, the emigrants were making their own prepara-
tions by recounting their 'yarns and adventures'. Anna Fowler found
herself trying to catch up with events the night before she was due to
disembark:

I am writing in my cabin kneeling down to a box, everybody
having turned in. I wanted to chronicle the events of the day
before going to bed as tomorrow I shall be busy packing and after
that I may have too much to think about to be able to write much.
    So endeth my voyage scribblings which have beguiled some of
my many sea-spent hours and I hope may afford you some little
amusement if you can make it out. (Anna Fowler 23 Sept. 1866)

Here Anna Fowler is signing off as the 'confusion' of disembarkation is
about to begin; the 'confusion' of embarkation which I looked at in an
earlier chapter is matched by the 'confusion' of getting off the ship, as
Richard Watt records: 'At the landing stage all was confusion and bustle'
(15 Aug. 1864). Such spatial and social confusion will prevent diary-
writing but will also, or so the diarist hopes, lead to a restoration of the

equilibrium promised by the narrative of emigration. The stable point of the European home and all that the concept of home implies will be replaced by the stable point of an Australian home; once the voyage is over, the emigrant has the right to presume that the gap between the point of departure and the point of arrival not only has been bridged but has been abolished.

The procedure at the end of the voyage seems on the whole to have been fairly standard; as Don Charlwood remarks: 'The arrival procedures, indeed the voyage by sail itself, changed remarkably little over the decades' (249). Once the ship was close to its destination it would signal for a pilot who would take command of the ship until it was anchored; the captain could be tolerably trusted to get the ship halfway round the world but it needed a specialist knowledge of the tides, the shoals, and the winds to get the ship into any particular port, and even here things might go wrong, as the unnamed male passenger arriving at Sydney on the *Kate* in 1853 recorded:

At 5 p.m. the Pilot came on board just as the gale sprung up with great force while we were encountering a great deal of difficulty to keep all snug. In making for anchorage after passing through the Heads the Ship struck her keel against a rock while boating a tack, and . . . some minutes was considered in imminent danger of a great disaster; all the passengers helped a hand with a strong arm and willing will to work the Ship, some-times in the greatest imaginable confusion, and of others in awful silence and anxious supense watching the result of a tack and for the Pilot's orders. At 6 p.m. we dropped anchors in Port Jackson, thus ending a very long passage amidst great apparent peril. (25 Oct. 1853)

Once the anchor was let go it might be some time before emigrants actually landed. The ship might need a steam tug to carry it to its berth for disembarkation, as in Sydney, Adelaide, and Brisbane, and time could be lost while the captain negotiated a rate with the tug or while the ship was being towed: 'we come to the end of our long journey after spending two days in attempts to get up the River but it was so shallow the Steam Tugg could go but a short Distance before we got aground this morning we were successful and was moored between 7 & 8 o'clock' (James Murray 17 Mar. 1854). Then there would be the wait for a health officer to clear the ship, and in cases where sickness was still on board, the emigrants could find themselves kept in quarantine for one or two weeks, a fate not avoided even by the illustrious SS *Great Britain*, as William Bray discovered:

> Arrived here yesterday in the Great Britain after a passage of 65 days from Liverpool. To day has been a very long and tedious day, indeed it has seemed the longest since we left the shores of happy Old England occassioned by the severity of the Quarantine Laws to which we have unfortunately subjected ourselves from our having had some 3 or 4 cases of small pox on board. (19 Aug. 1854)

The emigrants spent the day 'looking over on the land of promise, in full sight of Melbourne, but not allowed to put foot thereon' while the captain argued with the authorities. The next morning, however, he was persuaded to sail back the forty miles to the quarantine station at Port Phillip Heads: 'At 7 o'clock in the morning, Her Majestys Brig the "Fantome" 18 gun Man-of War frigate which lay anchored alongside of us finding that we had not obeyed orders sent us a message in the shape of a cannon ball which came whizzing about our ears and which fully satisfied the Captain that he must obey the orders' (20 Aug.). Even when the ship had been cleared by the health inspector, there was the visit of the immigration officers: 'About 10 a.m. the officials came on board, and called over the passengers' names, asking each individual as he passed, if he had any cause for complaint. Of course, everyone was only too eager to get the business over, and smothered his grumblings' (Richard Watt 15 Aug. 1864). And when all this had been completed and the passengers were free to leave, there was yet another wait for a steamer to take them ashore: 'About 6 O. C. thought we could see the smoke of a steamer coming to fetch us. It proved to be one but it did not come to us. The Custom's Officer said he thought we should not get one down to day, which rather damped our spirits' (George Randall 21 Oct. 1868).

Despite the number of stages involved between sighting land and spending a night on land, emigrants seem to have had a pretty keen idea of where the voyage ended. Overwhelmingly, the diaries end either with the anticipation of landing or with the end of the first day on shore when food and somewhere to sleep had been secured. Solomon Joseph was one of those who ended his diary while still on board ship: 'Sunday. – Muster roll called over to-day for the last time. Weather fine. Going on splendidly. All in high spirits at the idea of landing soon' (4 Sept. 1859).

[197]

Charles Bolton was another: 'All seem pretty active and in good spirits, at the prospect of being at the pier tomorrow' (22 May 1872). Diaries which end like this leave the reader, like the emigrants at sea, tantalised by the prospect of landing.

Gilbert McCaul's diary finishes at the end of the first day on land; having found his Uncle Bob in Collins Street earlier in the day ('a man with Red Check, short legs & tight pantaloons'), 'Gibbie' McCaul is taken out in the evening to celebrate the New Year, no doubt in Scottish style: 'Went to a large ball at night with uncle, a regular stunner   the people here are very gay just like London, and the finest climate imaginable, no idea of it at home   the heat is great but no closeness, quite bouyant both in Spirits and body   got to my bed about 6 o'clock next morning – so ended my first day' (31 Dec. 1855). Of course, it is quite useful to be able to end the diary on the last day of the year, the coming of the New Year would certainly reinforce the sense of a new life beginning. But the first day on land also seemed to provide a natural finishing point for many other diarists, among them this unnamed diarist arriving at Brisbane on the *Scottish Admiral*:

> at a ¼ to 4 we left the ship which had been our home for 13 weeks & arrived at Brisbane at 6.30 pm. A most miserable place   they took us in   we were to sleep in what they called the deptt   Tom & I had a look in and then went & got lodgings as it was worse than the ship bare boards to lie on and before 9 oclock every body that could get beds had done the same as we. We went to the Theatre in the evening & thus ended our voyage from England to Brisbane Australia. (18 Aug. 1883)

These two types of ending, the anticipation of landing and the first day on land, suggest that the ideal ending would be at a moment between the two, that moment, beloved of Pope John Paul II, of stepping on land, though whether or not emigrants also kissed the ground is not recorded. One of those who gets closest to ending his diary with stepping on land is Edward Cornell:

> This morning we got underway about 9 o'clock and about eleven a steam tug arrived on spec. and being employed soon brot us to our anchorage among the shipping. As soon as the ship was cleared the passengers friends were admitted on board, the bulwarks were crowded so I mounted on top of the [round]

'House' and had not long to wait before Fred bounced over the gangway and in the course of an hour I was once more treading on terra firma on 19th August, 1856.

This precise dating of 'treading on terra firma' signifies to Edward Cornell himself, if it does nothing for anyone else, that this is a very special moment, a moment to be recorded and remembered for a long time to come. Others ended their diaries with the same gesture: 'we got a boat to take us ashore, and landed at Wooloomooloo Bay at 12.45, midday, or about 2.40 a.m. Greenwich time' (J. R. Waight 30 July 1882); 'by eight o'clock 26 Jany we were once more able to step on land' (Marjory MacGillivray 25 Jan. 1894). The statement 'I was once more treading on terra firma on 19th August, 1856' is an ideal ending to the diary because it marks so clearly the end of the voyage.

Yet I am suspicious of the diaries here. I am suspicious for two reasons, the second of which I will come to in a moment. My first reason is this: there is nothing in the act of stepping out of a boat and onto land that materially warrants the kind of investment that emigrants make in that particular moment. It is true they are no longer bobbing up and down, and that they can now go out and buy fresh food without having to eat beef or potatoes that have been preserved for probably six months or more (there were reports of salt beef making at least a couple of round trips to Australia). But the emigrants are still confused, that first step on land being not quite the end of the voyage experience that it ought to be:

Thursday April 14th [1842] I went on shore yesterday, horribly disappointed with the place – confused. my feet very soon became tender – unable to walk – turned back to the wharf to return to the ship – was charged by the policeman with being intoxicated because I walked so roly – escaped him by explaining – returned to the Ship in a state of delirium tremens. (William Wills)

Stepping on land in itself does not provide somewhere to live, work, or friends. Stepping on land is more important as a symbolic moment than for any material benefits it offers.

I raised the possibility in Chapter 2 of seeing the voyage out as a liminal period, a stage in a rite of passage from one social condition to another. In rites of passage there is a structural parallelism between beginnings and endings, with rites of separation being balanced by corresponding rites of incorporation, and this kind of balancing of beginnings and endings is made explicit at the end of Amy Henning's diary: 'I feel almost inclined to go on writing my journal now I am on shore, I am got so into the way of it, but as it began with our first hour on the water it must end with the last' (22 Oct. 1854). In terms of rites of passage, if leaving Britain operates as a rite of separation, landing in Australia operates as a rite of incorporation; the emigrant achieves a new social status after successfully completing the transitional phase of the long voyage out. But I am sceptical of this too. Some emigrants certainly viewed the voyage out as a trial which would prepare them for life in Australia, though this sentiment is not widespread and is perhaps more often found in retrospect than at the time of migration. But the status achieved immediately on arrival in Australia is that of an 'immigrant' or even 'New Chum', both of which are themselves transitional statuses. In other words, seeing the voyage out as a transitional stage between two lives is a way of making sense of the experience of migration, but it is a cultural way of seeing which does not necessarily fit the circumstances of arrival. The voyage out is a story and as Louis Mink says of stories: 'Stories are not lived but told. Life has no beginnings, middles, or ends; there are meetings, but the start of an affair belongs to the story we tell ourselves later, and there are partings, but final partings only in the story' (557).

I suggested above that the diaries overwhelmingly end either with the anticipation of landing or with the end of the first day on shore when food and somewhere to sleep had been secured. This is true so far as the content of the diaries is concerned, but there is a third, wholly textual ending which is often found in conjunction with one of the other types of ending. By a textual ending I mean an ending through which the narrator signs off, as in the ending of James Murray's diary: 'took Lunch at Mr Mosswell's at 11. the End.' Writing 'the End' or 'Finis' is the same kind of ending as the 'That's All Folks' which concludes Bugs Bunny cartoons, an ending at the level of the narration rather than at the level of what is narrated. It was a fairly well-used device:

As I have brought the ship to an anchor I will now close my journal. (Jessie Campbell 27 Dec. 1840)

I do not intend to write any further, as the Journal of my *voyage* is now complete. (Arthur Manning 14 Feb. 1849)

At about 9 o'clock we dropped anchor at Wiliams Town and were

at Port Phillip or as it is now called Victoria. And do end my diary
of my voyage. (Thomas Severn 4 Dec. 1852)

Now that I arrived here the first thing that I had to think about
was work, and hoping that I would find something to keep me
going, I concluded my diary. (Samuel Shaw 19 Feb. 1878)

Such endings are due in part to the perceived or imaginary dialogue
between the diarist and her or his audience; they are the written
equivalent of a spoken goodbye or a wave of the hand: 'Adieu dear Girl I
close my Book' (Henry Widdowson 4 May 1826). But they are also
idealised endings, or perhaps, an idealisation of endings. As rituals they
attest to a desire for absolute endings, they are part of a departure and
arrival mentality; above all, they suggest that what has gone before will
be different from what follows.

And here we can talk not just in terms of the past of the voyage out,
but of the past as a past way of life. The investment made in the
beginning of the voyage as a break, as a leaving of Old England,
suddenly becomes not such a break after all and many of the diarists
write of the ship with fondness and are sad to leave:

Loth to leave the ship, seemed now like home, – & all the anxieties
of a new mode of life now to begin. (Theo West 19 Feb. 1854)

Altho' we were glad, heartily glad to get away from the old ship,
there was something of regret in parting with the faithful crew,
and the ship that had brought us so many thousands of miles and
had been our home for four months. (George Randall 21 Oct.
1868)

This is the 'home' aspect of the 'floating home' duality; but at this stage
the ship could also represent the home left behind in Britain: 'Although
glad to see dry land, I shall bid adieu to my snug little berth with regret –
as long as I am in the ship I feel in Old England   how then can I say
farewell without a tear when the link will be broken which binds me to
the land I love?' (Susan Meade 1 Aug. 1842). This was not necessarily a
universal sentiment, particularly when the voyage, as in the case of
John Joseland, had lasted almost five months, two months longer than
he might have expected it to last: 'I believe firmly that no body of
passengers ever left a ship with fewer regrets and a greater feeling of
disgust than we did' (John Joseland 14 July 1853). But there was a sense

that leaving the ship was also a final farewell to the old world. Writing 'The End' at a certain point in a diary was to turn psychologically from a past stretching back into the mists of memory to a future stretching out into the unknown.

*

I mentioned a little earlier that I was suspicious of the end of the voyage as an absolute ending for two reasons. The first, which I have just looked at, is that the mere act of stepping out of a boat onto land did not justify in material terms the kind of investment that emigrants made in that particular moment; the moment was symbolic, a ritualistic investment in the new life. The second reason for my suspicion, which I want to look at now, is that most diaries continued beyond the landing. I am not here referring to diaries by travellers or lifelong diarists which do not even hesitate at the landing; nor am I referring to those handful of diarists who, evidently having got into the habit of keeping a diary, decide to keep one running after arrival in Australia. In the first place I am thinking of those diaries which push on for a few more days in order, as it is sometimes put, to 'give an account of the place'.

After months at sea, many diarists use their diaries as a way of stimulating their sense of place. The only place they have been able to cite for the past three or more months has been the ship. Now the point on the map can at last correspond not to an undifferentiated stretch of water but to a place on land. The final entry of Francis Taylor's diary is a description of Adelaide: 'I cannot take my leave of my Log Book without a few concluding remarks upon the town and neighbourhood of Adelaide' (13 June 1850). Francis Taylor found Adelaide 'in a brisk flourishing condition, the town is in a very pretty part situated seven miles from the Port, and a road as level as a Floor.' Attitudes to Australia differed partly as a reflection of the economic conditions of the time; a growing town in 'a brisk flourishing condition' is better than a rundown town in a depression. But all these types of description had one thing in common: they all took as their point of reference the home country. Unlike the views of the coastline from on board ship which owed much to a landscape aesthetics based on the Alps, descriptions of towns depended much more closely on the everyday environment of the immigrants. These new arrivals were in transition from being outsiders, who could view the land as an object from which they were separated, to becoming insiders, for whom the environment represented somewhere to be inhabited; food had to be bought again, work had to be found. In such circumstances, it is not surprising newly arrived migrants should use familiar everyday co-ordinates to assess the new country.

There are two main types of familiar everyday co-ordinate. The first is that of the seasons. Francis Taylor's 'concluding remarks' note that 'it is now the middle of winter, but all kinds of vegetation contradicts the idea' (13 June 1850). Francis not only has to get used to June being winter, he is also baffled by grain being sown in winter. Such remarks are part of a discourse of colonial inversion, a feeling that in the Antipodes all kinds of things, including the seasons, are inverted: 'colonial narrative . . . told of a society characterised by inversion of the natural or metropolitan state of things, and could be used either to celebrate or to lament the consequences' (Goodman 102). Even by Francis Taylor's time such a discourse was a commonplace of remarks on Australia, but that still did not prevent a succession of immigrants using it in their diaries:

> Though it being mid-winter on arriving, everything bore the appearance of an English summer, men were scraping dust off the streets and all nature clothed in verdure. The grass ankle deep, grain ready for shooting, and garden produce abundant such as celery, radishes, letice, cabbages and potatoes, ripe apples and pears in abundance as well as mushrooms and flowers in full bloom. (Richard Skilbeck Aug. 1858)

It was in order to counter this 'unnatural' natural environment that some emigrants had converted their ship into what must have been more a floating aviary than a floating home:

> Now and then a blackbird, thrush or lark, a little more lively than his brothers, sends forth a note; but I am sorry to say that many of the birds have died from one cause or another, and their number is now hardly a tithe of that when we left Plymouth. I hope those left will reach Adelaide and enliven the hearts of many exiled from their native land. (Edward Lacey 8 Aug. 1862)

But if the natural environment baffled the familiar co-ordinates of home, the cultural environment of the cities could be more easily accommodated. Architecture, so far as it was based on British architecture, made the cities much less strange for British immigrants than the country around them: 'Melbourne is a good town, quite English, can scarcely fancy yourself 16 000 miles from home. English people, houses, shops and good wide streets, all quite like home. Everything very dear and out of town in every direction it looks more strange and foreign' (J. W. Reeves 13 Feb. 1857). While the country is 'strange and foreign', the city itself is 'quite English'. The same applied to Sydney, even though a comparison with London was not always to Sydney's advantage: 'Of course, the streets are not nearly so fine as the principal streets in London, nor are the shops, George St and Pitt St are the two principal streets and they are something similar to the Essex Road, Islington' (J. R. Waight 1882). This comparison is perhaps not flattering to Islington either. Melbourne rather than Sydney was praised for being so English: 'a very fine city – streets 2 miles length so busy active bustling – fine shops – & really splendid public buildings, altogether it reminded me more of London than any other city   it is certainly far before Dublin in every respect' (Elizabeth Ankatell 23 Mar. 1866). In the heyday of British municipal architecture, Melbourne out-Englished the English.

The underlying point, though, is that whether the countryside was foreign or the cities familiar, the co-ordinates against which both were being assessed were those the immigrants had brought with them from home. There is nothing surprising about this, but it does have implications for how far the voyage out or the landing marked a discontinuity. In a crucial sense, there is no break, and by employing the values and expectations of their home culture, immigrants are ensuring that they are always, to a very large extent, still at home. *MacKenzie's Australian Emigrant's Guide* (1852) summed up the emigrant experience like this:

> Emigrants from not finding everything exactly as they had been
> accustomed to at home, feel at first some little dissatisfaction,
> and, John Bull like, grumble; but always having, when
> industrious, plenty of choice food, this soon wears off, which is
> greatly aided by finding themselves surrounded by their own
> language, religion, laws, and monarchy. (8)

In his *Impressions of Australia Felix* (1845), R. Howitt coined the phrase 'home return anxiety' for immigrants whose only thought was of when they would be able to return home and impress their friends and relatives with how well they had done in the colony. 'Personally they are

abroad,' says Howitt, 'but mentally at home; living, moving and having
their existence amongst their friends and kindred' (in Reece 13). Yet in
a sense, all emigrants suffered from 'home return anxiety' by the very
fact that their comprehension of their new environment was through a
European cognitive set. And to the extent that the culture they came to
inhabit in Australia was also essentially a British culture, they
remained, as Howitt puts it, 'mentally at home'.

*

When emigrants stepped on land, they were not just leaving a temporary shipboard home, but, despite having made the move earlier when
waving goodbye to Old England, they also imagined themselves to be
stepping out of an old life into a new. As Edward Lacey put it: 'I must bid
a hasty farewell to my fellow passengers, pack up my traps, and prepare
to land in this new country where I have to commence life afresh and
where all are entire strangers' (25 Aug. 1862). Yet it is also clear that
emigrants once they became immigrants looked around for signs of
continuity. A city was praised for being like London; a countryside was
viewed with suspicion if it behaved differently from a British countryside. In general, what suited emigrants best and what they hoped for
was the discovery of continuities, and for British immigrants in British
colonies such continuities were not hard to find. When migrants talked
of new lives, they meant lives materially more prosperous than they had
been used to, but lives which were nonetheless continuous with the old;
to talk in terms of old and new was a symbolic gesture which con-
tradicted the ways in which immigrants remained mentally at home.

I made the point earlier that not all diaries end with arrival and some
diarists push on for a few more days in order to give an account of their
destination. Yet in another sense, even those diaries which conclude
with the diarist making that symbolic first step onto land have continued after disembarkation because accounts of disembarkation had to
be written-up later. Whereas a snapshot camera might have captured
the symbolic entry into the new life, the diary had to recreate that
moment after the event and with the emigrant already inside. The final
entry in William Reay's diary is undated although it deals solely with the
first day on land:

> I think I never [saw] anything in all my life to equal the Harbour it
> is something splendid   a great many people came to meet
> friends but we were disappointed at Jack not being there to meet

us and after almost all the passengers had gone away from the
ship I felt very soft in a strang[e] land but Jack was there at six in
the morning   he had being at Sydney and waited two Days so he
was forced to go away and come back in the morning   we three
went into town and got some tocker something that we had not
seen for a life time   salt butter

The reason, of course, why this entry is undated is that William Reay has
sensed the incongruity; while the events it deals with probably occurred
on 5 Dec. 1877, the date of its composition would have been some time
later. Such accounts are retrospective, being written up when the
'confusion' of recovering luggage and struggling through crowds had
been overcome and a new 'home', a site for writing, had been established. Isabella Turner admits as much in a similarly undated entry:

I must finish up this beautiful journal of mine now, the day
following the last on which I write on board ship I was in too
unsettled a state to write.
We have now been a week in Australia, but we have been going
about so much since we landed I could not get sitting down
properly to continue this. (Isabella Turner 1868)

In the same way as accounts of setting sail were dependent on establishing a space for writing, so too were accounts of leaving the ship. To
write 'I was once more treading on terra firma on 19th August, 1856'
was to write having reached a lodging-house or the house of a relative or
friend.
It follows, therefore, that if the moment of stepping on land
designates the end of one life and the beginning of the new, the diarist
has already begun the new life when she or he is writing about the end of
the old. A diarist may occasionally opt for simultaneous narration, as in
Mark Blasdall's final entry, 'A steamer makes its appearance while I am
writing' (1 July 1862), but such endings are the exception and most
diarists will be inhabiting a different time and space from that of the
persona making that giant step onto terra firma; while the diary may be
dealing with William Reay getting on land, it is written by an effaced
William Reay who is already relatively settled. This suggests that the
diary is being used by the migrant to add shape and significance to an
experience that has already passed. If this is so, it also confirms that the
break between the old and new lives is not as clean a break as it purports
to be; once again, the ending of a diary is an idealised ending. Indeed,

such breaks can only ever exist as cultural representations, and while the diarist is thinking in terms of endings and beginnings, she or he is also seeking and experiencing continuities. Like William Reay, she or he is perhaps already once again enjoying salt butter.

I have referred to Bunyan's *Pilgrim's Progress* several times in previous chapters because it was a journey narrative which would have been known by many of the emigrants; as a religious work it occupied a privileged place alongside the Bible in even working-class households. At the end of *Pilgrim's Progress*, Christian crosses the River of Death into the Celestial City. The narrator-dreamer, however, who has been following Christian along his path from the City of Destruction, is left stranded on the wrong side of the river; all he can do is gaze longingly at the sight of Christian entering the Celestial City, the endpoint of his pilgrimage:

> I saw in my dream that these two men [Christian and Hopeful] went in at the gate: and lo, as they entered, they were transfigured, and they had raiment put on that shone like gold . . .
> Now, just as the gates were opened to let in the men, I looked in after them, and, behold, the City shone like the sun; the streets also were paved with gold, and in them walked many men with crowns on their heads, palms in their hands, and golden harps to sing praises withal.
> There were also of them that had wings, and they answered one another without intermission, saying, Holy, holy, holy is the Lord. And after that they shut up the gates; which, when I had seen, I wished myself among them.

For Jonathan Rée *Pilgrim's Progress* is a journey-of-enlightenment story, though he does not specify whether it is a journey of enlightenment for Christian, the narrator-dreamer, or both. Certainly both reach the end of the journey and both can now look back on the journey and comprehend it as a story that can now be told; they have achieved that overview which Louis O. Mink terms the configurational mode of comprehension. There is now a beginning, middle, and end.

What troubles me about this as an explanation of the position of immigrants is that in *Pilgrim's Progress* only Christian actually enters the Celestial City; the narrator has to return, as it were, to the old life. Because of the popularity of *Pilgrim's Progress* in the nineteenth century, the parallel between emigration and the Christian journey-story is one that many emigrants would have made. So I believe I am not far wrong in suggesting that there is a hint of the ending of *Pilgrim's Progress* in the endings of some of the diaries, as here, for example, with the ending of the diary of Joseph Sams:

> The country here presented a very picturesque appearance and here we had the pleasure of seeing the first village on the New Land and a very pretty one it is with its hotel and baths, lighthouse etc. and sandy beach. On entering the heads on the left is the quarantine ground, it being a fine open bay . . . We landed at Sandridge Pier about 5 p.m. and I then wished the ship a good bye as far as inhabiting her went, and entered the great and prosperous city of Melbourne. (16 Nov. 1874)

Stretches of water, usually a river, are a common feature of so many stories because they lend themselves to the symbolism demanded by rites of passage. As Bunyan's Christian crosses the River of Death to reach the Celestial City, so Joseph Sams is entering a New Land. Yet nowhere does Joseph describe Melbourne from the inside. Although Joseph had already entered Melbourne before he wrote his final diary entry, the reader of the diary is left, like the narrator-dreamer in *Pilgrim's Progress*, outside looking in. It is as if the New Land can exist only as the New Land from a perspective prior to arrival.

Put simply, a diary tends during the voyage out towards a destination in which the emigrant has made a huge investment. Arrival at the destination ought to result in the kind of enlightenment Christian enjoys in reaching the Celestial City. Diarists are therefore anxious to end their diaries with that moment of stepping on land, a moment which will provide a suitable end to their narrative. However, in order to write up that moment the diarist needs already to have entered the Celestial City and begun the new life. On the other hand it is clear from the desire for continuity expressed in the diaries after landing that the concept of the new life no longer holds; however good Australia may be, the diarist has changed perspective from an outside observer to an insider who, by virtue of being a participant, no longer sees the land as a New Land. In order, therefore, to write the ending of the diary as if the goal of the journey has actually been reached, the diarist must write from a perspective prior to arrival. It is as if Christian has to cast himself as the narrator outside the city to go on seeing it as the Celestial City.

The ending of the diary of Richard Watt is exemplary in this respect.

We might reasonably have expected Richard Watt to conclude his diary on the evening of his first day on shore with Richard 'thanking Providence for His great mercy in preserving us over so dangerous a voyage' (15 Aug. 1864). Like some other diarists, however, he continues for another two days in order to give a description of Brisbane and the surrounding countryside. The passage which then ends the diary recreates, unconsciously no doubt, an idealised version of his arrival in Brisbane:

> On recrossing the river by the ferry I was much struck with the romantic appearance of everything on the banks, the city with all its glittering lights was reflected in the water, and the moon, being just at the full, brought out all the light and shadow of the hills dotted up the country, the curious immovable wavy white clouds encircling the heavens, made in effect the most perfect picture of the kind I ever beheld. This then is my arrival in Australia, a country that has occupied my imagination for many months. (17 Aug. 1864)

Like Christian in Bunyan's journey-story, Watt has arrived at the shining Celestial City, 'the city with all its glittering lights'. And yet this static endpoint to the journey, 'the most perfect picture of the kind I ever beheld', belongs more to someone who thinks himself back at sea than to someone who has already arrived at his destination. The 'curious immovable wavy white clouds' belong to Richard Watt the voyager who has just spent over three months at sea and who is once again on a boat looking towards the horizon. As a picture the whole depends on the perspective of a specific viewer, a bounding of space by the hills in the background and by the river in the foreground, a viewpoint which belongs very definitely to the outsider. Richard Watt is here writing Brisbane according to the cultural viewpoint of a prospective English settler rather than describing a place from the inside. To view the city Richard stands outside it, both physically and culturally, presenting Brisbane as a kind of stage, complete with footlights, back lights, and cloud-like curtains. He is mythologising the landscape in terms of his own journey and the kind of higher destiny to be found in journey-stories like *Pilgrim's Progress*, but to do it, even though he as narrator is clearly already back inside the city, Richard Watt has to adopt the perspective of himself back at sea on his way to Australia. Like Joseph Sams, Richard Watt can only imagine his destination as a Celestial City by imagining himself still on his journey;

he is both in and not in the Promised Land at the same time.

A more apt narrative model that applies to the immigrant at this stage is Coleridge's *Rime of the Ancient Mariner*. The Ancient Mariner undertakes a similar journey of enlightenment, but far from arriving at a self-sufficient destination where his wanderings will end, the mariner is condemned to travel from land to land continually telling and retelling the story of his journey. It is a story which leads to no final telling, no final destination. William Shennan, at the end of his diary, reaches a similar conclusion: 'it is a very wild place here nothing but hills on every side   I have had a hill in front of me sinse I left Plymouth and I beleive I shall never get to the head of it   so endeth my travels' (1870). The paradox of this extraordinary statement lies in the fact of immigrants wanting to believe in the myth of the new life while living what is demonstrably the old; their travels may be over, but they are still not at the Celestial City: like Coleridge's Ancient Mariner, William Shennan 'shall never get to the head of it'.

The diary here, as in many other ways that I have pointed out in the course of this study, allows migrants to hold together contradictory concepts. It makes possible the dialectic between the old and the new, the 'I shall never get to the head of it' and the 'So endeth my travels'. Emigrants wanted to believe in the myth of the New Land, but as this unusually perceptive entry in the diary of an unnamed male passenger on the *Ganges* testifies, they were unlikely to find it in Australia:

> I feel a strange sensation, a 'busy something' within me – a wish that I had been rather destined to accompany Cook, to whose course we have, on the whole, closely adhered, (a splendid navigator Cook was), instead of being in a passenger ship, and prepared, on again setting foot on land, to find the forms, modes, and shows of the old country. ('Life in an Emigrant Ship' 1 Oct 1863)

There are many who would argue that even Cook coasting up the eastern coast of what is now Australia was in search of a land that could never exist. Be that as it may, it is the endings of the journals, the writing of 'So endeth my travels' and the closing of the book, which allows British migrants who find themselves on land and surrounded by 'the forms, modes, and shows of the old country' to believe that they have, nonetheless, reached the New Country. White Australians are to this day trying to live with the implications of that belief.

Bibliography

Abbreviations: AJCP = Australian Joint Copying Project; ANMM = Australian National Maritime Museum; HRR = Historic Records Register; LTC = La Trobe Collection, State Library of Victoria, Melbourne; mfm = microfilm; ML = Mitchell Library, State Library of New South Wales; MMM = Merseyside Maritime Museum, Liverpool; ms = manuscript; NLA = National Library of Australia, Canberra; NMM = National Maritime Museum, Greenwich; OxL = John Oxley Library, Brisbane; PRONI = Public Record Office of Northern Ireland; SSGBP = SS Great Britain Project; ts = typescript.

Primary Sources

Manuscript

A, Mr. Diary on *Clifton*, Liverpool to Launceston, 1837–8. NLA ms 4058.

Allardyce, Hugh. Diary on SS *Great Britain*, Liverpool to Melbourne, 1860. NLA AJCP M2346.

Allbon, Elizabeth. Diary on *Samuel Plimsoll*, Plymouth to Sydney, 1879. NLA ms 1966.

Ankatell, Elizabeth. Diary on *Queen of Australia*, London to Melbourne, 1865–6. PRONI T1769/3 plus NLA AJCP M388 and M389.

Annison, G. Diary on *Emigrant*, London to Melbourne, 1853. NLA ms 3878.

Anon. Diary on *Calphurnia*, London to St Paul's Island, 1853. NLA ms 6119.

Anon. Diary on *Calphurnia*, St Paul's Island to Melbourne, 1853. NLA ms 4143 [continuation of above].

[211]

Anon. Diary on SS *Great Britain*, Liverpool to Melbourne, 1863. NLA ms 193 [in French].

Anon. Diary on SS *Great Britain*, Liverpool to Melbourne, 1863. SSGBP plus NLA AJCP M2346.

Anon. Diary on SS *Great Britain*, Liverpool to Melbourne, 1871. SSGBP plus NLA AJCP M2346.

Anon. Diary on *Kate*, London to Sydney, 1853. ANMM.

Anon. Diary on *Orient*, Plymouth to Adelaide, 1863. ANMM.

Anon. Diary on *Prince Albert*, London to Melbourne, 1852. NLA ms 1363.

Anon. Diary on *Scottish Admiral*, London to Brisbane, 1883. NLA ms 4100 and mfm G24,759.

Barringer, William. Diary on *Superb*, London to Melbourne, 1879. NLA ms 1105 [copy of *'Superb' Gazette*].

Barton, Mr. Diary on *Irene*, London to Adelaide, 1853. NLA ms 2893.

Bird, Edwin. Diary on *Marco Polo*, Liverpool to Melbourne, 1853. NLA ms 6064.

Blasdall, Mark. Diary on *City of Brisbane*, London to Brisbane, 1862. NLA ms 957 and mfm G24,760.

 Bloxsome, Oswald. Diary on *Florentia*, Plymouth to Sydney, 1838. NLA ms 336/1 and ts 336/2.

Blyth, Thomas Bolivar. Diary on *Tropic*, London to Hobart, 1846–7. NLA ms 2310.

Bolton, Charles Henry. Diary on *Lincolnshire*, London to Melbourne, 1872. NMM ms JOD/91.

Braine, Emily. Diary on *Eagle*, Liverpool to Melbourne, 1854–5. NLA ms 8413.

Bray, William. Diary on SS *Great Britain*, Liverpool to Melbourne, 1854. SSGBP plus NLA AJCP M2346 [includes a quarantine diary].

Brennand, Stephen. Diary on *Harbinger*, London to Adelaide, 1883. District Central Library, Rawtenstall plus NLA AJCP M977.

Brown, C. Diary on *Bon Vennue* (or *Ben Venue*?), London to Adelaide, 1858–9. NLA ms 4003 and mfm G7753.

Brown, John. Diary on unnamed ship to Adelaide/Melbourne/Sydney, 1840. NLA AJCP M849 [initial pages missing].

Buchan, Louise. Diary on SS *Great Britain*, Melbourne to Liverpool, 1872. SSGBP plus NLA AJCP M2346.

C., E. Diary on *Hesperus*, London to Adelaide, 1879. NLA ms 4056.

Cairnes, Claudius Beresford. Diary on *James Booth*, London to Melbourne, 1860–1. NLA ms 127.

Campbell, Jessie. Diary on *Blenheim*, Greenock to Wellington, 1840. NMM ms 70/129.

Cannan, Jane and David. Letters on *Hempsyke*, London to Melbourne, 1853. NLA ms 401.

Carter, John. Diary on *General Hewett*, Portsmouth to Sydney, 1844–5. NLA AJCP M1618.

Cashman, Denis. Diary on *Hougoumont*, London to Fremantle, 1867–8. Battye Library, Perth 555A.

Chambers, William. Diary on *Sobraon*, London to Melbourne, 1879. NLA ms 201.

Champion, Thomas. Diary on *Andromache*, London to Melbourne/ Sydney, 1841–2. NLA ms 1093.

Charlesworth, Alfred. Diary on *Columbus*, London to Auckland, 1875. NMM ts TRN/55 [contains two versions].

Clarke, Arthur. Diary on *Conflict*, Plymouth to Melbourne, 1868. NLA ms 6792.

Clarke, William. Diary on *Invercargill*, Greenock to Port Chalmers, 1879. NMM ms TRN/19.

Clifton, Louisa. Diary on *Parkfield*, London to Leschenault Bay (Western Australia), 1840–1. NLA ms 2801.

Cornell, Edward. Diary on *Red Jacket*, Liverpool to Melbourne, 1856. NMM ts TRN/20.

Coy, Thomas. Diary on SS *Doric*, London to Hobart, 1885. NLA ms 7932.

Curr, Henry. Diary on *Morning Light*, Liverpool to Melbourne, 1856. ANMM and MMM DX/908.

Davies, Thomas. Diary on *Lord Raglan*, Plymouth to Adelaide, 1854. NLA ms 200.

Deighton, John T. Diary on *Fred Warren*, Liverpool to Melbourne, 1867. MMM DX/651.

Dodds, Henry. Diary on *Frances*, Liverpool to Sydney, 1853. NLA ms 3850.

D'Ouseley, Rosamond. Diary on SS *Great Britain*, Liverpool to Melbourne, 1869. SSGBP plus NLA AJCP M2346.

Edelsten, Frederick A. Diary on *City of Adelaide*, London to Adelaide, 1867. NLA AJCP M837.

Elliott, Charles. Diary on *Prince of the Seas*, Liverpool to Melbourne, 1861. NLA AJCP M387.

Evans, Alf. Diary on SS *Fifeshire*, London to Fremantle, 1895. NLA ms 7163.

Forbes, J. D. Diary on *Guildford*, Chatham to Sydney, 1827. NLA ms 7565 [guard captain on convict ship].

Forwood, William Bower. Diary on *Red Jacket*, Liverpool to Melbourne, 1857–8. Liverpool Libraries and Information Services plus NLA AJCP M870.

Francis, Edwin. Diary on *Clara Symes*, Bristol to Melbourne, 1852–3. NLA ms 5768.

George. Diary on *Eusemere*, London to Melbourne, 1884–5. NLA ms 7873.

Good, Abijou. Diary on *Beejapore*, London to Rockhampton, 1863. NLA ms 513.

Gordon, James. Diary on *Eliza*, Cork to Sydney, 1832. ANMM [captain of convict ship].

Gosling, Francis. Diary on *Alexander*, London to Hobart/Sydney, 1835. ANMM.

Gratton, Annie. Diary on *Conway*, Liverpool to Melbourne, 1858. NLA ms 3304.

Greaves, George. Diary on SS *Great Britain*, Liverpool to Melbourne, 1867–8. SSGBP plus NLA AJCP M2346.

Hall, Edwin. Diary on *Yorkshire*, London to Melbourne, 1869–70. NLA ms 3688.

Hamilton, Andrew. Diary on *Birmingham*, Liverpool to Melbourne, 1852. NLA AJCP M862.

Hamilton, William. Diary on *North Briton*, Firth of Forth to Hobart/Sydney, 1837. NLA ms 2117.

Harbottle, William. Diary on *Scotia*, London to Sydney, 1848. NLA ms 828.

Harding, Henry. Diary on *Ida*, Liverpool to Melbourne, 1853. NLA AJCP M674.

Harvey, H. Letters on *Norfolk*, London to Melbourne, 1867–8. NLA ms 4009.

Haslett, S. T. 'Notes on the Passage Out,' *Calcutta*, 1842. NLA ms 7385.

Hedges, John. Diary on *Admiral Lyons*, Liverpool to Sydney, 1858–9. MMM DX/243/1.

Higgins, Henry. Diary on *Eurynome*, Liverpool to Melbourne, 1869–70. NLA ms 1057.

Higson, Daniel. Diary on SS *Great Britain*, Liverpool to Melbourne, 1869. The Harris Library, Preston plus NLA AJCP M2501.

Hoare, Frederick. Diary on *Red Jacket*, Liverpool to Melbourne, 1854. NLA AJCP M405 (also return voyage 1856).

Hodgson, Arthur. Diary on *Royal George*, Portsmouth to Sydney, 1839. NLA AJCP M675 (also return voyage 1848).

—. Diary on *Arbuthnot*, Plymouth to Sydney, 1849–50. NLA AJCP M790.

Hope, Louis. Diary on unnamed ship, Portsmouth to Sydney, 1843. NLA AJCP M980.

Hopkins, James. Diary on *Schomberg*, Liverpool to Melbourne, 1855. NMM ms XJOD/1.

Hufton, Edward. Diary on *Northbrook*, Plymouth to Sydney, 1879. NLA AJCP M2813.

Hughes, Joshua. Diary on *Montmorency*, Liverpool to Brisbane, 1863. Cumbria Record Office BDX 170 plus NLA AJCP M2078.

Hunt, Atlee. Diary on *Resolute*(?), Plymouth to Sydney, 1852–3. NLA ms 1100.

Jemima. Diary on *Star of the East*(?), Liverpool to Melbourne/Sydney, 1853. NLA AJCP M591.

Joseland, John. Diary on *Salsette*, Portsmouth to Melbourne, 1853. NMM ms 77/028.

Joseph, Solomon. Diary on *Morning Star*, Liverpool to Melbourne, 1859. NLA ms 6395.

Kennaway, William and Laurence. Diary on *Canterbury*, London to Lyttelton, 1851. NLA ms 4249. [published 1973]

Kershaw, George. Diary on *Columbine*, Liverpool to Sydney, 1841. ML mss FM4/1629 plus NLA AJCP M435.

Key, Benjamin. Diary on *Pestonjee Bomanjee*, London to Adelaide, 1838. ANMM.

Knight, Henry. Diary on *Java*, London to Sydney, 1852–3. NLA ms 3169.

Learmonth, Agnes. Diary on *Elizabeth Ann Bright*, Greenock to Brisbane, 1864. OxL OM83–17.

Loraine, William. Diary on *Lord Warden*, London to Melbourne (?), 1877. NLA AJCP M942 [died on board].

Lord, Richard. Diary on SS *Austral*, London to Melbourne/Sydney, 1882. NLA AJCP M1859.

Lovell, John. Diary on *Elizabeth*, Bristol to Melbourne, 1853. NLA AJCP M401 and NMM ms JOD/79 (crew member).

Ludlow, John. Diary on *Andromeda*, Portsmouth to Hobart, 1822–3. NLA ms 4166.

M, Mr. Diary on *La Hogue*, Plymouth to Sydney (?), 1877. ANMM.

MacAndrew, I. F. Diary on *Harbinger*, London to Adelaide, 1876–7. NLA ms 5521/1.

McCaul, Gilbert. Diary on *Sea Star*, Greenock to Melbourne, 1855. NLA mfm G21,338.

McDonald, Duncan. Diary on *Glen Ormond*, London to Adelaide, 1871. NLA ms 8156.

MacGillivray, Marjory Colquhoun. Diary on *Torrens*, London to Adelaide, 1893–4. NMM ms JOD/78 plus mfm SMF/89.

MacKenzie, John. Diary on *Robert Benn*, Greenock to Melbourne, 1841–2. NLA ms 685.

Maclean, Mary. Diary on *Africana*, Liverpool to Sydney, 1864–5. HRR 2544.

Manning, Arthur Wilcox. Diary on *Earl Grey*, Plymouth to Sydney, 1839–40. NLA ms 289.

Martin, John. Diary on *Mountstuart Elphinstone*, Cork to Sydney, 1849. PRONI D560.2 plus NLA AJCP M387 [state prisoner on convict ship].

Massingberd, Peregrine Langton. Diary on *Edward Lombe*, London to Hobart, 1832. NLA AJCP M719.

Mathew, Felton. Diary on *Morley*, Sheerness to Sydney, 1829. NLA ms 15.

Matthews, Daniel. Diary on SS *Somersetshire*, London to Melbourne, 1870. NLA ms 2195/3/1–4.

Meade, Henry White. Letter to Susan Meade on her marriage, 1 Aug. 1848. LTC ms 11382.

Meade, Susan. Diary on *Caledonia*, London to Melbourne, 1842. NLA ms 4053 plus LTC ms 11382.

Menzies, Margaret. Diary on *Earl Durham*, London to Sydney, 1838–9. NLA ms 3261 [wife of Robert Menzies].

Menzies, Dr. Robert. Diary on *Hope*, London to Sydney, 1836–7. NLA ms 3282 [husband of Margaret Menzies].

Miller, Thomas F. Diary on *Walmer Castle*, London to Melbourne, 1869–70. NMM ms JOD/180 plus ts TRN/180.

Mort, Thomas. Diary on *Superb*, Liverpool to Hobart/Sydney, 1837–8. NLA ms 3308.

Murray, James. Diary on *Hyderabad*, Southampton to Adelaide, 1853–4. ANMM.

Nichols, William. Diary on *James Gibb*, London to Sydney, 1849. NLA ms 8166.

Parrington, Joseph. Letter account of voyage on *Storm King*, London to Brisbane, 1869–70. NLA ms 1384 [part verse].

Pearson, George. Diary on *Lady Jocelyn*, London to Auckland, 1880–1. NLA AJCP M979.

Pegler, Edwin S. Diary on *Prince Albert*, London to Melbourne, 1852. NLA ms 3128.

Peters, Edmund. Diary on *Chowinghee*, Melbourne to London, 1853. NLA AJCP M830 [return trip].

Pillow, Samuel. Diary on *Digby*, Liverpool to Melbourne, 1853. PRONI T634 plus NLA ms 914 plus AJCP M388.

Randall, George. Diary on *Planet*, London to Brisbane, 1868. NLA ms 2107.

Rawson, Samuel. Diary on *Florentia*, Plymouth to Sydney, 1838. NLA ms 204/1.

Reay, William. Diary on *Parramatta*, London to Sydney, 1877. NLA ms 2586.

Reeves, J. W. Diary on *Queen of the West* (or *Queen of the North*), 1856. NLA ms 6442 plus HRR 541.

Ricou, J. P. Diary on *Indus*, London to Brisbane, 1872. NLA AJCP M437 plus M469.

Roberts, S. E. Diary on *Symmetry*, London to Adelaide, 1848. NLA ms 3272.

Ronald, Byron. Diary on *Heart of Oak*, Liverpool to Melbourne, 1853. NLA ms 2758 [brother of Janet and Helen].

Ronald, Helen. Diary on SS *Great Britain*, Liverpool to Melbourne, 1861. NLA ms 2758 [sister of Janet and Byron].

Ronald, Janet. Diary on *Invincible*, Liverpool to Melbourne, 1857. NLA ms 2758 [sister of Helen and Byron].

Saddington, Robert. Diary on SS *Great Britain*, Liverpool to Melbourne/Sydney, 1853. ANMM.

Sceales, John. Diary on *North Briton*, Leith to Hobart/Sydney, 1838–9. NLA ms 2717.

Severn, Thomas. Diary on *Prince Alfred*, London to Melbourne, 1852. NLA ms 710 plus NMM PST/42.

Shaw, Samuel. Diary on *Tyburnia*, Plymouth to Sydney, 1877–8. NLA ms 2829.

Shennan, William. Diary on *Crusader*, Plymouth to Melbourne, 1870. NLA ms 596.

Sheraton, Richard B. Diary on *Duke of Wellington*, Liverpool to Melbourne, 1852. NLA ms 4061.

Smith, Alexander. Diary on *Norfolk*, London to Melbourne, 1867. NLA ms 5599.

Smith, Rev. John Jennings. Diary on *Amelia Thompson*, Plymouth to Sydney, 1839. ANMM.

Stack, Mary. Diary on *Andromache*, Plymouth to Sydney, 1837. HRR 2201.

Stamp, Edward. Diary on *Tasman*, London to Melbourne, 1849. NLA ms 29.

Stapleton, Bryan. Diary on *True Briton*, Deal to Wellington, 1852. NLA ms 4054.

Steley, Maria. Diary on *Ariadne*, Liverpool to Brisbane, 1863–4. OxL OM71–14 plus M418.

Stobart, Rev. Henry. Diary on *Resolute*, Plymouth to Sydney, 1852–3. NLA ms 1033 plus AJCP M467.

Tait, Mr. Letter account of voyage on *North Briton*, Firth of Forth to Hobart/Sydney, 1837. NLA ms 1412.

Taylor, Francis C. Diary on *Stag*, London to Adelaide, 1850. NLA AJCP M2514 plus NMM ms JOD/75.

Taylor, Harriet. Diary on *Wilmot*, London to Sydney, 1839–40. NLA ms 2009.

Thompson, William. Diary on *Donald McKay*, Liverpool to Melbourne, 1857. LTC ms 5631.

Thornton, Frances. Diary on *Selkirkshire*, Glasgow to Rockhampton, 1882. Devon Record Office ms 877 M/F 1.

Thorpe, D. Losh. Diary on unnamed ship, London to Melbourne, 1888. NLA ms 2693.

Tindall, Grace. Diary on *Anna*(?), Liverpool to Sydney, 1856–7. NLA ms 3281.

Towle, Edward. Diary on SS *Great Britain*, Liverpool to Cape Town, 1852. NLA AJCP M2345 plus NMM NAI/2/24.

Townsend, William. Diary on *York*, London to Rio de Janeiro, 1825. NLA ms 112 [working passage as captain's clerk].

Turner, Alexander. Diary on *Eastern Monarch*, Greenock to Townsville, 1883. Scottish Record Office GDI/806 plus NLA AJCP M1131.

Turner, Isabella. Diary on *Wimmera*, London to Melbourne, 1868. NMM ts XJOD/6.

Vickers, Thomas Rogers. Diary on *Enterprise*, London to Adelaide, 1851–2. NLA ms 4220 [midshipman's log].

Waight, J. R. Diary on *Patriarch*, London to Sydney, 1882. NMM ms NAI/2/24.

Walker, James. Account of voyage on SS *Great Britain*, Liverpool to Melbourne, 1867–8. SSGBP plus NLA AJCP M2346.

Walpole, J. Kidd. Diary on *Andromache*, Plymouth to Sydney, 1837. NLA ms 4073.

Walpole, Margaret. Diary on SS *Pathan*, London to Albany, 1883. NLA ms 2209.

Ward, John. Diary kept on *Norfolk Island*, 1841–2. NLA ms 3275.

Watt, Richard. Diary on *Young Australia*, London to Brisbane, 1864. *Sea Breezes* no. 21 (1956); pp. 162–8, 250–6, 318–23, 408–15; no. 22 (1957); pp. 12–16, 82–92.

West, Theo. Diary on *Palmyra*, London to Sydney, 1853–4. NLA ms 3660.

Westmoreland, Charles. Diary on *Melpomene*, Plymouth to Rockhampton, 1882–3. NLA AJCP M2348.

White, James Espie. Diary on *Henry Fernie*, Liverpool to Melbourne, 1862. Edinburgh City Libraries plus NLA AJCP M864.

Whiting, E. Diary on *Henry*, London to Launceston, 1835–6. NLA ms 149.

Whitings, John Warren. Diary on *Lightning*, Liverpool to Melbourne, 1854. NLA ms 5071.

Whittingham, Henry. Diary on *Duke of Wellington*, London to Sydney, 1853. NLA ms 8433.

—. Letter book, 1852–69. NLA ms 8433.

Widdowson, Henry. Diary on *Albion*, London to Hobart, 1825–6. NLA AJCP M2116.

Wills, William Charles. Diary on *Louisa*, London to Sydney, 1841–2. Thomas Coram Foundation for Children, London plus NLA AJCP M934.

Withers, Alfred. Diary on *James Baines*, Liverpool to Melbourne, 1857. NMM ms JOD/171 plus mfm SMF/258.

Woolley, Harry. Diary on *Roman Emperor*, London to Sydney, 1850–1. NLA ms 955.

Published

Annual Reports of the Colonial Land and Emigration Commissioners 1840–1870. Rpt. as vols 10–18 of *British Parliamentary Papers: Emigration*. Shannon: Irish UP, 1969.

Anon. [Diary on *Ganges*, London to Auckland, 1863.] 'Life in an Emigrant Ship: Journal of a Voyage to New Zealand in Ship "Ganges" '. NLA ms 4145 [unnamed periodical].

Anon. [Diary on SS *Great Britain*, Liverpool to St Helena, 1852.] *Times*

Plymouth Any Port in Queensland 1848-18 1868

13 Nov. 1852: 8 plus Supplement 1.

C., N. [Diary on *Derwent*, Portsmouth to Adelaide, 1848–9] *Journal of a Voyage from England to Port Adelaide*. London: George Mann, 1849.

Campbell, Jessie. [Diary on *Blenheim*, Greenock to Wellington, 1840] *Women Under Sail*. Eds Basil Greenhill and Ann Giffard. Newton Abbot, Devon: David & Charles, 1974.

Canterbury Papers: Information Concerning the Principles, Objects, Plans and Proceedings of the Founders of the Settlement of Canterbury in New Zealand. London: np 1850.

Capper, John. *Philips' Emigrant's Guide to Australia*. 1856. Ed. D. J. Golding. Melbourne: Hawthorne Press, 1973.

Cook, Captain James. *The Voyage of the 'Endeavour'*. Ed. J. C. Beaglehole. Cambridge: CUP, 1955.

Corkhill, Robert. [Diary on *British Trident*, Liverpool to Melbourne, 1855.] *Digger* 13 Jan–16 Feb 1974; 16 Feb–23 Mar 1974.

Davis, Fanny. [Diary on *Conway*, Liverpool to Melbourne, 1858.] *The Long Farewell*. Ed. Don Charlwood. Ringwood, Vict.: Allen Lane, 1981.

Earp, G. Butler. *The Gold Colonies of Australia and Gold Seeker's Manual*. London: Routledge, 1853.

The Emigrant's Manual: Australia. Edinburgh: William and Robert Chambers, 1851.

Fenton, Elizabeth. [Diary on *Denmark Hill*, Mauritius to Hobart, 1829.] *The Journal of Mrs Fenton 1826–30*. London: Edward Arnold, 1901.

Fenwick, John. *The 'Lightning' Diary of John Fenwick*. [Diary on *Lightning*, Liverpool to Melbourne, 1854.] Ed. I. Wynd. Geelong: Geelong Historical Society, 1969.

Field, Barron (ed.), *Geographical Memoirs on New South Wales*. London: Murray, 1825.

First Annual Report of the British Ladies' Female Emigrant Society. London: British Ladies' Female Emigrant Society, 1850.

Fowler, Anna. [Diary on *Alfred Hawley*, London to Brisbane, 1866.] *A Victorian Engagement*. Ed. Bertram Hume. St Lucia, Qld.: University of Queensland Press, 1975.

Gouger, Robert. [Diary on *Africaine*, London to South Australia, 1836.] *The Voyage of the Africaine*. Ed. Penelope Hope. Melbourne: Heinemann, 1968.

Greenhalgh, William Culshaw. [Diary on *Marco Polo*, Liverpool to Melbourne, 1853.] *The Passage Makers*. Ed. M. K. Stammers.

[220]

Brighton: Teredo, 1978.

Griffiths, John. [Diary on *Euterpe*, London to Lyttelton, 1875–6.] *'Euterpe': Diaries, Letters & Logs of the 'Star of India' as a British Emigrant Ship*. Ed. Arnold Craig. San Diego, CA: Maritime Museum Association of San Diego, 1988.

Henning, Amy. [Diary on *Calcutta*, Southampton to Melbourne/ Sydney, 1854.] *The Sea Journals of Annie and Amy Henning*. Ed. Joan Thomas. Sydney: Halstead, 1984.

Henning, Annie. [Diary on SS *Great Britain*, Liverpool to Melbourne/ Sydney, 1853.] *The Sea Journals of Annie and Amy Henning*. Ed. Joan Thomas. Sydney: Halstead, 1984.

Henning, Rachel. *The Letters of Rachel Henning*. Sydney: Angus & Robertson,1986.

Hinshelwood, Mrs. Thomas. [Diary on *Nebo*, Glasgow to Rockhampton, 1883.] *Port of Melbourne Quarterly* Oct–Dec (1963), pp. 33–41; Jan–Mar (1964), pp. 32–7.

Hume, Walter. [Diary on *Pera*, *Bengal*, and *Madras*, Southampton to Sydney, 1862–3.] *A Victorian Engagement*. Ed. Bertram Hume. St Lucia, Qld.: University Of Queensland Press, 1975.

Johnstone, William. [Diary on *Arab*, London to Launceston, 1841–2.] *Women Under Sail*. Ed. Basil Greenhill and Ann Giffard. Newton Abbot, Devon: David & Charles, 1974.

Kingston, W. H. G. *The Emigrant Voyager's Manual*. London: Trelawney Saunders, 1850.

—. *The Emigrant's Home*. London: Groombridge, 1856.

—. *The Fortunes of the 'Ranger' and 'Crusader'*. London: Gall & Inglis, 1872.

—. *How to Emigrate*. London: Groombridge, 1855.

Lacey, Edward. [Diary on *Orient*, London to Adelaide, 1862.] *Diaries from the Days of Sail*. Ed. R. C. Bell. New York: Holt, 1974.

Lightoller, Dr. Henry Martin. [Diary on *Scottish Bard*, London to Rockhampton, 1878.] *Dog Watch* 20 (1963), pp. 19–32; 21 (1964), pp. 97–114.

Lister, George J. [Diary on *Euterpe*, London to Lyttelton, 1879.] *'Euterpe': Diaries, Letters & Logs of the 'Star of India' as a British Emigrant Ship*. Ed. Arnold Craig. San Diego, CA: Maritime Museum Association of San Diego, 1988.

McCrae, Georgiana. [Diary on *Argyle*, London to Melbourne, 1840–1.] *Georgiana's Journal*. Ed. Hugh McCrae. Sydney: Angus & Robertson, 1992.

MacKenzie, Eneas. *MacKenzie's Australian Emigrant's Guide*. London: MacKenzie, 1852.

Melchior, Moses. [Diary on *Gauntlet*, London to Melbourne, 1853.] *Dog Watch* 30 (1973), pp. 79–93.

Midgley, Sarah. [Diary on *Agnes*, Liverpool to Melbourne, 1851.] *The Diaries of Sarah Midgley and Richard Skilbeck 1851–1864*. Melbourne: Cassell, 1967.

Mitchell, Thomas. [Diary on *Othello*, London to Hobart/Sydney, 1833.] *Voyage of the 'Othello'*. Ed. C. M. and N. B. Abbott. York: William Sessions, 1988.

Moore, George Fletcher. [Diary] *Settlers: Being Extracts from the Journals and Letters of Early Colonists in Canada, Australia, South Africa, and New Zealand*. Ed. John Hale. London: Faber, 1950.

Prout, J. S. *An Illustrated Handbook of the Voyage to Australia and a Visit to the Gold Fields*. [London?], n.p., 1852?

Sams, Joseph. [Diary on *Northumberland*, London to Melbourne, 1874.] *The Diary of Joseph Sams*. Ed. Simon Braydon and Robert Songhurst. London: HMSO, 1982.

Sayer, Will. [Diary on *Samuel Plimsoll*, London to Sydney, 1876.] *The Diary of Will Sayer*. Parks, NSW: Parks & District Historical Society, 1989.

Sidney, Samuel. *The Three Colonies of Australia*. London: Ingram, Cooke, 1852.

Sidney's Australian Hand-Book: How to Settle and Succeed in Australia. London: Richardson, 1848.

Skilbeck, Richard. [Diary on *Salem*, Liverpool to Melbourne, 1858.] *The Diaries of Sarah Midgley and Richard Skilbeck 1851–1864*. Melbourne: Cassell, 1967.

Snell, Edward. [Diary on *Bolton*, London to Adelaide, 1849.] *The Life and Adventures of Edward Snell*. Ed. Tom Griffiths. Sydney: Angus & Robertson, 1988.

Stones, William. *New Zealand (the Land of Promise) and its Resources*. London: Shaw, Savill, 1859.

Sturt, Charles. *Two Expeditions into the Interior of Southern Australia*. London: Smith, Elder, 1833.

Taylor, Sophia. [Diary on *Candahar*, London to Adelaide, 1851.] *Sophy Under Sail*. Ed. Irene C. Taylor. Sydney: Hodder & Stoughton, 1969.

Thomas, Mary. [Diary on *Africaine*, London to South Australia, 1836.] *The Voyage of the Africaine*. Ed. Penelope Hope. Melbourne: Heinemann, 1968.

[222]

Trotter, Thomas. [Diary on *Duchess of Northumberland*, Cork to Sydney, 1836.] *A Diary by Thomas Trotter*. Stafford Heights, Qld.: Ted White, 1984.

Were, Jonathan Binns. [Diary on *William Metcalfe*, Plymouth to Melbourne, 1839.] *A Voyage from Plymouth to Melbourne in 1839*. Melbourne: J. B. Were & Son, 1964 plus NMM ts TRN/28.

Secondary Sources

Altick, Richard D. *The Shows of London*. Cambridge, MA: Harvard UP, 1978.

Andrews, Malcolm. *The Search for the Picturesque: Landscape Aesthetics and Tourism in Britain, 1760–1800*. Aldershot: Scolar, 1989.

Arnold, Craig (ed.), *'Euterpe': Diaries, Letters & Logs of the 'Star of India' as a British Emigrant Ship*. San Diego, CA: Maritime Museum Association of San Diego, 1988.

Arnold, Rollo. *The Farthest Promised Land*. Wellington: Victory UP, 1981.

Bach, John. *A Maritime History of Australia*. Melbourne: Nelson, 1976.

Baines, Dudley. *Emigration from Europe 1815–1930*. London: Macmillan, 1991.

Ball, Adrian, and Diana Wright. *SS Great Britain*. Newton Abbot, Devon: David & Charles, 1981.

Barrell, John. *The Idea of Landscape and the Sense of Place 1730–1840*. Cambridge: Cambridge UP, 1972.

Bell, R. C. (ed.), *Diaries from the Days of Sail*. New York: Holt, 1974.

Benveniste, Emile. *Problems in General Linguistics*. Trans. Mary Elizabeth Meek. Coral Gables, FL: University of Miami Press, 1971.

Birch, Brian P. 'British Evaluations of the Forest Openings and Prairie Edges of the North–Central States, 1800–1850'. *The Frontier: Comparative Studies* vol. 2. Ed. William W. Savage, Jr., and Stephen I. Thompson. Norman, OK: University of Oklahoma Press, 1979 pp. 167–92.

Bishop, Peter. *The Myth of Shangri-La: Tibet, Travel Writing and the Western Creation of Sacred Landscape*. London: Athlone, 1989.

Borrie, W. D. 'The Population'. *Australian Society*. Ed. Keith Hancock. Cambridge: Cambridge UP, 1989.

Brooks, Peter. *Reading for the Plot: Design and Intention in Narrative*. Oxford: Oxford UP, 1984.

Brown, Martyn. *Australia Bound! The Story of West Country Con-*

nections, 1688–1888. Bradford on Avon: Ex Libris, 1988.

Bunkers, Suzanne L. 'Midwestern diaries and journals: what women were (not) saying in the late 1800s', *Studies in Autobiography*. Ed. James Olney. Oxford: Oxford UP, 1988, pp. 190–210.

Buzard, James. *The Beaten Track: European Tourism, Literature, and the Ways to 'Culture' 1800–1918*. Oxford: Oxford UP, 1993.

Carter, Paul. *Living in a New Country: History, Travelling and Language*. London: Faber, 1992.

—. *The Road to Botany Bay: An Essay in Spatial History*. London: Faber, 1987.

Castro, Brian. *Birds of Passage*. Sydney: Allen & Unwin, 1983.

Certeau, Michel de. *The Practice of Everyday Life*. Trans. Steven F. Rendall. Berkeley, CA: University of California Press, 1984.

Charlwood, Don. *The Long Farewell: Settlers Under Sail*. Melbourne: Allen Lane, 1981.

Clarke, Patricia. *The Governesses: Letters from the Colonies 1862–1882*. London: Hutchinson, 1985.

—, and Dale Spender. *Life Lines: Australian Women's Letters and Diaries*. Sydney: Allen & Unwin, 1992.

Cochrane, Peter, and David Goodman. 'The Great Australian Journey: Cultural Logic and Nationalism in the Postmodern Era.' *Australian Historical Studies* 23.91 (1988), pp. 21–44.

Coleman, Terry. *Passage to America*. London: Hutchinson, 1972.

Colligan, Mimi. 'Canvas and wax: images of information in Australian panoramas and waxworks 1849–1920'. Diss. Monash University, 1987.

Cosgrove, Denis E. 'Prospect, perspective and the evolution of the landscape idea'. *Transactions, the Institute of British Geographers* 10 (1985), pp. 45–62.

—. *Social Formation and Symbolic Landscape*. London: Croom Helm, 1984.

Cressy, David. *Coming Over: Migration and Communication between England and New England in the Seventeenth Century*. Cambridge: Cambridge UP, 1987.

Dening, Greg. *Mr Bligh's Bad Language: Passion, Power and Theatre on the Bounty*. Cambridge: Cambridge UP, 1992.

Donaldson, Ian, and Tamsin Donaldson (eds), *Seeing the First Australians*. Sydney: Allen & Unwin, 1985.

Donaldson, Marsha. 'Shipboard accounts of voyages 1840–1900'. *Proceedings of the 1991 Hawkes Bay Genealogy Conference*. pp. 89–104.

Erickson, Charlotte (ed), *Emigration from Europe 1815–1914*: Select Documents. London: A & C Black, 1976.

—. *Invisible Immigrants: The Adaptation of English and Scottish Immigrants in 19th Century America*. Leicester: Leicester UP, 1972.

Field, Trevor. *Form and Function in the Diary Novel*. Basingstoke: Macmillan, 1989.

Fiske, John, Bob Hodge, and Graeme Turner. *Myths of Oz: Reading Australian Popular Culture*. Sydney: Allen & Unwin, 1987.

Fitzpatrick, David. ' "Oceans of consolation": letters and Irish immigration to Australasia'. *Visible Immigrants*. Ed. David Fitzpatrick, pp. 47–86.

—. ' "Over the foaming billows": the organisation of Irish emigration to Australia'. *Poor Australian Immigrants in the Nineteenth Century*. Ed. Eric Richards, pp. 133–52.

— (ed.), *Home or Away? Immigrants in Colonial Australia*. Canberra: Research School of Social Sciences, Australian National University, 1992.

—. *Visible Immigrants: Neglected Sources for the History of Australian Immigration*. Canberra: Research School of Social Sciences, Australian National University, 1989.

Fletcher, John. 'German diaries, Australiana and literary manuscripts (1550–1850) in Australia'. *Australian Universities Modern Language Association* 45 (1976), pp. 36–53.

Foucault, Michel. *Discipline and Punish: The Birth of the Prison*. Trans. Alan Sheridan. 1975. Harmondsworth: Penguin, 1979.

Frost, Lucy. *No Place for a Nervous Lady: Voices from the Australian Bush*. Melbourne: McPhee Gribble; Melbourne: Penguin, 1984.

Frow, John. 'Michel de Certeau and the Practice of Representation'. *Cultural Studies* 5.1 (1991): pp. 52–60.

Garrett, Richard. *The Search for Prosperity: Emigration from Britain 1815–1930*. London: Wayland, 1973.

Gennep, Arnold van. *The Rites of Passage*. London: Routledge, 1960.

Gibson, Ross. *The Diminishing Paradise: Changing Literary Perceptions of Australia*. Sydney: Angus & Robertson, 1984.

—. *South of the West: Postcolonialism and the Narrative Construction of Australia*. Bloomington and Indianapolis, IN: Indiana UP, 1992.

Goodman, David. 'Gold fields/golden fields: the language of agrarianism and the Victorian gold rush'. *Australian Historical Studies* 23.90 (1988), pp. 19–41.

—. 'Reading gold-rush travellers' narratives', *Australian Cultural*

History 10 (1991), pp. 99–112.

Gothard, Janice. ' "Pity the poor immigrant": assisted single female migration to colonial Australia'. *Poor Australian Immigrants in the Nineteenth Century*. Ed. Eric Richards, pp. 97–116.

Greenhill, Basil (ed.), *The Great Migration: Crossing the Atlantic under Sail*. London: HMSO, 1968.

—, and Ann Giffard. *Travelling by Sea in the Nineteenth Century: Interior Design in Victorian Passenger Ships*. London: A & C Black, 1972.

—. *Women under Sail: Letters and Journals Concerning Eight Women Travelling or Working in Sailing Vessels between 1829 and 1949*. Newton Abbot, Devon: David & Charles, 1974.

Hale, John (ed.), *Settlers: Being Extracts from the Journals and Letters of Early Colonists in Canada, Australia, South Africa, and New Zealand*. London: Faber, 1950.

Hampsten, Elizabeth. *Read This Only to Yourself: The Private Writings of Midwestern Women 1880–1910*. Bloomington, IN: Indiana UP, 1982.

—. 'Tell me all you know: reading letters and diaries of rural women.' *Teaching Women's Literature from a Regional Perspective*. Ed. L. Hoffman and D. Rosenfeld. NY: MLA, 1982, pp. 55–63.

Harper, Marjory. *Emigration from North-East England* vol. 1. Aberdeen: Aberdeen UP, 1988.

Himmelfarb, Gertrude. *The Idea of Poverty: England in the Early Industrial Age*. New York: Knopf, 1984.

Hogan, Rebecca. 'Engendered autobiographies: the diary as a feminine form'. *Prose Studies* 14 (1991), pp. 95–107.

Hope, Penelope. *The Voyage of the Africaine*. Melbourne: Heinemann Educational Australia, 1968.

Hyde, Ralph. *Gilded Scenes and Shining Prospects: Panoramic Views of British Towns 1575–1900*. New Haven, CT: Yale Centre for British Art, 1985.

—. *Panoramania! The Art and Entertainment of the 'All-Embracing' View*. London: Trefoil, 1988.

Jupp, James (ed.), *An Encyclopedia of the Australian People*. Sydney: Angus & Robertson, 1988.

Letts Keep a Diary: A History of Diary Keeping in Great Britain from 16th–20th Century. London: Charles Letts, 1987.

Lloyd, Lewis. *Australians from Wales*. Caernarfon: Gwynedd Archives, 1988.

Lyons, Martin, and Lucy Taksa. *Australian Readers Remember: An Oral History of Reading 1890–1930*. Melbourne: Oxford UP, 1992.

Lyotard, Jean-François. *The Post-Modern Condition: A Report on Knowledge*. Trans. Geoff Bennington and Brian Massumi. Manchester: Manchester UP,1986.

MacDonagh, Oliver. *A Pattern of Government Growth: The Passenger Acts and their Enforcement*. London: MacGibbon & Kee, 1961.

MacDonald, Charlotte. *A Woman of Good Character: Single Women as Immigrant Settlers in Nineteenth-Century New Zealand*. Wellington: Allen & Unwin; Wellington: Bridget Williams, 1990.

Martin, Stephen. *A New Land: European Perceptions of Australia 1788–1850*. Sydney: Allen & Unwin, 1993.

Mayne, Alan. 'An Italian Traveller in the Antipodes: an Historical Rite of Passage', *Australian Cultural History* 10 (1991), pp. 58–68.

Mink, Louis O. 'History and Fiction as Modes of Comprehension'. *New Literary History* 1 (1970), pp. 541–58.

—. 'Narrative Form and Cognitive Instrument'. *The Writing of History: Literary Form and Historical Understanding*. Ed. Robert H. Canary and Henry Kozicki. Madison, WI: University of Wisconsin Press, 1978, pp. 129–49.

Moore, Bryce, Helen Garwood, and Nancy Lutton. *The Voyage Out: 100 Years of Sea Travel to Australia*. Fremantle: Fremantle Arts Press, 1991.

Moorhouse, Frank. *Tales of Mystery and Romance*. 1977; rpt. Sydney: Angus & Robertson, 1988.

Nadel, George. *Australia's Colonial Culture: Ideas, Men and Institutions in Mid-Nineteenth Century Eastern Australia*. Cambridge, MA: Harvard UP, 1957.

Nicholson, Ian. *Log of Logs: A Catalogue of Logs, Journals, Shipboard Diaries, Letters, and All Forms of Voyage Narratives for Australia and New Zealand, and Surrounding Oceans*. 2 vols. Aranda, ACT: Roebuck Society, n.d. and 1993.

Nunn, Pamela Gerrish. 'Look homeward angel: Marshall Claxton's emigrant'. *Art Bulletin of Victoria* 32 (1991): 1–20.

O'Farrell, Patrick. *The Irish in Australia*. Sydney: NSW UP, 1986.

—. *Letters from Irish Australia 1825–1929*. Sydney: NSW UP; Belfast: Ulster Historical Foundation, 1984.

Pearson, Michael. 'Travellers, Journeys, Tourists: The Meanings of Journeys'. *Australian Cultural History* 10 (1991), pp. 125–34.

Pratt, Mary Louise. *Imperial Eyes: Travel Writing and Trans-*

culturation. London: Routledge, 1992.

—. 'Scratches on the face of the country; or, what Mr. Barrow saw in the land of the Bushman'. *Critical Inquiry* 12 (1985–6), pp. 119–43.

Rée, Jonathan. *Philosophical Tales: An Essay on Philosophy and Literature*. London: Methuen, 1987.

Reece, Bob. *Australia the Beckoning Continent: Nineteenth-Century Emigration Literature*. London: Institute of Commonwealth Studies, University of London, 1988.

Renza, Louis A. 'The veto of the imagination: a theory of auto-biography'. *Autobiography: Essays Theoretical and Critical*. Ed. James Olney. Princeton, NJ: Princeton UP, 1980. 268–95.

Richards, Eric. 'Annals of the Australian immigrant'. *Visible Immigrants*. Ed. David Fitzpatrick, pp. 7–22.

—. 'British poverty and Australian immigration in the nineteenth century'. *Poor Australian Immigrants in the Nineteenth Century*. Ed. Eric Richards, pp. 1–30.

—. 'Return migration and migrant strategies in colonial Australia'. *Home or Away? Immigrants in Colonial Australia*. Ed. David Fitzpatrick, pp. 64–104.

—. 'Voices of British and Irish migrants in nineteenth-century Australia'. *Migrants, Emigrants and Immigrants: A Social History of Migration*. Eds Colin G. Pooley and Ian D. White. London: Routledge, 1991, pp. 19–41.

— (ed.). *Poor Australian Immigrants in the Nineteenth Century*. Canberra: Research School of Social Sciences, Australian National University, 1991.

Rickard, John. *Australia: A Cultural History*. London: Longman, 1988.

Robson, L. L. *The Convict Settlers of Australia*. Melbourne: Melbourne UP, 1965.

Rowley, Sue. 'The journey's end: women's mobility and confinement'. *Australian Cultural History* 10 (1991): 69–83.

Ryan, Simon. 'Exploring aesthetics: the picturesque appropriation of land in journals of Australian exploration'. *Australian Literary Studies* 15 (1992), pp. 282–93.

Savill, David. *Sail to New Zealand: The Story of Shaw, Savill & Co 1858–1882*. London: Hale, 1986.

Schofield, R. S. 'Dimensions of illiteracy, 1750–1850'. *Explorations in Economic History* 10.4 (1973), pp. 437–454.

Seddon, George. 'The evolution of perceptual attitudes'. *Man and Landscape in Australia*. Ed. George Seddon and Mari Davis.

Canberra: Australian Government Publishing Service, 1976, pp. 9–46.

Sherington, Geoffrey. *Australia's Immigrants 1788–1978*. Sydney: Allen & Unwin, 1980.

Simmons, Jack. *The Victorian Railway*. London: Thames and Hudson, 1991.

Smith, Bernard. *European Vision and the South Pacific*. New Haven: Yale UP,1985.

Stammers, Michael K. *The Passage Makers*. Brighton: Teredo, 1978.

Staniforth, Mark. 'Deficiency disorder: evidence of the occurrence of scurvy on convict and emigrant ships to Australia 1837–1839'. *The Great Circle* 13.2 (1991), pp. 119–32.

Todorov, Tzvetan. *The Poetics of Prose*. Trans. Richard Howard. Ithaca, NY: Cornell UP, 1977.

Turner, Victor. 'Social dramas and stories about them'. *Critical Inquiry* 7 (1980): 141–68.

Vincent, David. *Bread, Knowledge and Freedom: A Study of Nineteenth-Century Working Class Autobiography*. London: Europa, 1981.

Webb, R. K. *The British Working Class Reader 1790–1848: Literacy and Social Tension*. London: Allen & Unwin, 1955.

White, Richard. *Inventing Australia: Images and Identity 1688–1980*. Sydney: Allen & Unwin, 1981.

Williams, Michael. 'Non–British immigration to Australia during the nineteenth century'. *Studies in Overseas Settlement and Population*. Ed. Anthony Lemon and Norman Pollock. London: Longman, 1980, pp. 187–206.

Woolcock, Helen R. *Rights of Passage: Emigration to Australia in the Nineteenth Century*. London: Tavistock, 1986.

Yi–Fu Tuan. 'Space and place: Humanistic perspective.' *Progress in Geography: International Reviews of Current Research* vol. 6. Eds Christopher Board *et al*. London: Edward Arnold, 1974, pp. 211–52.

Index

For names of individual diarists, see under *diarists*.

[230]

Index

Index

Index

Hampsten, Elizabeth, 101
Harris, Alexander, *Martin Beck*, 84
Himmelfarb, Gertrude, 132
Hogan, Rebecca, 89, 90
home, *see* space, domestic

journal-letters, 26, 30, 46
journey-stories, 51–3, 56, 58, 65–8,
    73, 82, 95, 192–4, 209

Kingston, W. H. G.
    Emigrant Voyager's Manual, 36–7,
        57, 97
    *Fortunes of the 'Ranger' and
        'Crusader', The*, 82, 85
    How to Emigrate, 185, 186–7

'land of promise', 184–9, 191
letters home, 26–30, 41, 43, 46, 58;
    see also journal-letters
Letts diaries, 22, 29
libraries
    class bias, 12–14
    gender bias, 14–15
    ethnic bias, 15–16
literacy
    convicts, 6
    emigrants, 11, 12–13, 18
Lyotard, Jean-François, 87

McCubbin, Frederick, *The Pioneer*,
    182
MacDonald, Charlotte, 56, 70, 71
maps, 91–7
matrons, 70–1, 139, 153
Mayne, Alan, 100
Merseyside Maritime Museum, 192
Mink, Louis O., 194, 200, 207
Moore, Bryce, 5, 74, 75

New Zealand, 163, 176, 186, 191
Nicholson, Ian, 11, 15

panoramas, 176–80, 182

photography, 1–3, 41, 167, 178, 205
Pratt, Mary Louise, 78, 82, 83, 85,
    138–9, 174, 177
Prout, John Skinner, 180

quarantine, 188, 196–7

Rée, Jonathan, 158, 192–4, 207
Renza, Louis A., 146–7
rites of passage, 55–6, 177, 199–200,
    208
route to Australia, 8, 90–7
Rowley, Sue, 68

Seddon, George, 173
Shakespeare, William, *Richard II*,
    53–4
shipboard life
    accommodation, 61–5, 69–70,
        110–13, 118, 135–6
    advice to readers, 38–40, 80–2
    calms, 23, 105
    captain's table, 112, 113, 115–16
    cleaning, 139, 141
    cooking, 126, 127, 129, 150–2
    crossing the line, 55
    daily routine, 125, 139–42
    deaths, 83, 156
    dietary, 136–8
    gender roles, 63–4, 72–3, 149–54;
        see also women
    lice, 130
    mess system, 124–9
    monotony, 21, 92–3, 96, 97–103,
        105, 154
    pastimes, 98, 117, 140–1
        catching birds, 24, 79, 80
        catching sharks, 82–3, 85
        dancing, 66, 72, 130–1, 132
        reading, 117, 119, 140–1, 156
        singing, 91–2, 132, 141, 156
    sewing, 151–2, 153
    paying one's footing, 117
    position reports, 91–2

[234]

Index

religious services, 116
seasickness, 20, 29, 49–50, 58
seeing a ship, 27, 91, 103
sickness, 69, 143, 159
storms, 103–4, 152–3, 157–8, 159
washing, 81, 151
yarning, 85–9
space
    diary, 100, 102
    domestic, 57–73, 101–2, 103–6,
        135–6, 144, 201, 204–5
    geographical, 90–7, 202
    social, 110–34, 144

surgeons, 71, 111, 119, 125, 143

Todorov, Tzvetan, 100
Turner, Victor, 55

Vincent, David, 13, 14

women, 14–15, 16, 52, 63–4, 68–73,
    88, 139–40, 144, 152–4, 173
Woolcock, Helen, 125, 139

Yi-Fu Tuan, 96–7